Pete "Snakey Jake" Johnson

Pete Johnson is a musician with a long career in blues music, specialising in the country blues of the Twenties and Thirties. He is also an acknowledged connoisseur of vintage guitars and an innovator in the field of sound systems.

Sandra Gibson

Sandra Gibson is a writer with a special interest in art and music. She has written promotional material for art exhibitions and reviews for *Art Of England, The Nerve* and *Circa* magazines. She also writes poetry and fiction and is currently completing a novel.

AIN'T BAD FOR A PINK!

The life of bluesman Pete 'Snakey Jake' Johnson

Grey-dawn motorways and yachts on silver seas; whisky with Peter Green and slide guitar with Son House; coffins riding the flood waters of Albany and moonlight on the railway line: the life of bluesman Pete "Snakey Jake" Johnson.

Sandra Gibson

Written from conversations with Pete Johnson and friends.

Matador
5 Weir Road
Kibworth Beauchamp
Leicester LE8 0LQ, UK
Tel: (+44) 116 279 2299
Fax: (+44) 116 279 2277
Email: books@troubador.co.uk
Web: www.troubador.co.uk/matador

ISBN 978 1848766 655

British Library Cataloguing in Publication Data.
A catalogue record for this book is available from the British Library.

Typeset in 12pt Palatino by Troubador Publishing Ltd, Leicester, UK

Matador is an imprint of Troubador Publishing Ltd

Printed in Great Britain by the MPG Books Group, Bodmin and Kings Lynn

This book is dedicated to Dobro

Dobro is the name given to the type of resonator guitar I so admire. It's a contraction of Dopyera Brothers coined when their company was set up in 1928. I named my dog Dobro and one day recently he was a bit lively and I kept having to call him to me. I soon noticed that people passing by were smiling and acknowledging me. I later discovered that "Dzien dobry" is a Polish greeting and "Dobry den" is a Czech greeting – hence my popularity with the local immigrants!

So the dedication has three aspects.

CONTENTS

Prologue

On Thursday 12th March 1998, at Whippoorwill Studios, Smyrna, Georgia, I recorded a CD of country blues songs: the pinnacle in a long career as a musician and a tribute to the bluesmen I admire. It was all finished in four hours on my mother's birthday and this convergence of important event and significant date created the pivotal moment at which I started to assess my life.

This book is about a lad from Crewe who loved the blues. And it's about those about me and the times we had and it's about the music. That's it, really.

SECTION ONE

From Bridget's Barn To The Brunswick:

A Tug Of Love

My early years were mauled by powerfully emotional experiences propelling me towards the inevitable. I was like a rugby player running with the ball, temporarily slowed down by counter forces but certain of reaching the touchline.

The Influence Of Affluence

I was born in Crewe in 1949, within the echoes of World War II and within the sounds of the steam trains giving the town its heavy metallic life. There was a moment in my infancy that caught the social and economic change I would inherit: my earliest memory, aged two, is of a vast, unrecognizable object that blinded me with its whiteness. My mother, my father and their three sons were gazing in awe at that powerful symbol of affluence and renewal, only understandable, only remarkable, in the context of the Fifties.

A bath. A bath in its own room.

I had been born into an era of state welfare and educational and economic opportunity which was to transform the lives of ordinary people. My hands, now sticky with Farley's Rusks, would soon dance across a guitar and within two decades steer my first yacht.

Bibles And Brakes

Personal memories of my grandparents are vivid though few. Grandma Sophia Johnson had been abandoned by her husband in the 1920s – this was never spoken about – and was supported at all levels by the Christadelphian Church. I remember her in two modes: as part of the nineteenth century – old and frail, her mass of grey hair down her back and coiling out of the bed, reading, according to Christadelphian tradition, seventeen chapters – why *seventeen*? – from the Bible every day, or part of the twentieth century – screaming about with me in my Turner Climax to visit her sister in Timbrell Avenue for tea and cakes.

I still have Sophia's recipe for pickled eggs.

If Sophia was from Dickens, granddad Rafe Billington was from *The Wind in the Willows.* What they shared was a love of speed. He was a Class 1 train driver who broke more than a time record for travelling from Carlisle to Crewe: all the crockery on the train smashed, so fiercely were the brakes applied on arrival. Ralph's vehicular prowess extended to the road. He had an open Austin Seven: a yellow model he drove like a train. His handlebar moustache flapping in the breeze, he'd be honking the horn, expecting everyone to get out of the way. Two of his fingers were missing – lost when some machinery backfired at the site of a rail crash. He used the stump of one of them to pack his pipe down, even when it was lit! I inherited my grandfather's liking for fast cars but also something far more serious. He had Dupuytren's Contracture, a syndrome inherited from the Vikings from which I also suffer. It causes the tendons in the hand to contract so that it looks arthritic and clawlike, I remember my grandfather's hands looking this way. Dupuytren's Contracture has severe implications for a musician as we shall see.

Ralph's wife Minnie – my maternal grandmother – is associated in my mind with a cosy kitchen in Ruskin Road, Crewe, redolent of hot pot. Being profoundly deaf didn't stop her lipreading six conversations simultaneously.

In Tandem

I've often wondered why my grandfather John Johnson left his family: was he traumatised by the Great War or by the aftermath? What made him unable to cope with family life? I don't know what became of him but poverty filled the gap he left. Nevertheless, partly because of the kindness of the Church, his family lived a respectable and religious life.

Looking at the evidence, I don't think that cowardice was much of a *motif* in the Johnson family. My father Norman Johnson was conscripted in 1940 and went to fight in Africa, Italy and Europe. His brother Mont had a different kind of courage: he was a conscientious objector and went to prison for his beliefs. My father always felt disappointed that he had lacked what he regarded as Mont's superior courage yet after his death I discovered he was probably the most decorated and longest serving private in the Second World War, resisting promotion at all costs so that his decisions could not affect many lives. He always shrugged off his role[1] in the war, saying, "I was just a surveyor." But what did this mean? It meant he did a dangerously exposed front line job gauging enemy fire. He was unimpressed by the trinkets of glory; my mother picked up his medals and he gave them to his first son Ralph to swap for cigarette cards. Being a painter and decorator in civilian life with an interest in buildings and art, he valued far more a set of unsent architectural postcards from every place he passed through. The only other statement he made about his army service was: "The army taught me to smoke." He described a room with a false floor: the officers were above the floor, the men beneath. They were planning manoeuvres. The men were instructed to blow smoke through allocated gaps in the floor to represent gun emplacements – a ludicrous activity worthy of Spike Milligan.

I would describe my father as an intelligent man whose lack of education wasn't his fault. It was to be the next generation that would benefit from universal education regardless of class or wealth. I feel I inherited strength, determination and courage from my father but I didn't absorb his religious beliefs and to be fair I wasn't pressurised to do so. Ideological clashes between us did occur but this was later when I reached adolescence determined to be a rock musician. In view of his impoverished early life, it was understandable that my father would want economic stability and respectability for his three sons. We forget how shocking my ambition was – being in a rock 'n' roll band was like being an outlaw. Parents in the post-war era became increasingly alarmed at the emergence of a youth culture with its own views on music, politics and – worst of all – sex.

My mother, Albina Betsy Boswell Billington, came from a more economically sound background than my father and was privately educated. She was a resourceful, energetic woman who bought her own house – the basis of her hairdressing business – whilst her husband was in the army. A wartime photograph shows her looking like Vera Lynn, upwardly mobile in a fur coat without fear of censure or failure. She was certainly no ordinary housewife; both she and my father had been racing cyclists of some repute. Their common interest had neutralised the social differences between them and people said they were made for each other. This was a modern relationship: they never argued; they *discussed* things. I inherited my mother's business acumen and resilience – I ran my own business and owned a house at an early age as she did – and I was also influenced by her feminism in my choice of women.

But my mother dominated my life in a more profound sense. When I was three and a half my childhood ended. I watched an ambulance drive away – my mother had collapsed in the street – and although my infant's mind was probably as interested in the vehicle as it was distressed by the event, that was the beginning of twelve years of anguished uncertainty and the feeling of death hovering over everything. From the point when the ambulance disappeared with my mother – and my childhood – I had to learn to be self-reliant.

In spite of bouts of illness caused by heart problems, my mother was fabulous – full of positivity, pulling her business together every time she came out of hospital. Sometimes, I would help by shampooing hair and I often created chaos in this feminine world. During my travels I caught a grass snake; I drank the milk from my flask and put it in, cycled home, handed the flask to my mother for rinsing and out it slithered in a flash of caught light. You can imagine her reaction!

I've always been a practical joker; it's a good safety valve and became part of my entertainer's resources. I developed a few of these survival techniques negotiating the precisely defined territories of Crewe. You had to run like hell when you saw the Black Backs Gang – their coarse kneelength trousers exposing red-raw fighting knees. If you were cornered the best technique was to create a spectacular and noisy diversion; I've spent my life fighting The Black Backs Gang in one guise or another.

People ask about my musical genes: my mother was a reasonable pianist but I can't find any other musical aptitude in previous generations. From my infancy I was encouraged to enter talent contests in Rhyl, winning prizes for my singing. My mother had a freer, more liberal attitude than my father had; for her it was about achieving what you wanted to do – even being a musician! She didn't actively oppose my father – they were totally in love – but her influence at a more subtle level modified the tension between father and son, and she was always fully behind my ambitions.

But in spite of the many good times, my mother's illness gnawed at my childhood years. She was in and out of hospital for more than a decade but I can recall no one specific occasion. All visits were one generic visit: or, rather, a feeling, an overwhelming feeling, of the impossibility of communication, such was the dominating force of the hospital and the emotional power of unspoken thoughts. Out of hospital my mother was unstoppable – demanding that I push her up the bank at Queen's Park. Quite a challenge for a child.

Albina Betsy Boswell Billington, my mother, was the first woman in the UK to have open heart surgery. She had two problems which had to be dealt with sequentially. Stenosis is the narrowing of the artery so this had to be opened up in order to fix a breech in the mitral valve. This was when I was about eleven. The first operation was not successful; the periods in hospital got longer until she was permanently there. The journeys – an hour each way – to the hospital in Wythenshaw were horrendous and made worse by other events. My father had knocked a child over and although it was not his fault, he never got over it and wouldn't drive a car. So we went by scooter. In addition to this my eldest brother Ralph had been seriously injured in a motorcycle accident and was simultaneously in hospital in Oswestry. The memory of the danger and glacial misery of those winter visits: my father's worry about his wife and son, my lack of clothing and the ill-fitting crash helmet I borrowed, the icy conditions when we would repeatedly fall off, still makes me cry. One night it was so cold I couldn't hold the coins when we stopped at a petrol station for fuel we couldn't afford.

Layin' On A Coolin' Board (2)

My mother died when I was fifteen. She died on the operating table during her second heart operation. I was in bed; Ralph told me. Although we had lived with the possibility of her death for so long, that was and still is the worst, emptiest, moment in my life. Your mind can't accept the finality of death. My father had such an unreserved faith in medicine that his optimism must have given me hope. Besides: she had survived other operations and this one might have changed things for the better.

When I saw my mother at the mortuary I didn't want to touch her. I knew her organs had been removed – even her eyes would have gone to research – and the mortician had created false colour in her face and an unnatural smile. I was offended because she looked too happy and because it was a con. My mother was an eyeless, hollow carcass. How could she smile?

I became a recluse, playing guitar in my bedroom so the empty feeling wouldn't kick in. I'd played a guitar since the age of eight; it was like meditation. People – relatives – came and offered help. We hadn't seen them in ages then they sat there smoking in that way people do when they don't know what to do or say. I have no visual memories of the funeral; I was very emotionally disturbed and that was the time I stopped singing hymns. If you're not religious the service holds no meaning for you and no comfort. My mother wasn't a poor sinner needing forgiveness; she hadn't slipped away into the next room; we wouldn't meet again in any bright land.

She had gone.

Socks And Hymns

They told me off after the funeral for going to my bedroom to play guitar but I carried on. Mum used to love it. The blues became my bereavement counsellor – I needed one. I was fifteen years old, falling out with my father – we were both on short fuses, neither of us mentioning my mother or her death – and in trouble at school for not singing hymns and wearing odd socks. Oh – and a few other things like being disruptive and not doing enough work. The elitist grammar school I attended had no interest in my emotional state. I wasn't being eccentric or difficult; we weren't too poor to own socks but no-one considered sock pairing in our mourning household. I told my teachers that if I ever met God I'd headbutt him and then ask the questions – their hymns had no comfort for me and neither had they. I sank my fury into playing music I could most identify with as my only means of expression.

So, I would sit in my bedroom: eleven and a half stone, muscular, needing to shave, my mousey hair growing longer than school allowed, wearing blue jeans, a loose sweater and Cuban heeled shoes, playing an almost unplayable twelve string. The action was very hard. Linda bought it because I thought it was a Martin and therefore a bargain. Wrong. I'd never seen one, of course, or any other quality guitar and there had been no musical advice forthcoming from the blonde salesgirl from Bossons and Doig either. They sold tellies and all sorts of stuff as well as instruments.

Or I would plug in a budget priced Broadway into a Watkins Dominator: early Sixties blue and cream, with flecks in the blue and gold bars. There was a V front with angled speakers for a better spread of sound. Classic, rare and collectible these days. Or I would haul my gear onto the handlebars of my bike and cycle to Wrinehill to rehearse my band. Or I would thump any kid who spoke badly about his mother. That was how I survived.

The blonde bombshell who sold me the twelve string eventually specialised in music: she went to sell records in Breeden and Middleton: from Hightown to High Street.

Believing that we would all be reunited, Mum didn't want us to be unhappy about her death or for there to be a sad place for us to visit. She left generous, uplifting letters full of love and containing no self pity – to be opened posthumously – and she wanted her ashes thrown to the winds.

We'll Meet Again (3)

Darling,

Goodbye dear don't worry I shall be waiting for you and I want you to know that this 25 yrs have been the happiest in my life.

What happens today is what has got to be, but I have plenty to look after me until you come.

Dearest heart I am with you wherever you go and whatever you do so you are not alone. We have good children Norman and give them my love won't you, tell them not to worry after all it was my own choice.

The only regret is that I cannot spend a few more happy happy years with you. But dearest carry on, put the carpet down and so on it will help to keep us together and me happy.

In a few years maybe you will be able to find someone else to keep you company during the latter years.

Well dearest Goodbye for now, but if it is predicted that I am not to come back to you I will say Goodbye till I see you again. I have always loved you. I shall go on loving you they say until Eternity but it will be beyond that. Our happy married life has been so wonderful. Sweetheart Goodbye.

Your Loving and Devoted Wife

xxxxxx

PS.
Ralph x
Roger x
Peter x.

The Amazing Exploding Guitar

There were only two preoccupations in my early years: my mother's illness and playing the guitar. When she died, the music occupied the centre. I was fortunate enough to have had the redemptive power of music in my life for a long time. The blues resonated with my emotions in a positive way and the song that best expressed my sense of loss was Sleepy John Estes' "I'd Been Well Warned": a song about losing your best friend – in his case, his eyesight.

A musician is more likely to remember his first guitar than his first lover. When I was eight I bought a handmade guitar from a friend of my brother for a pound. It lasted twelve months: long enough for me to learn all the major chords from a book. Then, as if overstimulated from the intensive learning, it split asunder!

Bridget's Barn

Six months later I persuaded my two brothers to buy me a guitar for

Christmas. This was a Spanish guitar which I played at my first gig: a concert at Edleston Road School when I was nine, in front of my class. I played "I Believe" – Frankie Laine's hit – noting that it went down very well with the girls. I always had an ear for a big song and you can't imagine a mid-twentieth century western without his voice on the soundtrack. Interestingly, Tex Ritter sang the soundtrack song for High Noon but Frankie's version was the bigger hit.

Aged twelve I bought an electric guitar from someone from Willaston who played in The Four Falcons. I remember the name because I just couldn't get rid of it off the case. I started my own band – can't remember the name – with school friends who all lived at Wrinehill, rehearsing in Bridget's Barn on a smallholding there. By now my band had developed a style of music derived from Chuck Berry, doing blues and slide in a rocky style at the school garden party, Betley Village Hall and Wistaston Memorial Hall. And the girls would jive and when they twirled round you could see stocking tops if your eyes caught the moment.

Leadbelly, Mississippi Fred McDowell And The Honeydripper

About this time, on my paper round, I was immobilised by the sound of loud, unfamiliar music coming from one of the suburban houses. It caught me in the solar plexus and in the balls; it took me out of my time and out of my place. This wasn't anything from the *Top Twenty*; it was a raw, uncompromising sound from the edge of the world.

Leadbelly.

From that Damascene moment when I heard the powerful voice and the twelve string guitar on "Black Girl", the course of my life was fixed. I became a blues musician and Huddie accompanied me through the early turbulent times.

By this age I had been listening to music by Sonny Terry and Brownie McGhee, Josh White and Leadbelly available – bizarrely – in a series for sale at Woolworth's for pocket money. But this was blues music directed at a white audience; it hadn't prepared me for the heart-stopping sounds coming from that British window. None of my peers knew this music although the currently popular Lonnie Donegan did sing Leadbelly numbers. As far as authentic blues music was concerned there was virtually a desert. Fortunately for me it turned out that Bert Bellamy, whose window it was, had hundreds of blues records, many bought from Pete Russell's record shop. The address is burnt into my brain: 24 Market Avenue, Plymouth. I began to buy all my records from this shop; I still play this rare and precious collection.

Like many people from Crewe, Bert, originally from Liverpool, worked on the railway, where he had a clerical job. He looked like a white black man and favoured the early blues music that I so admired and like his friend Fred Watts, he was interested in big band jazz as well. I would go to Bert's house regularly on Tuesday and Thursday evenings to listen to blues records and get information. It became a social event when my girlfriend Linda came – though she was more into jazz – and Bert's wife joined us. A nourishing time and occasionally, blues musicians stopped at Bert's house.

Bert Bellamy and Fred Watts – also the owner of a fine record collection – both wrote articles about music: Fred for a small magazine attached to a jazz shop in London and Bert for *Blues Unlimited*, a magazine reputed to be "the daddy of all blues magazines" (4) founded in 1963 and edited by Mike Leadbitter, an authority on post-war blues. Leadbitter also edited a collection of the magazine's articles in a book: *Nothing but the Blues* published in 1971. They knew everyone in the business and took me to gigs in Manchester at the Guild Hall, Club 43, and the Free Trade Hall where they had backstage passes. Through this connection, I was not only able to hear live blues – I could actually meet the American bluesmen who were enjoying fame because of the currently awakened interest in their music. Big stars like Jimmy Witherspoon: a great big black man who smoked dope and drank with Bert, with whom he stayed. Everything about him was big – what an amazing, booming jazz voice he had! A big, big voice. We saw him in Club 43 in 1962/63 and I had the privilege of cooking him a full English. Fred Watts also got to know Jimmy Witherspoon very well.

Halfway Down The Stairs

My musical awakening began during World War II in my childhood home in Goostrey, Cheshire. This was the age of radio and we relied on it for news of the war. It was always on and I could hear it in bed. But one particular night I found myself halfway down the stairs listening intently to what turned out to be a Jelly Roll Morton number: "The Naked Dance". Although from a respectable Creole family whose business was timber, Jelly Roll Morton played music in brothels and the reference is to the way the whores danced for their clients. This was heady stuff for a twelve year old and after that I listened to every jazz programme on the radio and started collecting records.

Jazz led me to country music: Jimmie Rodgers was a particular favourite and country music led to blues, especially Leadbelly, together with Big Bill Broonzy, Muddy Waters and Lightnin' Hopkins. Josh White was a softer-voiced singer who used to guide blind performers about. That's how he learnt guitar.

You had to do a lot of sorting out to find them.

I also followed the swing music of the contemporary big bands at the Royal Festival Hall. I saw Louis Armstrong at Bellevue, Manchester in 1956 or 1957. A coach trip had been organized from Breeden and Middleton's – the record shop in High Street, Crewe. I attended both houses; Armstrong varied his repertoire for the second house. I saw The Saints Jazz Band at Crewe's Royal Hotel but the band members were displeased because of all the talking.

The first blues performers I saw included Chris Barber and Sonny Terry and Brownie McGhee at Manchester's Free Trade Hall where a mixture of jazz and blues was on the bill. This was in the early Sixties; possibly before that. Then there was a memorable trip to London's Hammersmith Odeon. I was able to get a ticket from someone who had a spare ticket because he had fallen out with his girlfriend. There were all these old-timers playing steel guitars. Someone had shone them up and they dazzled you. I saw Bukka White, Son House and Skip James.

I have a photograph with me and Bert on either side of Jimmy Witherspoon, one of my favourite performers. He was a very friendly man. I got to know him well.

The friendship between me and Jimmy was to lead to some interesting situations. I was in London to see a concert and afterwards I wanted to see

Jimmy's second set at Ronnie Scott's. I knew I would have some difficulty getting in because I wasn't a member and sure enough, I did. However, just at the crucial moment, when I was standing in the entrance hall a door opened and Jimmy shouted, "My man! He's with me!" *So I was allowed in. On another occasion I took Bert Bellamy to a record shop in Salford owned by Barry Ansell, a man who was associated with putting on shows in Manchester. Jimmy Witherspoon was in there with Ernie Garside, who ran Club 43 and was responsible for booking blues artists such as Jimmy to come over from the States. This was how Bert met Jimmy who subsequently stayed with him and ate a breakfast cooked for him by Pete Johnson.*

Musically speaking, I would describe Jimmy Witherspoon as what you would call a blues shouter. He was very loud; it was developed to overcome a big band sound. Joe Turner was another one – he used to sing in a café while waiting on – and so was Jimmy Rushing. He was with the Basie band. Unfortunately Jimmy got throat cancer and didn't get the high notes after that though he lived on a while.

I also met Sleepy John Estes, his harmonica player Hammie Nixon and Yank Rachell the mandolin player. I do regret the fact that I didn't get a photograph taken. John Estes did look sleepy and Lightnin' Hopkins said, "Poor old Sleepy's a very sick man." *But Sleepy John was musically marvellous. I had quite a good talk with Lightnin' Hopkins. He was supposed to be a man who was quite reticent. I asked him about travelling – he didn't like flying much and wrote a song about it! I've got nearly all of his records. I met John Lee Hooker but was not so keen on the white bluesmen he played with. John Lee was a stammerer. T-Bone Walker was another bluesman I got to know quite well.*

I have two photographs of JB Lenoir: one with Bert Bellamy; the other with me. The poignant fact is that these photographs were taken on the night before Bert's death.

Incidentally, I once saw Bojangles dance at a Louis Armstrong concert. Apparently he had a lot of trouble with his stump bleeding.

Fred Watts. (5)

The age profile of the audiences at these early Sixties gigs was older than anything I had come across. These were *beatniks* – already creating a moral panic in the press – and I remember the heavy smell of marijuana, the tailored beards and baggy sweaters. In spite of the eighteen years age limit I got away with it because I looked older than my thirteen years and because I was with Bert.

It was at Manchester's Free Trade Hall that I met Mississippi Fred McDowell – a musician who used to say, "I do not play no rock 'n' roll y'all. I jus' play jus' straight an' natchel blue" – and saw for the first time an open-tuned slide guitar. I didn't know his reputation at the time: that Alan Lomax had said, for example, "In him the great tradition of the blues runs pure and deep" or that I would share the feelings Fred had expressed about the blues: "I'd get the sound of it in my head, then I'd do it my way from what I remembered" or that he played but didn't own a guitar until he was thirty-seven whilst I had one when I was eight. I wasn't aware of any of that then: I just observed his self-contained dignity and listened to his strong, penetrating voice and insistent slide playing. I still can't believe Fred McDowell let me play his guitar! Perhaps he was somehow repaying the white man who gave him his first guitar. Fred offered to get me a drink and when I accepted he passed me a whisky bottle. "No thank you – I meant a beer!" So he got me a beer. And there was more: a man who looked like a boxing promoter was watching me play. This was pianist Roosevelt "The Honey-Dripper" Sykes, a cigar-smoking man with puffy eyes and rings on his deft fingers, whose career as a thundering boogie pianist and reputation for *risqué* lyrics was to span seven decades. His fleshy, urbane presence formed a contrast to the lean, serious McDowell.

"Ain't bad for a pink!" he said – a comment I have treasured ever since.

Mississippi Fred McDowell drained the rejected whisky bottle in one swallow and went on stage. These bluesmen had generous hearts.

Sleepy John Estes

At this age I also met Sleepy John Estes, another bluesman who, like Mississippi John Hurt, Son House and Skip James, had been brought out of obscurity to tour Europe. Lean, gaunt and still, with John it was the voice rather than the guitar playing that impressed. Sleepy John was one of the best blues poets: the sounds he made were penetratingly expressive of life's harshness. I later found out that John's slicing, suffering voice had set the pace for work gangs when he was the leader of a railroad maintenance crew and that Big Bill Broonzy had described him, "crying the blues". He had enough reason to. He lost one eye aged six when someone threw a rock at him and the other when he was fifty-one in 1950. He was rediscovered living in extreme poverty in Brownsville, Tennessee in 1962. It was believed that John, whose voice sounded so old, was dead! But fortunately Big Joe Williams told researchers where he was living.

Like many black musicians, he had been an itinerant performer in the Southern states, had done some recording in 1929 and 1930 and returned to sharecropping in 1941 when shellac rationing, followed by the recording ban, cut short musical careers.

Georges Adins (6) gives a filmic description of a fallow cotton field with an apparently abandoned cabin in the distance, and then the appearance of the elusive John Estes who lived there with his wife and five children. Adins was shocked by the extreme poverty and fear he found there. He was asked to buy food for the family and describes how John's visits – to the laundry, to the car wash – become an occasion to stop work and play the blues. Joe Boyd (7) writes about fetching Sleepy John and Hammie Nixon, threadbare and carrying cardboard suitcases tied up with string, from the Cornell Folk Festival in Ithaca, New York after their first appearance in front of a white audience. John Estes went on to tour Europe and Japan and appeared at the Newport Festival in 1964.

Estes' songs and performances and those of fellow musicians: the plaintive mandolin of Yank Rachell and the driving force of Hammie Nixon's harmonica, have been much admired by reputable black and white musicians. "Slow Consumption" has been covered by Ry Cooder and "Floating Bridge" by Eric Clapton. The Blues Band did "Someday Baby" and Taj Mahal also covered some of his songs. "I'd Been Well Warned" was to become part of my repertoire from early on in my career. This is one of the bluest of blues songs. I've modified the words for the contemporary audience, to emphasise the most poignant aspects and altered the playing to suit the way I do things, with no disrespect intended.

Sleepy John Estes did keep falling asleep.

Wear A Hat

Fred Watts has the signed programme from the time we met Sister Rosetta Tharpe at a blues festival at the Free Trade Hall, Manchester: a powerful, formidable presence and a link with gospel. Like Son House she had experienced tension between her religious background and vocation as a gospel singer, and her liking for singing jazz and blues: the devil's music. This must have been difficult because her husband was a preacher who became tense if she didn't wear a hat in church. She played a Gibson electric guitar and was an early exponent of soul, regarded as second only to Mahalia Jackson. By the time she got to her third marriage, 25,000 people attended her wedding. She influenced both Elvis Presley and Johnny Cash. (8)

Sonny And Brownie And John Lee

I also met Sonny Terry and Brownie McGhee and John Lee Hooker in those early days. I was to support Sonny Terry and Brownie McGhee when they did later tours in the UK, appearing with them at The Placemate in Newcastle, at The Place in Hanley, at Manchester University, and in Sheffield in the late Sixties.

Sonny and Brownie were amongst the earliest blues performers to tour Europe; they first came over in the Fifties, then in 1962 when I met them, in 1967 when I supported them and in 1970. Both had long-established and distinguished careers. Just as slide extends the range of an acoustic guitarist, the harmonica extends the range of a singer. Sonny's harp playing complemented and extended his vocal range. By vocalising through the instrument, he intensified the moaning sounds, punctuating it with loud hollers between blasts. Traditional call and response. He could reproduce the whistles and train rhythms so common, so evocative in blues music. Before he met Brownie, Sonny used to play on street corners with Blind Boy Fuller and the Reverend Gary Davis. He later became linked with popular mainstream culture, appearing on Broadway in *Finian's Rainbow* in 1946 and in the mid Fifties both he and Brownie appeared in the

Broadway production of Tennessee Williams's *Cat on a Hot Tin Roof.* He also ventured into the folk arena with Pete Seeger and Woody Guthrie.

Brownie played acoustic guitar and also sang. Critics have referred to the "Piedmont-style musical interplay" of the partnership which exploited the finger picking technique of this style. Piedmont blues – from the area extending from central Georgia to central Virginia, between the Atlantic coast and the Appalachians – was popularised by such performers as Blind Boy Fuller, Blind Blake, Blind Willie McTell, the Reverend Gary Davis, Etta Baker and Elizabeth Cotton. It incorporated elements from city and country, from black and white: ragtime, blues, country dance songs, early string bands and pop songs from the early twentieth century. Some would maintain that this music has more 'white' elements in it than the Delta blues and demographically speaking, this would make sense. I've always admired the finger picking style used by such musicians as Blind Blake, who incorporated ragtime piano rhythms and chord changes into guitar playing: the left hand piano rhythms produced by the thumb and the right hand piano melody by the fingers.

Brownie also ventured into the popular limelight by appearing in Langston Hughes' play, *Simply Heaven,* in films and on TV. The willingness of Sonny and Brownie to be open-minded about the way they earned a living was important in popularising the blues in Europe and the UK, and in linking the blues with the folk boom as well as kindling an interest within the pop *genre.* They brought what I would call commercial country blues music, doing gigs in all the popular venues and discos, performing cabaret blues effortlessly and brilliantly – almost without thinking about it. They made the blues accessible to a wider, mostly white audience for whom the duo had cleaned up their act. Brownie McGhee had originally been known as the second Blind Boy Fuller – a far cry from the toned down versions of the Reverend Gary Davis and Big Bill Broonzy numbers he was now playing. But you couldn't condemn the commercial instinct of bluesmen to capitalise on the enthusiasm for their music by touring and appearing at festivals. It was better than picking cotton. Ghettoised as "race music", acceptance into mainstream music and its financial rewards had been previously denied to their work.

The Blues Revival

But for some less worldly than Sonny and Brownie, the glare of publicity in the Sixties at events like Newport must have been a shock and a pressure. The critics at the time didn't take this into account. John Hurt stole the show at Newport nevertheless. Joe Boyd (9) writes about the tension between the desire of white audiences to hear 'authentic' blues and the attempts of the blues singers to be 'up to date'. This lead to the absurdity of having snappily clad blues singers dressed as sharecroppers. When Muddy Waters first came to the UK he played an electric guitar and British fans were shocked. By the time he returned in 1962 he had relearned some earlier acoustic material. The same attitude gave rise to the cries of "Judas!" when Dylan went electric. (10)

The blues revival had the effect of exposing black musicians to more liberal attitudes. One bluesman, Champion Jack Dupree, an ex-boxer who served his country in World War II and became a Japanese prisoner of war, sought a life in England and Europe to escape the pressure of segregation in America. He had good reason: born in New Orleans in 1909, Jack Dupree was orphaned when his parents died in a fire allegedly set by the Ku Klux Klan and was brought up in the Coloured Waifs Home for Boys, as was Louis Armstrong.

Blues And Pop

"These English boys want to play the blues so bad. And they play it so bad."
Sonny Boy Williamson. (11)

Parallel to this, pop music had exploded in Liverpool in the early Sixties. In addition to consumer articles unavailable in post-war austerity Britain, the "Cunard Yanks" sailing between Merseyside and New York had brought in equally unavailable jazz and blues records. The influence of black music soon penetrated pop bands such as the Rolling Stones, The Yardbirds and The Animals. One of the best interviews I experienced was with WRFG: Radio Free Georgia in 1998. The interviewer was enthusiastic and interested in what I had to say and he had things to contribute as well. He mentioned the Stones cutting their first album at Chess Studios, Chicago, and said that such blues virtuosos as Sonny Boy Williamson, Muddy Waters and Howling Wolf would be "hanging around". I had to disagree: I am entirely certain of the musical superiority of these bluesmen and insisted that it would have been the Stones who were doing the "hanging around" – mentally at least. You only have to listen to what Keith Richards had to say about the musical stature of these men to know this.

Son House

I never met Sonny Boy Williamson but all the blues musicians I did meet – leagues ahead of me musically – would be complimentary about a little white boy singing the blues. Brownie McGhee said he liked the way I changed my turnarounds and the way I tried to do jazzier chords. He spoke to me as a fellow musician. When I played with Son House he was equally complimentary and very helpful. I met him in 1967 or 1968 and he taught me how to play slide. When I appeared on WRGF thirty years later, I performed Son House's song, "Death Letter" – long part of my own repertoire – in tribute to him. Son House was criticised in the British music press for poor performances at that time and I was very angry about this. I supported him on several of these dates. I was there. He was old and ill and frail but he gave you the main line into his suffering: his music showing Southern gospel and spiritual influences, his whole body pushing the feeling and sound into the steel guitar, his right hand flailing and pulling the strings while his left hand worked with precision, moving the slide up and down. The audiences were fine. What right had some acnied kid from *Melody Maker* to slate him when he was a hero?

A pastor by the age of twenty, Son House had fallen from grace by falling for an older woman, developing a liking for corn whisky and picking up a guitar to play what the church regarded as the devil's music. Son House was possessed by the music, not the devil, but perhaps they were one and the same to him. Like Leadbelly, he spent some time in jail.

I feel honoured that the man with long feet and hands who played with Charley Patton and influenced Robert Johnson and Muddy Waters also took the trouble to teach me.

From listening to interviews I have done, remembering my first encounters with blues musicians, I know that the young Pete Johnson didn't possess the clear musical and historical perspective I have now. He was living it all; he wasn't contemplating it and anyway, perspectives require distance. But remembering and talking about the great blues legends I have met, drunk with, cooked for, smoked with and learnt from, is still a humbling experience for me even after all these years.

Tribute

Without the committed interest of Fred Watts and Bert Bellamy, I wouldn't have had these unique experiences or such access to blues music on record. Now that music is instantly accessible through downloading, it's hard to imagine the effort – and the relative cost – required in the early Sixties to enjoy the blues. Mainstream popular music of the Fifties and early Sixties sounded very sugary and tame but it was readily available on the radio, as sheet music and on 78s. Its subject matter was acceptable: sentimental ballads, novelty songs, coins in fountains, rings on fingers ... whilst for many, the blues represented something raw and sexually menacing. Tin Pan Alley didn't make too many references to rampant sex or blokes being visited at the gallows or dying mothers comforting their children or slain pimps or lovers at the morgue. Even black people were shunning it as being embarrassing because it said something about their past and current oppression. It was the white kids, mainly from the student community, who took to the blues and it's really strange to see the newsreels of these – often suited – audiences of polite middle class kids. Bert and Fred, older and engaged in working class employment and family life in a northern industrial town, were unusual. Meeting Bert (and then Fred) through Leadbelly's music was to be the first of many musical convergences in my life. Such events require a prior effort as well as luck. In my case I had the temerity, aged thirteen, to ask about the music; I was already spending my pocket money on what was available to me in Woolworth's and this opened the door for Bert's effort in encouraging and educating me.

Bert Bellamy died aged fifty when I was eighteen. It was a shock. I'm still listening to music from his record collection given to me by his widow. I'm grateful to him.

Girls

One of my reasons for picking up a guitar was to impress girls and it worked. I used to go to the air raid shelters opposite the entrance to the Queen's Park – this would be the late Fifties/ early Sixties – and there was a lot going on sexually even before the sexual revolution. At this time a glimpse of stocking top and being allowed to touch a girl's breast was quite something. But it was all a bit furtive and tense. Within five or six years it was to be miniskirts, see-through tops, nipple counts and free love. Young people had been liberated from periodic anxiety by the Pill.

From the age of fifteen I had a regular girlfriend who eventually became my first wife but I'd also had a lot of sexual adventures, aided and abetted by my opportunistic libido, my musician's charisma and the freedom of my movements as a performer. Interestingly, although my father knew something of my philandering ways, he was never judgmental.

I had my first girlfriend when I was about thirteen. We sometimes had the house to ourselves and one day she called me to the bathroom. She was naked. Nothing came of the invitation because I was too scared. I had heard my brother talking to my father about "having to get married".

But mostly I was shocked by the pubic hair.

Whilst a student in Manchester I enjoyed a hedonistic lifestyle and a new kind of freedom in which the women had the sexual confidence to do the choosing. I would crash at one flat or another in the area, depending on where I had been playing music. I recall being friendly with a good-looking guy with a fashionable Mexican moustache who was older than me – about twenty-three years old – and he took me to a student flat to meet two nice girls. The foursome split into two twosomes and the settee was arranged to provide two 'compartments', with me and the Derbyshire girl on the side nearest the fire, and the Geordie lass and the hunk on the other side. A little later in the night I was woken by the request, "He's gone to sleep; can I join you?" Being a magnanimous chap I had to say yes. I ended up living part of my time with both girls. It was all very light-hearted and simple.

I met a girl with an Alpha Romeo and hundred quid shoes during my days at university. She was very keen on me so I let her be my roadie and she drove me to gigs in her exceptional car. One weekend she invited me to stay at her house for the weekend; her parents were away and we would have the place to ourselves. Talk about culture shock! Her huge place at Alderley Edge was like Buckingham Palace. We were standing in the ballroom; there was a horse running about in a paddock at the back. "Would you like a swim?" my hostess asked. I couldn't see any pool. She pressed a button and the ballroom floor slowly moved to reveal a swimming pool below. But where was James Bond?

Interestingly enough, I'd long had the habit of visiting stately homes – with a tent! Yet this visit to the mansions of Cheshire brought out the angry young man in me. I was a communist at that time – against wealth and privilege; supporting Castro and the underdog and involved in student protests. But I didn't terminate the visit; I wasn't puritanical about wealth. Though I never was impressed by it *per se*, that didn't stop me having and enjoying yachts and fast cars for a while! And I remember well how lovely my roadie looked in her expensive underwear.

My father remarried when I was twenty-two but before then he had had a couple of relationships. Aged nineteen, I arrived home late one night, undressed without switching on the light and got into my bunk bed. It was already warm and occupied – by a beautiful girl. "I've always wanted a brother!" was the cheerful welcome.

She turned out to be the daughter of the woman from Blackpool my father was seeing. To add to the incestuous nature of things, this brotherless blonde had already had a fling with Melvyn, my drummer-to-be whom I already knew and whose band had played at Blackpool. I remember picking her up from Crewe station on my scooter. She played with my bits all the way to Wistaston. Unfortunately – perhaps fortunately – my father severed the Blackpool connection.

Another encounter had less auspicious beginnings. I had a mutually hostile relationship with one of the women where I worked. Part of the management consultancy training included in-service courses which involved stopping in hotels. On the last night of the last course, one of the women persuaded me to dance with the woman I disliked. The chemistry took over. The next day, during the car journey back, the matchmaker turned to speak to the happy couple we had become in the back of the car. "I can't talk now; I've got my mouth full!" said the lady.

My present wife Zoe had been part of my social circle since our Edleston Road School days. I'd known her since we were nine. Unusually for the area, she came from a middle class background and lived in a big house in Walthall Street, Crewe. Her upbringing was free, bohemian and intellectual. And a bit wild. She had total freedom to do what other kids couldn't do. I remember going to her house, where she had her own bedroom in the attic. It was painted red and black and she was allowed to entertain friends: there were settees and CND pictures and posters of political heroes and we played records and had discussions. It was like a youth club. We were great friends and by the age of thirteen or fourteen we were going out together in a foursome.

Zoe's father was a schoolteacher and a considerable classical pianist; she herself had eclectic musical tastes and was musically influenced by her uncle. She collected records by Dave Brubeck, MJQ, Thelonious Monk and Big Bill Broonzy among others, and she also enjoyed listening to my blues records. This was at a time when most of her contemporaries were listening to The Searchers and The Hollies.

As often happens during the experimental period of adolescence, we swapped partners and drifted apart when she started doing festivals, and later on going to the Twisted Wheel in Manchester and taking poppers. Our musical tastes were too divergent. Zoe was intimidated by my intensity and busy finding herself. She was like a butterfly. Although she and I remained great friends, it was inevitable that I should end up with her more mature friend.

So by the age of twenty-one I was married and living in Sandbach with my first wife Linda, a raunchy, sexy woman with an hourglass figure and nice breasts. I started going out with her about the time my mother died and I became very attached to her. She was sexually approachable and with her I had the combination of domestic stability and intimate good times that I needed after such an uncertain home life. Linda was the first girl I had seen topless; this was on a Cornish beach in the days before beach nudity was acceptable.

Intensity Of Need

At that time I was physically quite immature; Pete Johnson terrified me with his sexual intensity. I felt he was desperately in need of love and attention and was substituting sex for this. Linda was stable and motherly and more physically mature than I was and I think she was what Pete needed at that time. His mother was very ill and his home life was affected by this. He was essentially conservative and shy but became an intense, angry young man. A lot of his behaviour was bravado and this is more true now than when he was young. The emotional trauma of his mother's illness and death was not handled at all – it wasn't that it was badly handled – it was just not handled. He's psychologically stuck in his bereavement.

Zoe Johnson. (12)

For A While The Balance Was Right

In those days I was more than happy to go along with Pete. Because of his adventurousness I had adventures. I was the domestically stable one: a bit staid even. I deny the beach nudity, by the way. My relationship with Pete made me independent; I had soon learnt not to rely on him. In the early days in Manchester clubs with Bert Bellamy, Pete used to leave me in the audience and go backstage with Bert to meet blues singers. He'd be gone for ages – he used to watch from the wings and when he appeared at the end of the performance he'd be surprised that I was anxious. But for a while the balance was right; we needed one another. He lifted excitement into my life and I gave him stability. He had lost his mother and I feel that if that hadn't happened he wouldn't have turned to me. I sort of replaced her.

Linda Johnson. (13)

One night my wife appeared at a party dressed as Morticia Addams. Another woman was also dressed as Morticia. The second Morticia vowed to the first Morticia that she would get me off her. A couple of years into the marriage, this is what happened though it didn't cause a divorce at that time.

"I'm A Little Pimp With My Hair Gassed Back"

Finding the lyrics to "Mississippi Queen" whilst looking for something else reminded me of a heavy rock band called Axe – something to do with Plum – that I was in briefly round about 1966-67, before I went to Manchester University. Plum, an instinctive heavy rocker, was someone I'd known for a while who was to play an important part in my future business. Axe had a good lead guitarist in Pete Trotman, who went on to play in a well-regarded band called Strife, with Paul Elson and there was Phil Simcock on drums, Plum on bass and me on vocals and slide guitar. Ozzie was our roadie. The Frank Zappa number, "I'm A Little Pimp With My Hair Gassed Back" is one I remember from the set and Plum always did "Rock Me Baby" and songs of that ilk. I left after a few gigs – it was fun rehearsing but I wasn't into the music. Being the least experienced player in the band, I had the least influence over anything.

Some of the guitar playing in heavy rock is skilful but I didn't and don't find it melodic. I don't like distorted guitar sounds – it's too much of a manufactured noise. If I play electric guitar it's clean, the same as an acoustic guitar. With regard to virtuosity, as far as I'm concerned it's not the number of notes – it's the economy of notes, the spaces between the sounds that matter and heavy rock goes for a continuous sound. The exception would be a band called Spooky Tooth; their music had lots of gaps in it and if I'd wanted heavy rock, I'd have gone that way. Their version of "I Am The Walrus" is memorable.

A Banned Band

From early on in my career I attended jam nights at various clubs and pubs. One was held on Sunday nights at the Oddfellows Club in Edleston

Road, Crewe. Every musician in the area would be in there if they weren't gigging. There would be a sort of rota and then people did additional turns as well. Axe did a rendition of Edgar Broughton's "Out Demons Out" and it created a riot, with people stamping and making a noise. We were subsequently banned from every working man's club in the area.

Axe wasn't really a family band!

Bubonic Monk

You don't often see someone wearing evening dress and sandals. When I saw a bloke wearing evening dress and sandals *whilst riding a bike* I was intrigued. I liked his style. I later discovered that I also liked his music. Pete Whittingham – Whitty – was to become my most important musical collaborator and friend.

A daft little trio: Bubonic Monk, that also pre-dated my time at university and ran parallel to my solo work at various folk clubs, consisted of me, Pete Whittingham and John Billington. We all had pseudonyms: I was Rabid Wank'ard, Whitty was Foam Leg and John was Sir Bubon the Bongo, because he talked as if he had a plum in his mouth. It lasted about a year and during that time the band experimented with various types of instrument. As well as the basic guitar (Pete Whittingham) and slide guitar (me) there would be sitar, mandolin, banjo – a very rare four stringed banjo that Whitty eventually incorporated into the Skunk Band – and bongos (John Billington) all adding to the variety of sound textures. Whitty was far more folkie than me but not into that feeble crap that some people liked to listen to. He was more influenced by the Gaelic folk songs he had learnt in Ireland and also did a bit of contemporary stuff like Dylan and Neil Young. He had a fabulous voice; it sort of floated and the Irish Celtic flavours would come through, but he was also a great Stones and Pete Townsend fan so he incorporated this tremendous drive into his playing as well. He had less finesse than me but he was a fantastic singer-songwriter. We would also do a sort of acoustic psychedelic music with Pink Floyd songs from

Atom Heart Mother. We took it in turns to take the lead in singing, depending on whether it was a hard, harsh song or a gentle melodic song, harmonising naturally and this also carried on into our later band: two different voices and two different guitars. The harmonies were instinctive; we never had to work anything out.

Brahms And Lissed

I've subsequently done duos with Des Parton and enjoyed it but it's professional hard work. With Whitty and the music and a bottle of cider it was a party. We had this musicians' chemistry – we just sang like brothers having a bit of fun and the musical performance was almost a casual thing. Whitty and I started performing together in local pubs – the first acoustic evening being at the Chetwode Arms on Hightown, Crewe. Other places we appeared at included The Albion in Mill Street and the smallest pub in Crewe, on Wistaston Road. No payment was involved; it was just an extension of our social life but we soon built up a band of followers. Whitty would come to our house in Sandbach to put our set together and we eventually called our musical duo Brahms and Lissed, combining blues from my side and Gaelic and pop from his side. He had written some songs and I arranged them. We never had rehearsals because we rehearsed all the time, in effect.

Fellow Performers

Pubs weren't the only venues. The existing folk clubs were established before the folk boom and I had performed on my own in clubs such as the one held on Sunday nights at The Brunswick on Nantwich Road, Crewe and various blues venues. If I appeared at a folk club it would be as a floor singer; if I appeared at a blues club I would be a support act. I would have been about seventeen or eighteen at the time. How sniffy the folk *aficionados* were about music other than folk! I had to learn some folk songs in order to be tolerated. Yet modern folk music was allowed and I think Paul Simon once performed there in his "Homeward Bound" days. There are whole chat rooms debating which grim northern station his song is based on. Interviewed in 1990 (14) Simon said he wrote it at Liverpool. But that didn't stop them putting up a plaque at Widnes.

Anybody from Crewe just knows it had to be Crewe station.

Bert Jansch also appeared at The Brunswick – I really enjoyed his songs, though I was more impressed by John Renbourn as a player. I performed with both of them and with Davey Graham. Jansch's first album, released in 1965, sold 150,000 copies. He later went on to form Pentangle with Renbourn, Jacqui McShee, Danny Thompson and Terry Cox, performing an eclectic programme of music referred to as "folk baroque", each musician bringing their own influence: traditional, jazz, early music, blues and contemporary. Davey Graham was also an eclectic musician who incorporated folk, jazz, blues, Eastern European and North African music into his work. He was far ahead of his time; the early Sixties albums now acknowledged as folk-blues classics were described in the recent *Guardian* (15) obituary as "delayed time-bombs; their initial impact may not have been enormous but the long-term effect was remarkable". The band I formed in the early Seventies drew music from many influences and was part of this vibrant, influential and transformative movement.

Wizz Jones also played at The Brunswick and Brian Golby – with whom Wizz went on to specialise in country music – was another performer from those days. Wizz was a great blues lover at the top of his profession, influenced by Broonzy, Alexis Corner, Davey Graham and Ewan MacColl, and influencing Clapton and Renbourn in their early days. As was customary, he had done the European busk and had travelled to North Africa. He stayed with me a couple of times at the house in Wistaston Avenue where I lived with my father. I first met Wizz Jones at a gig in Stoke and the second time I met him I played with him, also in Stoke. I found some notes pertaining to a performance by (probably) Wizz Jones at (probably) the Stoke Guitar Club. I had written down how to play the different parts whilst closely watching and listening. There was no other way of finding out.

It's reminiscent of me getting the early bus to school so I could talk to Keith Haines – no longer at school and a skilled musician – about playing chords. Keith played with a successful band: Gary B. Goode and the Hot

Rods on the same bill as The Beatles. He graduated from skiffle to rock 'n' roll and eventually to jazz.

Bands

As well as solo performances, I was supporting some quite high profile bands such as Trader Horne, The Incredible String Band and Pentangle. Other performers included Dave Swarbrick: a virtuoso fiddle player who was to become a member of Fairport Convention, Son House and Peter Green from the early incarnation of Fleetwood Mac. This was a time when folk became folk rock and I'd be helping with lists of performers for gigs. I always put myself down to support; it was cheap and easy. I needed no equipment to move onto stage – just me and two microphones. In an electric band everyone needs an amplifier. I wasn't competing with these bands because I'm doing blues and they're doing folk rock. There's also variety for the audience. Sometimes I'd do an extra solo slot in a room off – there were lots of different rooms in the university buildings and many possibilities after the bands had finished. I was also playing with Stefan Grossman at Manchester University, at Keele and other big folk clubs as a support act during the late Sixties and early Seventies. He had a thorough grounding in the country blues, having studied with the Reverend Gary Davis for eight years and then with Mississippi John Hurt, Son House, Skip James and Fred McDowell. Stefan Grossman and I both did solo acoustic blues. He was technically much better, certainly in the Sixties; I'd caught up a bit by the Seventies.

Martin Carthy was another musician at the top of his prowess I met and played with. He was a solo performer before he joined Steeleye Span. It felt good to be accepted by players of this calibre. You always expected them to be miles better than you were but it was not always the case. So it gave you confidence. I also supported Ian Campbell at the Brunswick.

But my allegiance to the blues was paramount and I did find some of the folkies precious and pretentious, I must say. I was once representing The Brunswick playing my Dobro in the Best of the North West: a competition for folk singers. I looked around and saw a lot of pullovers.

"You put your fingers in your ears and I'll sing. I'm from Crewe – we do things differently there."

Musical Networking

As a pedestrian or cyclist when I was very young, I attended youth clubs in the west end of town as well as the south end of town. As soon as I was old enough I had a scooter and a motorbike. I could be a mod or a rocker depending on my mood! At seventeen I got a sports car which allowed me to extend my territory and from then on I made an effort to play clubs as far away as possible: Poynton, Leek, Macclesfield, Whitmore, Chester, Manchester, Bolton, Sheffield, Barnard Castle, London, Cornwall... performing two or three nights a week. The moment you perform you've made contact with everyone present and indirectly with the people they know. That's how people get to know about you and that's how you get to know about other potential venues. There were territories not strictly associated with musical circles. I'd been halfway round the country with Ralph, at a very early age: climbing and caving in Bristol, the Mendips, Derbyshire, Lancashire, Yorkshire, North Wales and Snowdonia, so this extended my circuit as well. Flying with Phil Brightman meant I could play gigs at the Flying Club at Sleep in Shropshire.

I remember one Moss Side, Manchester, club in particular: a pub in Denmark Street that might have been called The Denmark – the local of predominantly black drinkers. I would receive £10-£15 a night and a hat would also be passed round, some of the punters showing their appreciation by putting drugs into it. In those days I was not interested in drugs so a friend of mine would sell them and we'd share the cash.

The Cornish Connection

Pilgrimages to Cornwall started six weeks after my seventeenth birthday when I passed my test. The folk scene there was thriving in the mid Sixties and I did gigs at Mevagissey and The Folk Cottage in Mitchell near Newquay and became quite well known in the area. The Folk Cottage was a derelict house with a pit to piss in. It was during one of these gigs that I met Clive Palmer: Billy Connolly's banjo hero and one of the founder members of the psychedelic folk group, the Incredible String Band, formed in 1965. Their first album, recorded in 1966 had been *Melody Maker's* Folk Album of the Year and one of its tracks: "October Song" had been praised by Dylan. At that time – about 1969 – Clive had a four man band called – perversely – The Stockroom Five, specialising in jug band music and white blues. He eventually went on to do traditional acoustic music. Four decades later he came into the shop with Fluff (Claire Smith) who was playing with ISB in its most recent incarnation. He looked at me and said: "Dobro – voice – Mitchell – Cornwall." I think that about covered it.

Images From A Darkling Plain

I was once asked to leave a folk club because I fell off my stool: they thought I was drunk. I wasn't drunk: I had fallen asleep from boredom. I loathed folk music and bottom of the pile was the sea shanty. From the age of fifteen I visited many, many folk clubs with Pete and although a lot of the music was folk, I was also able to enjoy slide guitar which was Pete's passion. We went to see Ry Cooder and that really knocked me out. I liked music that was on the jazz/blues part of the spectrum. I listened to Leadbelly, Charlie Parker and Oscar Peterson.

An enduring memory of those times was riding pillion and holding Pete's precious guitar propped between him and me, travelling to live gigs anywhere and everywhere. Later, when we became joint owners of a Turner Climax I still had to hold the guitar because there was nowhere to put it. When we reached our destination – often Cornwall – we would look for local musical venues. It was on a visit to Cornwall that we met The Stockroom Five performing upstairs in a barn. I was very, very tired but afraid of falling asleep because of the spiders! I'd sat through various acts but Stockroom Five were electrifying. They brought me out of it.

At the end of gigs musicians used to do a bit of jamming, swapping addresses and songs and we were the last to go – at between 12.30 and 1.00. It was a strange night; there was a mist rising high enough to conceal the car. We fumbled about until we found it, then once inside I stood up like Boadicea to guide Pete out of the parking area. Anyone seeing this would think I was a strange apparition with only head and shoulders showing, moving slowly through the mist.

But everything was about Pete and his guitar. I remember key images rather than the whole thing: moments like Mevagissey town hall where they had miked up Pete's guitar. The moment he strummed the first note a hand reached out to whip the mic away because it was so powerful, the whole room vibrated.

Linda Johnson. **(16)**

Meeting Slade

The Cornish connection enabled me to meet Slade in 1971. We went down there to do a sound system for Strife, their support band. We put the PA system we had built into a JU 250 van and got as far as Cheltenham before it blew up. The van, that is. We had to transfer this massive PA to a rented van then we set off again, eventually arriving at the venue near St Ives. Noddy Holder was there but it was his guitarist Dave who looked at our equipment and uttered those immortal lines, "You can't put that there." After a bit of consternation and discussion the reason for this was revealed: "Because we're having a party and you're invited!" Strife were welcome – and this was the essence of our time with Slade – to use the PA Slade were using. So the gig became part of the party and the party became part of the gig. We were in familiar territory.

Then it was time to drive back to Cheltenham and tow the other van back to Crewe. It's amazing how we took long journeys, mishaps, changes of plan, impromptu parties and lack of sleep all in our stride. But when you're young these are adventures. Driving on the motorway with me in the hired van and Plum in the exploded JU 250 van, I became aware that the van I was towing was swaying across three lanes and dragging the vehicle I was driving with it. Plum had gone to sleep! In those days there was far less traffic on the roads. At Keele Bank things slowed down and I was able to stop. Fortunately.

When we eventually got back to Crewe we found that the hire van was as knackered as the JU 250 through carrying so much weight. Absolutely knackered: the brakes were fading with the exertion of the journey. I took the van to the Crewe branch of the national van hire firm, told them it was not fit to drive back to Cheltenham and got my money back. Plum had also disconnected the speedo so we only had to pay the mileage from Cheltenham to Crewe. I felt I could justify some dishonesty with big companies.

The Wayfarer: A Little Piano Player

This early period of intense musicianship had another strand. I was asked to run a blues night – my own blues night with acts to support me – by the proprietors of The Wayfarer, the night club in Nantwich which later became Gregory's. I've played gigs at this venue in all its manifestations; when I played at The Wayfarer I did solo performances but also played with the bands. As a slide player you could guest with anyone in those days. If, on my musical travels, I came across someone talented, I would book them. Other artists would be booked by the management, who knew somebody in Jimmy Powell's band. My support acts included Long John Baldry, Jimmy Powell – a man with a gun belt full of harmonicas – Elton John and Rod Stewart. On one occasion I was being supported by Jimmy Powell and the Five Dimensions when, as often happened, Long John Baldry was the guest singer and Reg Dwight – soon to be known as Elton John – was playing the piano. He was just a little piano player then. This seems strange now but it is less surprising when you realise that this particular ensemble was based on harmonica, guitar and two high-profile singers. The Elton John charisma could hardly develop in those circumstances but things would soon change for him.

I've met many musicians destined for fame – an autograph book of mine would have been like a bible – but I've usually found the famous fairly human and ordinary; besides, with important exceptions, I didn't usually rate their ability higher than my own. I had come across David Bowie and Marc Bolan when I played a folk club in London in the days before I went to university. It's strange to think of these mega stars as young teenagers negotiating – as I did – the lonely road of the floor singer. David Bowie is a good singer-songwriter who had concepts that were ahead of his time, combining theatricality with pop music, creating stage personae and extending the range of what was permissible. It's taken until now for young men to use guyliner! He was at the forefront of the space age with songs like "Major Tom", which had a futuristic feel of 2001 about it. His songs were cleverly written and original. He was the Dylan of pop music.

The Hot Rods

In 1970 when I was 21 I played with the Hot Rods (not the same band that had played at The Majestic) who had a residency at The Wayfarer. Roy Tatler – a great whisky lover who eventually settled in the Scilly Isles – was on rhythm guitar and vocals; I played bass guitar and Gary Burgess – alias Spadge, alias Gary B. Goode – was the singer and excellent frontman. Jonty Ellwood was on lead guitar and there were a variety of drummers including Reg Banks. Reg was to manage my Hanley shop and has had a subsequent career in retail, now dealing in vintage instruments. I was with the Hot Rods for about a year. Before then I'd played with Jonty Ellwood in daft duos at private parties for people who seemed to be millionaires. That's how it seemed to a working class lad.

Versatility

Pete Johnson played bass – he'd never played bass in his life! He used to wear a long morning coat, a T-shirt and a dickie bow. But the thing you noticed most were these silver wellies. It made sense when you realised he kept a bottle of beer in each one.

Jonty Ellwood. (17)

The Loneliness Of The Dobro Player

From an age that has experienced heavy metal, thrash and punk it's impossible to imagine what a culture shock the blues was, even as late as the Sixties. It was as if punk happened then, if you want some idea of the impact.

My taste in music didn't endear me to the folk enthusiasts, who said I had a good folk voice and should stick to sea shanties, nor did it qualify me for a stint in Hamburg. My music was not popular except to a niche audience, generally older than me. Although it is folk music the folkies didn't embrace it; what I brought was a world away from Jansch, Renbourn, Davey Graham or Martin Carthy. My voice wasn't liked; my music wasn't liked. Resonator guitars were another rarity and I had a Dobro; if the majority hadn't heard the blues I played, they certainly wouldn't know about slide guitar. In spite of opposition in folk circles I gradually introduced blues songs but it was a lonely field. In those days I was aware of only one good slide player in the UK: Sam Mitchell. He owned a National and I met him once.

These days, since the success of *Brothers In Arms* by Dire Straits everyone knows from the cover what a Dobro looks like and it's known as a Mark Knopfler guitar, even though he only used it on one track.

First Resonations And The Bolivian Coke Spoon

My interest in musical instruments *per se* began when I was fifteen. I've never been without a resonator guitar since. It was an unconventional choice but resonators have a modern *art deco* appearance, a unique tone and a wider range than either electric or ordinary wooden acoustic guitars. People who love them get dramatic about them; one note from a Dobro "that weird, crude, evocative plunk, full of wonderful echoes and overtones" (18) evokes a whole culture. Mike Harding introduced his Dobro as "my Barnsley Fighting Guitar" and it does have an edge of danger.

It's loud, too, and you seem to be able to get almost the same volume from a single string as you can from a whole chord…when I applied the old brass slide – Lord above, is that my train I hear a-coming? There ought to be a health warning stuck on the side; persons of a nervous disposition should on no account play this instrument anywhere near a crossroads after eleven o'clock at night…there's something about the things and people are going to keep on buying them…if anybody wants me, I'll be sitting on the porch with no shoes…

Rick Batey. (19)

Although resonators were aimed at Hawaiian musicians and guitarists in white dance orchestras, they were taken up by bluesmen, hillbillies, and jazz musicians. I was in good company!

I found my first vintage guitar in a garage belonging to my friend's father. The garage door was open to reveal piles of stuff and I noticed the edge of something under a pile of paint tins. With some difficulty I managed to extricate it from its grave; the barely-recognizable object was the squashed skeleton of a resonator guitar. I recognized it because I had seen Son House play a National and I'd also seen pictures in blues books. It wasn't the sort of thing you saw in a shop, unless it was a junk shop. Without knowing something about them you'd think they were a bit of a toy. But this was a Dobro – or the basis of one – and I had known the whole from the tiny part showing from beneath the tins. The resonator was there but squashed; the spider's web was there but a pencil was holding the strings up; the bridge was missing; a name had been deeply burnt into the wood with a soldering iron.

It was in pretty bad shape.

I swapped my car radio for it, took it home and assembled the bits. I knew that there were still some parts missing so I went back to the garage. Sure enough: there was the brass cover plate – likewise all squashed – and the two eyes. A man who worked in Rolls Royce sorted the cover plate and then the corroded silver work went to Niphos in Hope Street (aptly named) to be re-plated with copper, then nickel. I wanted it to look like a Russell Hobbs kettle: a duller shine than chrome which is a flashy surface thing. Nickel has depth and class. Armed with my intuition and my love of music, I put a veneer over the head stock to cover the burnt-in name and also replaced a part that was missing in the back. When asked the price for his work, the man from Niphos said, "Put it all together and play me a tune."

So I did.

I sold this guitar more than ten years ago to an international bio chemist who kept in touch for ages and brought me a coke spoon from Bolivia. The guitar goes all round the world with him; it could so easily have rotted away in that long-ago garage.

An Odd Couple

At the beginning of the Seventies I had a residential at a Congleton pub and that's how I met Des, my life long friend and occasional musical collaborator.

Way Ahead Of His Time

Pete, in those days was a dapper young businessman with a job. When I first heard Pete play all those years ago I'd never seen anyone play like that before. It was quite moving. He was way ahead of his time. Nowadays, perhaps for the past, say, fifteen years, there is more appreciation for that type of music but he was so ahead of his time. There has been a bond between us ever since.

Des Parton. (20)

Guitars And Stop Watches

There's a 1901 notice from the London & North Western Railway which states: "It is forbidden for vagrants, beggars, itinerant musicians and females of doubtful reputation to enter these premises. By order".

You'd think that it had been "by order" of my father. In the opposite corner to my musical passion was my father's continued disapproval of it. When my mother died the subtle moderating influence she had over my father went, and things became very fraught between us over my yet to be decided future. I wanted to be a musician; I *was* a musician. Every home had a piano in those days but I wanted to play the guitar and this made me a renegade. If my music had been classical then perhaps his antagonism would have been less strong, but this was rock 'n' roll and the guitar was already my downfall, seducing me from studying for my O-levels or becoming a committed athlete. My relationship with

Nantwich and Acton Grammar School was equally turbulent; I was troubled and rebellious and class-conscious. Aged sixteen, things came to a head and I floored my father – something to do with me not coming up to expectations and his guilt about my troubled home life. Perhaps if we had talked about my mother, things would have been easier but I was too aggressive and strong-willed to fit into school life any longer, and that wasn't his fault. I was effectively if not officially expelled: refused entry into the Upper Sixth in spite of my remarkable prowess in athletics.

I am sorry to have to advise you that his behaviour here, his aggressive attitude to authority and his influence on his fellows, make it impossible for us to accept him for an Advanced course. (21)

I was a rebel with a cause: to me the school was riddled with class prejudice. I came from working class Crewe, not rural, well-heeled Nantwich. My school hadn't caught up with the new spirit of educational equality for all; it was still imbued with the values of privilege and the prejudice of class.

The school spat me out and partly in deference to my father I went to college to do A levels, then joined the Civil Service where even the considerable amount of horseplay and foreplay in the Filing Room could never compensate for the boredom of such a job. This was *Billy Liar* territory and I left after a year. I considered joining the Forces: all three invited me for interview; all three accepted me. One of the things we had to do was to give a talk. I suppose they were interested in communication skills and individual interests as well as political beliefs. I talked about the blues and slavery. The reason I didn't join up was because you had to sign up for sixteen years and that was too long. But it was interesting to see the same hierarchical attitudes in school, in the Civil Service and in the Forces. At one point I was shown into the officers' mess on my own where it was silver service with half a dozen people waiting on me. In all the services I found the sergeants' mess level more comfortable socially.

Throughout my white collar days I was playing music but I was trying to find work I liked and which would give me the security my father valued so much. That's how I ended up at Manchester University enrolled for a

B.Ed. following my two brothers who were both teachers. I left within a year after a dispute over leadership styles. My tutor was in favour of 'progressive' approaches to education and I had a more authoritarian position with regard to the tough kids at my teaching placement. Subsequently running a business and a band my instinct was reinforced: there has to be a chief and rules and everyone has to be clear where they stand.

Frustrating career-wise, fortunately my time at Manchester flowed musically.

After Manchester, I was getting into that morningless condition that afflicts the unemployed: late nights and up after midday. This offended my father's sense of the way things should be. He arranged for me to go and work on the bins. I quite enjoyed it; I was physically strong; I enjoyed being out of doors and I had the incentive of finishing by 2.00 and 11.00 on Fridays. All for a fairly decent wage and plenty of time for music. It was not the most pleasant job; the night soil run: I couldn't hack that. The worst thing was a bloke eating a pork pie after we'd just finished collecting shit! I did the job for two months and then went to work at Calmic as a Works Study Officer. When asked why I should get the job, I answered that I had the "air apparent" for it and I think this witty answer clinched things. I was then made redundant and went to work at Ideal Standard in Middlewich. Theoretically excellent, I failed on the practical side of my Industrial Degree. Why was this? I was hopeless at stopwatching and observing peoples' work rates. I felt it wasn't possible to do this unless you'd actually done the job yourself.

By anyone's standards I was upwardly mobile: a homeowner with a respectable job, married to a teacher. I had conformed, with some difficulty, to my father's ideals as well as keeping faith with the music.

However, I was again made redundant. Both redundancies were carried out on the last in first out principle and I found myself on the dole. I had failed to fit in with the educational establishment and the economics of management consultancy had also ejected me. It was at this moment that the musical imperative took over and my career went in a more conducive direction. With hindsight it seems obvious that I was always going to spend every waking moment on music and music-related activities: the karma was just so strong. The jerky rhythms of recent times were about to end.

Cabinets And Coffins: A Plum Business

There was an important convergence: aged twenty-two, I once again came across David Ernest Barrow – a man I had known since the age of fifteen – at the dole office. Plum was out of prison; I was out of work. During the time in the mid Sixties when we were going to The Oddfellows on a Sunday evening with our rock band Axe, along with most of the other local musicians, I realised that there was a potential market amongst this fraternity for repairing and supplying equipment. I had the eye for a good venture and a good musical purchase and Plum had the practical skills. Here was an opportunity for collaboration: making, hiring and selling speaker cabinets. So we started a partnership using Plum's front room in Ford Lane. We subsequently took over a workshop in Hewitt Street, just off Nantwich Road – where, incidentally, coffins used to be manufactured. Eventually, in 1971, premises on Nantwich Road were taken on the proceeds of the Hewitt Street business and I came off the dole. We had started with nothing but built up the business steadily and gradually: buying and selling guitars, making and selling speakers and hiring out sound systems. We bartered speaker boxes for instruments from other shops; we made equipment for local bands and I continued to collect guitars. In those days they were not worth a great deal but I saw a future in it. I used to go to Birmingham and Manchester to buy and I would buy to order as well. Once a month there were enough orders from Crewe musicians to warrant a 5 a.m. journey to London. A thousand pounds would eventually convert into fifteen hundred pounds worth of sales. Plum thought I was off on a nice day out: a view that was to lead to a rift between us.

Orders flooded in and I continued to travel about to buy for people. Everybody wanted to play in a band and there were plenty of local venues in those days. And young people had money.

Endings

Loss has been tangible in each decade of my being and has set the tone of my life. Music is by nature emotional and intuitive. As a musician I am particularly open to emotional involvement, so separation is always going to hit me hard.

In my infancy it was Uncle Willie Billington: my father's best friend and my favourite uncle. My favourite storytelling war hero of an uncle. Willie had received the equivalent of a George Cross in Greece, had founded a motorcycle display team and was a Regimental Sergeant Major in the Commandos. Aged forty-two he had come home to his mother's house to die. It was all in the air: not quite spoken and not quite clear, yet I knew something hushed and momentous was going on. When he died he was laid out in his mother's bay-fronted net-curtained front room in Ruskin Road and there was something important to see but they wouldn't let me see him. Even though I was on my father's shoulders. His was the biggest military funeral held in Crewe.

I was three years old.

It was shortly after this that my mother collapsed. Twelve years later she died. Three years after that Bert Bellamy suddenly died. His was the first death associated with the musical side of my life; there were to be many more.

In my twenties my father became ill coincidentally with having his teeth out. Feeling awful he sought medical opinion and was sent for radiotherapy at Christie's. His terminal illness – diagnosed as cancer of the chest cavity – lasted for nine months, though he was originally given three months. I accompanied him when he went for treatment and me and my stepmother Vera looked after him at home. I was his youngest son but I had to be the man. I became *his* father though he was too proud to allow me to nurse him. Vera did that but I administered his medicine in the last few weeks of his life. While my father was dying we became extremely close and he divulged things he wouldn't have said; I'm more emotional about it now than I was then. He who had such a strong constitution became a frail little thing with everything drawn in and a grey skeletal face. My father died in my arms; I was helping him to breathe and get his medication down when the terrible guttural struggle suddenly stopped.

"He's gone – thankfully," I said.

I regret not giving him more morphine in the last days. His final two and a half weeks were spent in a coma. In fact, if I'd known more and been stronger he'd have died two months earlier.

Mother had died unseen in a hospital; I'd been prevented from seeing my uncle laid out in a front room. But *this* death was in my arms. I felt it; I heard it; I was strong enough to deal with it because I had to be. I didn't want to see my father again but I went to the mortuary for Vera's sake. Like with my mother, they'd done a face job but his 'smile' was more of a grimace – well there hadn't been much in his life to make him smile.

My mother's death left me an angry teenager; my father's death left me grown-up. I was official and controlled at his funeral; I had to be because everyone else was crying on my shoulder. Wearing his suit, I found myself in his role. Like my father I have found myself in situations where I had to take responsibility for what was happening, where people were relying on me to sort things out.

My father hadn't lived to see the ultimate success of my business. He had been really upset when I opened a music shop instead of carrying on with a career in management consultancy or sport – my music still meant nothing to him. But before he died I had already begun to make serious money. Partly for his sake, I bought a Volvo 3 litre – almost a Rolls Royce to Norman Johnson and a very posh car in its day – and I took him all over the place in it. He must have realised that I had made a success of something.

The death of my father in 1972 marked the end of an era that had seen the establishment of a viable and growing sound system business called Custom Amplification with branches in Crewe and Hanley, an embryonic business in vintage guitars, the purchase of a house in Sandbach, my marriage to Linda and a burgeoning musical career.

The main strands of my life had been established from my childhood: the seductive, though limited power of luxury, self-reliance, confronting bullying, the precariousness of life.

And the blues.

1972 saw the inauguration of Snakey Jake's Dead Skunk Band.

Notes: Section One

(1) War has its ironies. Whilst my uncle struggled with the moral issues of pacifism and my father fretted about being responsible for making life and death decisions and saw unspeakable sights, Fred Watts was kept in a reserved occupation. And that occupation was…making coffins.

(2) Quoted from Son House's "Death Letter".

(3) From an undated letter Bina left for her husband.

(4) From website: bluesandrhythm.co.uk

(5) Fred Watts, interviewed by Sandra Gibson, 2006.

(6) *Jazz Journal* August 1963.

(7) Joe Boyd: *White Bicycles*, published by Serpent's Tail, 2005.

(8) Woman's Hour item, BBC Radio Four, 16th July 2009.

(9) Joe Boyd: *White Bicycles*, published by Serpent's Tail, 2005.

(10) Carl Palmer: *Rock & Roll, an unruly history*, published by Harmony Books, 1995.

(11) Quoted in *Rock & Roll, an unruly history* by Carl Palmer, published by Harmony Books, 1995.

(12) Zoe Johnson, interviewed by Sandra Gibson 26th April 2007.

(13) Linda Johnson, interviewed by Sandra Gibson 4th November 2008.

(14) *Song Talk* magazine.

(15) Robin Denselow, *The Guardian*, Wednesday 17th December 2008.

(16) Linda Johnson, interviewed by Sandra Gibson 4th November 2008.

(17) Jonty Ellwood, from a conversation with Sandra Gibson, 28th March 2010.

(18) Review by Rick Batey in *Guitarist* 1990.

(19) Ibid.

(20) Des Parton, interviewed by Sandra Gibson May 2006.

(21) Headmaster, Nantwich and Acton Grammar School, letter dated 20th June 1966.

SECTION TWO

In The Wake Of One Long Party

The next section of my life was like a pinball machine: perpetual motion through bizarre, colourful spaces, bouncing between extremes: farce and tragedy, wealth and bankruptcy, authority and hedonism, disintegration and survival.

It was touch and go. But the music never stopped.

Skunking

Mixing Pleasure With Business

Since 1972 my music shop has been the hub of a wide and loose social, musical and economic network. The music, the business and the lifestyle were so intertwined that a bit of exploratory strumming soon became a full-on session and people hired amps and bought guitars to a background of jamming and horseplay.

There's a photo of me standing over a tuba. The tuba is standing in a bath full of soapy water. Drunken shenanigans? Well – there was plenty of that but this time there was a serious purpose. I wouldn't abuse a musical instrument; I was just using the best method to clean the tuba. But I was also aware of how bizarre it was and I had fun doing it. This image, though taken in recent years, captures the ethos of our musical life.

There were plenty of ways to mix business with pleasure. A young punk band used to hire equipment from the shop. They were not that organized and took on a girl to manage them who had an unusual way of negotiating the deal. She had only a tenner to pay for £15 worth of equipment. "I'll settle for a blow job then!" I said jokingly. The plucky girl took me up on the offer and did an expert job cheerfully and thoroughly. I remembered her for some time because she left a reminder. She had bitten me, as I was able to remind her twenty-five years later when she revisited me – her bartering punk days long gone. She was now an Oxbridge lecturer.

Pinned Against The Wall

Outside pursuits impinged on life at the shop in a farcical way. I once had an eight-man, fully supplied inflatable life raft stored in my upstairs office. It had a painter line and it was this that Whitty became drunkenly fixated upon. "It's a painter line. I'm a painter – it must be mine!" Whitty

– a talented artist – was pointing unsteadily at the painter line: "I'm a painter – it must be mine!" Within moments he and Slim and Shep and Deannie were in cartoon land: pinned against the wall by this gigantic, rapidly inflating raft. Whitty hadn't been able to resist pulling the painter line. Well who could?

Special Brew

When I first met Pete Johnson he had the Nantwich Road shop and his entourage consisted of Slim, Shep, Al Dean, Plum and Pete Whittingham. My early memories are graphic. The group favoured tea as a beverage – as long as it had whisky added. In one of the milk bottles scattered about the place, overturned and now containing rancid yoghurt, Boomtown the Rat was to be seen: quite dead but a dominating presence.

I also remember Plum's reputation for taking a dump in your speaker cabinet if he didn't like you. I was initiated into Special Brew as a result of knowing Pete Johnson, It was de rigueur *in the shop in those days: warm, flat Special Brew* a la *Keith Richards before breakfast.*

John Darlington. (1)

It Wasn't Just the Dog

I used to go to Pete's shop on Nantwich Road to buy guitar strings during the school lunch hour. In those days Pete Johnson had a big dog – an Alsatian Old English cross: a formidable big dog. But it wasn't just the dog that was intimidating for me as a fifteen year-old entering the shop for the first time. There were people in there, drinking and raucous, most of the times I went. There was no sense you were a customer. It was like walking into a crowd of Hell's Angels or Motorhead's dressing room. One of them – Mick Wicklow – looked like Lemmy. It was blokes and beards and beer, playing and singing. Not your average people. It was a masculine world: the world of the alpha male and I was only a lad.

Andy Boote. (2)

Carry On

Some days, being in the shop was like being in a *Carry On* film. A prim and proper girl rented one of the upstairs rooms. One evening there was a timid knocking on my door: Miss Prim was standing there, looking anxious. "Have you seen my pussy?" she asked. It was difficult keeping a straight face.

One of my partners did secretarial work for me. There was some confusion about the dress code and I found it pretty hard to concentrate with her dressed in a waitress outfit! Pretty hard. She seduced me over my tax returns. The short skirt and dark stockings were every man's fantasy and appropriateness didn't seem to come into it! I enjoy the memory.

There were plenty of opportunities for, well, opportunistic sex. Imagine the scene at breakfast in a posh hotel: me casually dressed in jeans and my partner with dishevelled, uncombed hair, wearing her evening gown. This generous girl had asked me to chauffeur her to and from a works do. Realizing that I would be unable to relax and drink because I was 'on duty' she spontaneously booked us a room for the night. There was another escapade with a girl who was not as big as she appeared: she kept a ferret down her tee-shirt. I had somehow ended up in her flat, unfortunately unable to raise more than a smile because my in-laws lived across the road. The *impasse* was overcome by the sexual dexterity of this animal lover.

The ferret was safely stowed.

You never know what will happen after a performance or how you will store a memory of a good time. A woman helped me carry my stuff back from a gig. I invited her in for coffee and one thing led to another. She stayed the night. It was obvious that she was a married woman so the relationship had to end, as far as I was concerned. But she had the most amazing nipples…I can still see them now. Amazing.

Snakey Jake's Dead Skunk Band

Snakey Jake's Dead Skunk Band evolved out of these circumstances at the Nantwich Road shop and was more than the sum total of its four musicians. There was already an embryonic band: most of the original line-up were musicians who worked for me, and Pete Whittingham wanted me to join because we were already musical partners. Initially I felt like an adjunct but I played for fun. Whitty and I became the front men playing guitar and writing and arranging songs. Alan Dean was the bassist and Melvin Allan – the only one who didn't work in the shop – played drums. The Skunk Band soon had my stamp on it and all the songs we played came from my musical background and approach, apart from the original material. I'm still surprised that this happened because I always doubted my abilities. Still do.

People ask about the name. The three Johnson brothers were always known as "Jake" and the rest refers to a Loudon Wainwright III country song about a dead skunk in the middle of the road stinking to high heaven – a song that had the distinction of being number one in Little Rock, Arkansas for six weeks. I wonder why.

The essence of the Skunk Band was variety and Leadbelly was a strong influence in that respect, but we were also bang up-to-date with numbers from Pink Floyd's *Atom Heart Mother* such as "Fat Old Sun" and "If". We never aimed to sound like any other band but drew together the strands from my early musical experiences: amalgamating elements of pop, rock, folk, folk-rock, blues and original material with Vaudeville and Whitty's Celtic connection. Our covers were not so much covers as re-interpretations and some people preferred our version to the original. We could adapt our music to our mood, the mood of the audience, the current composition of the band – all of this. We could edge it with blues, popularise it, folk-rock it or ham it up. We could emphasise the melodic, the raucous, the humorous, the rhythmic or the pathetic. We could be lyrical-emotional, drunken-sentimental, and bawdy-hilarious. We were rhythmic rock-basic or floating tuneful harmony. The band did well and received critical acclaim.

Another aspect of the Skunk Band was its theatricality. In spite of the anarchic behaviour I always had a professional attitude towards public performances. I believed you shouldn't go on stage wearing what you arrived in. Our dressing up was part of the performance and not a fashion statement. Phil Doody remembers a bass player who wore one glove. There were a lot of these idiosyncratic performance details and Phil probably wouldn't have remembered him otherwise. Incidentally, the most valued item in the auction of Michael Jackson memorabilia on 22nd November 2009 was the rhinestone-studded glove – just the one – he wore in the Motown 25 celebration in 1983 where he first did his famous moonwalk. It fetched $420,000 from a Hong Kong buyer.

There's a black and white photo of me in my Skunk Band suit: slightly shabby, moth-eaten and with wide lapels. The £2.50 Oxfam label was attached for years, until Mick Wicklow borrowed it for a respectable do at the Civic Hall, Nantwich. The shop threw in the bowler hat I'm also wearing. To complete the parody there's a quaver-shaped diamante brooch on the lapel which also failed to survive Mick's evening out. What is evident is not so much the outfit, as the single-minded concentration on my face as I play the music. Our dressing up had a humorous edge but we were always serious about the music – which isn't the same as being solemn. I still have a great big kipper tie Cathy made for me. Whitty painted a Rubens nude with a skunk tail on it – it's a classic. Eugene bought two ties and hand-painted one with a Dobro logo, the other with a National logo. The occasion was the Resonator Show but he was too ill to go. I've worn the Dobro tie for Skunking. I have been known to wear one tie at the front and one at the back.

There's another photo – again black and white – of Pete Whittingham at the microphone wearing a plaid dressing gown. When he was drunk we dressed him up and put makeup on him. This photograph has poignancy, actually: it captures a sad clown moment.

Marking the transition between private person and public performer – a common enough convention – is psychologically as well as visually important as preparation and announcement. As the pop explosion progressed bands increased the gap between their ordinary life and their stage life. Pink Floyd were taking pop performance into the realm of spectacle. As things escalated some musicians wore the sort of makeup that completely masked their identity. King Crimson started their show in Hanley with a screen showing waves crashing on a beach then one by one the musicians came on the stage, starting with the drummer, thus creating suspense. At the end of the show it all happened in reverse. There was a standing ovation and the audience started stamping their feet for an encore. This was impossible, of course: in those circumstances you can't do a conventional encore because you would have to recreate the world you had just dissolved. A Shakespearian actor can't come back and say a few lines once the play is over. It would be absurd and it would break the spell.

Other bands introduced ritual destruction into their act. The Who routinely smashed up their instruments. It wasn't just gimmicky sensationalism; according to them it was like sacrificing an animal. During their debut on American TV Keith Moon blew up his drums, setting fire to Townsend's hair and causing Miss Bette Davis to faint – a delirious moment. Jimi Hendrix set fire to his guitar. He needn't have bothered – he already had! Personally though, I feel that any musician worth his salt wouldn't destroy his instrument. Perhaps in his case he did it because he didn't like what he had become: you have to remember what Jimi said about his commercial success when he cut short "Hey Joe" on *The Lulu Show* (1969) before launching into Cream's "Sunshine Of Your Love".

The Skunk Band didn't go to such lengths – shows and sacrificial goats cost money for one thing but we weren't the sort of band to make such a demarcation between ourselves and the audience or put ourselves into a situation where we couldn't be spontaneous about encores.

In all bands with longevity, people come and go, drift in and hang about, fall over, fall out, start their own band…die. I've always said that I could assemble the Skunk Band at a moment's notice because I've built up a large loose network of musicians I can call on. The Skunk Band had at least five phases – not that anyone was counting – and the fluidity was part of its vitality and success. Most of the musicians I called in had heard the set and knew the feel of it. When I was billed as "Pete 'Snakey Jake' Johnson & Special Friends", this was a reference to the wide musical circle I could call on for support.

Parallel Performer

A steady girlfriend of the time was a performer in her own right: she was a model with an almost professional attitude to nudity and a relationship with the camera that brought this out. Photos reveal her fun-loving, mischievous nature and her slim, smooth body. She obviously enjoys the fantasy role playing afforded by the fetishist clothing and accessories. The nicest, most erotic photograph shows her in a white satin bodice with one breast almost covered. She is looking away from the camera, which in other photos she defiantly confronts. In another photo she is sitting on my friend Keith Brammer – lucky him! But all you can see of him are his oily hands. He is obliterated by her full-frontal pose; her relationship is with the camera, not him or the person behind the camera. She is a woman quite comfortable in the nude yet not aggressively sexual, having an ethereal quality: varied moods flickering over her. Chameleon is a good description: she could easily and instinctively blend in with whichever crowd or boyfriend she was with, and could and should have been an actress. Talk about multitasking: she could do regional accents and monologues, strip and tell jokes all at the same time.

The Crown in Audlem used to hold a weekly disco for which I did the sound equipment. It was the end of the night and people were lingering for a late night drink. Someone remarked that "The Stripper" had tempted no dancers; my girlfriend said she would dance to it so someone put the record on again. She wore a long evening gown and she started to dance. Sexy and erotically teasing, she was very accurate in her timing and by the end of the record she had skillfully removed her dress to reveal she was wearing nothing underneath and had everything to show. Then she walked slowly to the bar, sat down and ordered a drink.

She had style.

Never seen a landlord more delighted. He invited her to dance at The Crown professionally but this resulted in an interesting demarcation between the amateur and the professional. What had been excellent as a spontaneous gesture became banal in different circumstances. She wore a bathing suit and managed not to look sexy or dance sexily in it. Perhaps the amateur performance came from the heart; the professional dancing from the head.

I remembered this when I went to Hooters in the US: a well-known establishment famous for its sexy girls. I beg to differ: they wore sports clothes and very firm bras.

Strangely enough, a later girlfriend illustrated a different side of this audience-orientated behaviour. She favoured public sex but it wasn't public because no-one knew what we were doing on the park bench! She had had sexy glamour photos taken before she met me and one of the studies is very revealing but not in the sense you would think. The photograph I have of her is professionally posed and very static. It's arty and in a *fin de siecle* setting: she leans on the mantelpiece of an Edwardian tiled grate. There is a conch shell – a typical piece of erotica – on the mantelpiece and an oval-shaped mirror above, which doesn't reflect her face, or anything else. She is dressed in a pair of brief knickers, and a sheer flimsy calf-length black skirt through which you can see her suspenders. Her dark stockings have seams and she wears high-heeled shoes: not stilettos as in the early Sixties, but something more of the New Look Fifties style. Her top is see-through and she is wearing a black bra. She has a beautiful hourglass figure but the setting and the stillness in the body give a feeling of detachment, amplified by the fact we don't see the face. The whole effect is one of the artful use of fetishist clothes and items, to produce an erotic tableau. But it's depersonalized because you can't see the face. She has turned her back on the viewer. Did she dress up entirely for herself?

Whilst with me she changed her image and took to wearing neutral, unisex clothing but I don't know why.

Chameleon

Our band was subsidised by a side band called Chameleon that did regular gigs for money so that the weekly wage would be fairly stable. The line-up was Pete Whittingham and me in our usual roles on guitar and vocals, Melvyn on drums and Keith Brammer on bass guitar. He was a fellow sportsman who'd played in a band with Geoff Ambrose: the owner of Speedway Motorcycles. Al Dean had a position in another band anyway. Chameleon was fun; it had a popular, commercial bias and was conceived as a local way to supplement earnings without involving the Skunk Band. In order to raise the status of the main band I had to separate it from the undiscriminating need to get paid. I sought gigs further afield and I was choosy and uncompromising in order to get the band into the proper circuits.

Your Morning Call, Sir

I decided the most important thing in running a band was being straight: I was the chief and people had to be professional about things. It might not have looked that way on the surface, when I was digging Whitty out of the pub but underneath things were tightly run. It was the same with the business – otherwise we wouldn't have been so successful. And somehow it all worked because there was consensus; we were all mates; we had a good time. I don't think I saw myself as a conventional boss – I was a communist at heart in those days. I'd leave Whitty in charge and he'd sell one packet of strings and then disappear to Holland's to buy cooking sherry or I'd arrive back to be told by Shep and Dean that he'd gone across to The Barrel. On one occasion I got them to dress up in white coats and go and fetch him as if they were carting him off to an asylum. There were always practical jokes going on. But the work got done; the music got played.

Phil Grice – Gricey – is a good example of what I mean. He was a good guitarist who stuck with pop and didn't become part of the Skunk Band but he worked at the shop. He was possibly the laziest lad I've ever met, and I had to go and dig him out of bed, cup of tea at the ready, if I wanted him to come to work. I am, and was then, very tolerant of erratic timekeeping as long as the priority work was done. Plum was similarly poor at morning timekeeping. Once the business was really up and running you had to have a bit of a hierarchy though the rules weren't conventional. They were based on friendship and good will and flexibility.

Making A Snake

I recall the amount of preparation that had to go into equipment for gigs. One night we were making a "snake" for an important gig the next day. It involved

32 channels, 64 plugs and 3 soldered joints per plug. We were doing this upstairs at Nantwich Road and it was going to take all night.

With a big bag of grass.

Anyway – it got late and I had to let my wife know I wouldn't be home. We didn't have a phone so I had to phone the old lady next door. She was religious and squeaky and I got the old spliff giggles and I couldn't communicate with her for laughing and in the end I couldn't leave the message. I think it was a crucial moment in relation to my wife. We were in two different worlds. There are pivotal moments when you start working in the business. You get a different outlook on life and that separates you from other people.

Wayne Davies (Slim). (3)

Plum: Not One Drop Spilt

I had a long acquaintance with Plum; he went in and out of my life even after we had split up as business partners. I admired his practical skills and thought his strengths were complementary to my own; the original partnership was a sound idea in more ways than one. Unfortunately he didn't know how I operated. He thought my lucrative visits to cities like Manchester, Liverpool and London to buy stuff for customers were pleasure trips and believing this he rightly felt resentful. He certainly hadn't rated my input – in fact he probably thought there was no input from me. So he wanted to split up. Plum kept Hewitt Street and I had Nantwich Road; I retained the Custom Amplification trade name and Plum renamed his section: Air. We had a share-out of stock and there was some animosity between us, but only initially. He continued making and supplying cabinets and if I wanted a cabinet I might have it off him but I was much more interested in retail than manufacture. Hewitt Street was in effect a wholesale factory shop. If Plum had listened to me I could have made it into a manufacturing unit but at the end of the day Plum was only interested in having just enough money for his present needs and never worried about the future: he just spent the money without considering tax or VAT or money for materials. Unfortunately his practical excellence was not enough to compensate for his lack of business acumen and he went bankrupt within six months. Meanwhile I had a growing business in vintage guitars which Gordon-Smith was advertising.

Plum could be very generous; he had a heart of gold and a head of lead; if you needed £100 he'd give it you, but he might have to consider robbing it from someone else! He was very keen on live music and would both perform and encourage others to perform. Everyone remembers the famous occasion when Plum was playing at The Royal. The worse for wear – he fell off the stage onto the dance floor – holding his beer intact whilst all the time his bass guitar was feeding back. With not a drop spilt. Not one drop.

Plum went off to Rhyl doing what he was good at: getting by, helping to run a night club, building bars, doing sound systems. He also dealt in cars, mainly cheap knackers. He was a survivor.

In the Eighties Plum lived in a caravan at the back of the premises, did repairs and ran the shop, freeing me up to go sailing. I rented a double garage behind the shop and Plum started to do some installation work again. I could offer customised PA systems: I did the assessment of needs, the negotiation and the selling then all I had to do was tell Plum what was required and he would build it, drive it to the place needing it and install it. Job done. The building would fall down before one of Plum's installations would budge! We supplied customised equipment for all the local clubs and dozens in the Potteries. When the clubs went into decline we started getting our own equipment back in the shop for resale.

There was the notion of a separate company: Decibel Sounds. It was to be the heir to Air! But before that could happen we split up again, this time for different reasons: we'd had a robbery and the tools went and the garage was no longer available for rent. So Plum went to Rhyl again. Then back he came and I re-employed him and he looked after the shop and did repairs as before. I think he latched on to me because I was stable and settled. People can only do this if they know this about you – they need to be able to predict.

But his enthusiasm for live music endured.

Come On Down

He was totally enthusiastic about live music and used to encourage people to have a go. Plum would drive up in his tiny car, with his big belly and he'd say, "Come on down – I'll get you a drum kit." He was just so keen for people to play. He'd resurrect Jam Night anywhere and he'd encourage young lads to play. He did the sound at The Limelight when it first opened.

Andy Smith. (4)

Ozzie: Spraying It Around

My business and musical career wouldn't have survived without people on hand to make stuff and shift stuff and set up stuff – unconventional characters who didn't quite fit in anywhere else and who contributed to the anarchic times. Sometimes when you visited Plum's workshop you'd feel rain. You'd look up and there would be Ozzie: a character who looked like Roger Daltrey – a Roger Daltrey who'd been kicked all round a football pitch – and he'd be pissing on you from the exposed beams. An old prison trick. The showers were even more tropical when Plum joined in.

Anyone buying a cabinet made by Ozzie and Plum got more than they paid for. They left charming messages on the inside such as, "Fuck off – don't be nosy!" or rude nudes – Ozzie could draw – or solid bodily substances. They didn't believe in customer care. You'd borrow the van and find the windscreen wipers wouldn't budge. Ozzie had left a heavy present on the windscreen: a huge dark turd that gradually became more pliable as the rain did its job until liquid shit was flying everywhere. What a journey that was.

But I could be basic with my practical joking as well. Whilst shooting on Beattock Moor with my dog Rafe I met a dog handler who admired his obedience. He asked me how I achieved it. "Oh – I give him the occasional wank," I said. The next time I met the dog handler he had been handling dogs in more ways than one. "You know what you told me to do? Well it didn't work," he said.

I kept a very straight face.

Ozzie – Keith Osbourne – wasn't a musician but he would be a roadie. You had to keep an eye on him because he attracted mither. One night he and I were leaving Gorstey Hall after doing the sound system for a band. It was quite late on; we'd had a few drinks and Ozzie decided to piss on me. Soon it was pee wars round and round a parked car, both of us trying to score hits. The car was a Rolls Royce. It was the Mayor of Crewe's Rolls Royce. There was a woman sitting in it wearing a very big necklace. The Mayoress of Crewe! She was sitting very still. Very, very still.

Things were always rather primitive with Ozzie.

Melvyn Allen: Drumming For Pete

Melvyn started his working life as an apprentice engineer at Rollmakers. He enjoyed the theory but disliked the practical work so he left and became a drummer – part of the first Skunk Band line-up, earning enough to keep the wolf from the door. He used to have a Ludwig Super Classic '63 kit, like the Beatles. I have a very high estimation of him: he's the best drummer I've ever heard. He can do a bass drum roll on a single bass drum faster than anyone on a double bass drum and various famous drummers have been mesmerised by him. Melvyn's drumming had loads of volume because he learnt his technique from a jazz drummer. He's the only one I know who can do a drum solo which sounds like music, not just drumming.

I've also valued his loyalty. Melvyn had the opportunity to join Tony McPhee and the Groundhogs at the time they were backing John Lee Hooker. Both John Lee and Champion Jack Dupree regarded them highly and they had toured with the Stones.

"I drum for Pete," Melvyn said.

Melvyn was the only member of the band I allowed to smoke on stage. This was because Melvyn Allen smoking a cigarette had great theatrical potential. The cigarette would move slowly from one side of his mouth to the other, the ash still intact, such was his dynamic control.

Al Dean

Like policemen, drummers and bass players come as a pair. Al came with Melvyn and became the Skunk Band's bass player. He had served an apprenticeship as an electrician. An innovative musician, he was also excellent as a sound engineer. Al and I went separate ways musically when he went down the pop and R & B route coincidentally with the demise of Nantwich Road. This split is understandable; I could no longer afford to employ anyone and people had to seek their main chance in order to survive financially. At one point Melvyn, Al Dean, an organist called Kenny Jones and a lead singer called Chris Steele – a melodic Joe Cocker – together with Phil Grice and Phil Colclough were in a band called Mustard. Mustard did the gruelling Hamburg stint. Years later, Melvyn, Al Dean and John Darlington went to South Africa and Kenny Jones was their contact there, having emigrated some years earlier.

I can't help noticing how extensive and kaleidoscopic musical networks are and how many of my musical friends and acquaintances emigrated or died young. Chris Steele – the singer with Mustard – went to New Zealand where he had a successful career in light entertainment. He unfortunately died of cancer. John Billington – an early musical acquaintance and long-time friend – also went to New Zealand. He became a film cameraman and covered the Balkans War. He died accidentally in 2009 when he missed his footing getting onto his yacht from his dinghy. His body was found in the sea.

Al Dean, a very competent musician, went on to have local commercial success, with Big Blue House and with The Holding Company. His latest band is Flight 505. He still builds PA systems and has personally built a luxury studio. He also supplies the sound systems for the Audlem Proms and organizes the Nantwich Blues Festival with Phil Martin.

What To Do With Celery (5)

Phil Doody is a drummer. From time to time your band gets stranded in hostile terrain and you need someone to rescue you. He was the one who towed us back safely from the red light district in Leeds – of which more later. On a recent visit to the shop he described some of the times he spent with us in the Skunking days as "a lifetime in a day". There was a gig at the Joiner's Arms, Chorley. Phil had been drinking hard and became violently ill. So the band shared his packed lunch! When Al Dean saw the celery he didn't know whether to eat it or smoke it – according to Phil. The pub had accommodation for bands: a sort of communal dormitory and when it was time to go to bed Phil was surprised when no-one wanted to share with him. Could it have been the smell of *eau de puke*? Shep's excuse was that he always slept at the foot of *my* bed, "like a faithful dog".

Everyone Loved Pete

When the folk club at The Brunswick first opened Whitty and I influenced others to look at musical roots. By the time we supported the inauguration of the Sandbach Folk Club in 1972, Pete Whittingham and I had done quite a lot to establish acoustic music in the area. That occasion was effectively the outing of the Skunk Band, a bringing together of our combined musical influences: myself, Whitty, Melvyn and Al. The heart of the band was the musical compatibility between Whitty and I, combining and balancing my blues and his folk-rock; his songwriting and my arranging: a compatibility that found its voice in our instinctive harmonising. We were part of the musical trends of the Sixties and Seventies, encompassing an acoustic revival that manifested in folk rock, psychedelic folk and a growing interest in the blues, as well as traditional folk and a pop explosion with blues influences. I was keener to honour the earlier manifestations of the blues from the Twenties and Thirties rather than the later urban blues exemplified by the Chicago musicians. We pushed out the boundaries with our combination of material and we also did comedy numbers – unusual in a young band.

Pete, an artist, a lyrical musician with a good sense of humour, was also a wild, hard-drinking man, loved by all who met him though he could have mood swings that frightened people. This was to have a future influence on the potential of the band.

Hectic Times

I had a friend called Pat whom I met at school. Together we would go to The Twisted Wheel at Manchester or The Torch at Tunstall where we took substances. We were also part of the Northwich Art College scene and that's how Pat met Whitty, whom she married. Everyone was in love with Pete Whittingham but he was a hopeless case and these were hectic times. Whitty would fall asleep in people's gardens or in baths; people would step over him or even on him; they would pee on him.

The two Petes had met and started playing together. Whitty was the only one Pete was able to play with spontaneously; they created wonderful harmonies; they were fabulous together; the banter between them was part of the act as well.

It's such a tragedy that Whitty was too drunk all the time but Pete let it slip as well. But it could never have worked with Whitty – not in his destiny. He was your classic talented, gifted, artistic person, doomed to die early. Pete's never found anybody to replace Whitty. He's tried very hard but I think it's as a solo performer that Pete's talent lies.

Zoe Johnson. (6)

Grand Junction

I watched the Skunk Band perform numbers by Ry Cooder, Little Feat, Mississippi John Hurt, Leadbelly and others at the original Grand Junction in Market Street, Crewe. The line-up was Pete Johnson, Pete Whittingham, Melvyn (on drums) and Al Dean. I'd never heard anything like it. I was listening to Hawkwind, Queen and The Sensational Alex Harvey Band at the time and although I was blown away by Pete's music I found it difficult to change my musical tastes. But I'd never heard anything like it.

John Darlington. (7)

Thriving Business

The first phase of the Skunk Band lasted about two years until 1975. By this time the business was doing well and the prosperity made everything easier with regard to equipment, reliable transport etc. and I owned an expensive house. I don't know if this relative wealth created complacency or if the fact that it allowed me to spend money on sporting activities caused a waning of interest in the band. Perhaps things needed to change; you can't stay the same musically without becoming stale and boring. Anyway, I took up Enduro riding, flying and sailing. I was extremely busy with my business: I was selling guitars for £500 and £800 and my shop turned over £89,000 in 1979. It was unheard of for a provincial shop to import from abroad in the Seventies, but I was importing stuff from Yorkville Sound in Canada, Electro-Harmonix in New York and Gruhn guitars from Nashville. I would regularly go to the airport to pick up a thousand quid's worth of pedals – now known as stomp boxes. The biggest amp sales were in Traynor Amplification which came from Yorkville Sound.

My business activities were attracting attention from the authorities; they were on my back. They thought I was laundering drugs money but nothing could be further from the truth. Fortunately I was always one step ahead of them: my books were impeccable.

My Way, Cadnant, See Feder And Huff Of Arklow

For someone who has stayed put in Crewe I've had a lot to do with mobility: cycles, motorbikes, cars, skis, planes, parachutes, boats and yachts. The yachts I owned reflected the youthful times of good money and each had its own character. My first boat was a motor yacht: *My Way*. I bought it in Swansea in the mid Seventies. I saw it; I wanted it but I hadn't got the ready cash and I was anxious in case it was sold in the meantime.

Des Parton invited me to have a drink in the town centre. This was unusual since we drank in The Barrel. Anyway, he went to the building society and when he got back to the pub he handed me two thousand quid in cash. I could buy the boat outright. I had only mentioned it in passing but he must have sensed my longing. I was able to have the boat because of his sensitivity and generosity. He was able to let me have the money because of his chart success but he didn't have to – he could have spent it on himself. Over the years I repaid him with guitars and a little money. I kept *My Way* for five years.

I inherited some money from my Auntie Betty and bought a fishing boat that had been used during the Royal Investiture to take the Prince of Wales round Caernarvon harbour. It was called *Cadnant.* When I had a problem with *Cadnant* I sold it and bought *Sea Feather*, originally called *See Feder*. The name was anglicised, not changed, because in the folklore of the sea that would have been unlucky. It had been bought in 1936 for Luftwaffe pilots on holiday and for training the Hitler Youth. I didn't have any objection to the boat's provenance: the Germans made some damn good stuff. After the war it became a windfall yacht to be taken by the British Navy which used such vessels as sail trainers. Government cuts in the 1970s occasioned their sale and this one, the *Sea Feather,* ended up virtually as scrap, in a boatyard in Beaumaris. A friend of mine helped me to renovate it; he loved that boat. At that time he owned a famous yacht called *Huff of Arklow* which had won lots of races in its time. Its designer was Uffa Fox who also built unsinkable lifeboats for World War II.

My friend was also trying to break into corporate entertaining: we both had classic yachts with interesting histories and his business plan included me and *Sea Feather*. The Scottish Tourist Board had already granted a site for the two boats. The idea was to set up sailing holidays and trips for underprivileged kids from the area round the American submarine base at Dunoon.

Through a friend of Des, I was offered £10,000 as a start figure for what would probably have been the first makeover programme on television. The plan was to follow the steps in the regeneration of *Sea Feather.* When we went to *The Boat Show* people were falling over themselves to contribute, to help, to get a mention.

Unfortunately, the owner of *Huff of Arklow* scuppered the deal by interfering behind the scenes, trying to get his own yacht in on the action. He insisted that the first documentary should record *him* chainsawing off the near-perfect deck of *his* boat and replacing it with teak. Not exactly riveting TV and not surprisingly the film company withdrew the offer.

The renovation of *Sea Feather* took two years. Owing to the aborted makeover programme, I had to finance it all myself. I worked at weekends and could take time off from my business in Edleston Road because Plum was able to take over. *Sea Feather* was a classic yacht: beautiful, and more beautiful than *Arklow*.

Once seaworthy, I sailed *Sea Feather* past the Beaumaris boatyard, just to snub them. They had no faith it would go into water again. I sailed to Holyhead where I kept it for a while. Then I took it back to Northwich via the Manchester Ship Canal and Weaver navigation.

Partings

Interest in the Skunk Band waned for Whitty as well. His restlessness took him and his new partner Cathy off to live in Aberystwyth. His wife Pat had been unable to put up with his chaotic, unreliable and sometimes violent ways and had taken their three children to Australia. Without telling him.

He was an angel but when he was drunk he could be an animal. He was terrible to Pat – they had three kids and he used to spend all the money on drink. She decided to leave him and take the kids to Australia. We all knew but we kept the secret. My God, she was brave. She's never regretted it; nor the kids.

Zoe Johnson. **(8)**

"Beat It"

Wayne Davies – Slim – worked for me from 1975 to 1979 doing various jobs, such as helping build cabinets and sound systems. He was into heavy rock and motorbikes and a lively social life. Like all my employees he worked on a fairly casual basis. At the end of the Seventies he took up a job with the MOD. Slim's band was called Barracuda.

Meeting Eddie Van Halen

I got my first guitar off Pete. It was a Grant Stratocaster Copy: an imitation of a Fender Stratocaster. My music is heavy rock although I did sometimes get roped into playing with the Skunk Band; I think every musician round here did.

I used to have a lot to do with Gordon-Smith Guitars – still do. I get my paint and lacquer from them. They made guitars to order; they made me two guitars: a Flying V and an Explorer.

At that time Eddie Van Halen had just broken into the big time. His band was supporting Black Sabbath at the Vic in Hanley and Eddie had gone to Pete's other shop in Hanley, so we got a 'phone call in Crewe asking us if we'd got any valve amps. Someone brought him in. He played everything – every guitar and every amp in the shop. What Eddie was playing in the shop was pretty mind-blowing. He's an amazing guitarist and one of the first to do "tapping" – you tap the strings instead of using a plectrum.

He bought my Explorer and about eight valve amps and offered Pete some tickets for the Hanley gig. "No thanks, I've already heard you!" was Pete's reply. So I had the tickets. I had them because I wanted to hear Black Sabbath. Van Halen toured with Black Sabbath and became mega famous after that. They blew Black Sabbath away.

To get to the point of the story: it is alleged that the guitar solo on Michael Jackson's "Beat It" from the Thriller *album is played by Eddie Van Halen using my Explorer.*

Using my Explorer!

Wayne Davies (Slim). (9)

Stolen Goods

Being in the shop was like living in a sitcom: dramas just walked in. I had a phone call from a lad whose car had been stolen. It had been stolen with one of my amps in it. The next day I had another phone call, this time from a bloke in a pub who said he had an amp and was I interested? I certainly was. I knew which amp it would be. "Fetch it in," I said.

"I think we're about to get someone in here returning one of ours," I said to Slim.

I recognised the FAL: a Futuristic Age Limited amp immediately.

"How much will you give me for it?" this little skinny guy asked.

"Nothing. It's already mine," I said.

He went to pick it up. He had a nerve. As usual, the shop was full of blokes who worked with me and blokes – big broad biker types – visiting me.

"Leave it there!"

"But it's me job!" I had to admire his amoral criminal logic.

"It's my amp. You'll have to fight me for it."

At that he left. He was persistent but not totally stupid – or so I thought. That was the end of it as far as I was concerned.

But that wasn't the end of it. The police prosecuted him for the theft of the car and the amp and I had to appear as a witness for the prosecution at Mold County Court. I was asked if I recognised him and of course I did. The farcical thing was that the skinny guy was conducting his own defence. "How did you recognise me?" he asked, leaning on the dock. "The heavily tattooed forearms are a bit of a giveaway," I said, "- yes – the ones you're trying to cover up now!" And sure enough that's what he was ineptly trying to do.

He got sent down.

I've got used to incompetent criminals. A Welsh guy staying with John Darlington brought a guitar in to sell. I could tell at a glance that it was JD's guitar but I let the drama unfold.

"It's a guitar like JD's – I'm selling it for a hundred quid."

"That's a good price," I said. "Just a minute," I said, "that *is* JD's guitar."

"Oh…I'll take it to him," he blustered.

"No," I said, "JD comes in here often. It'll be here for him when he comes."

"No I'll take it to him," says Taff. I was hoping that the verbal wrestling would do the trick, without having to resort to something more physical.

"Do you want to go out wearing it?" I said. "Get out before I phone the police."

So Taff goes.

Then JD arrives in tears. I let him go on for five minutes, then produce the Stratocaster from behind the piano.

But fancy bringing the stolen guitar to me – JD's friend! I might not recognize people but I'm an expert when it comes to recognizing guitars.

Lines From Eric The Red

Eric visited the Nantwich Road shop from time to time. He drove a series of trucks and then a Winnebago in which he travelled to the US to buy guitars. Each time he came I would buy up to six expensive guitars. He always used to ask to go upstairs to the office to do business. Then he'd spread out lines of cocaine for me and Whitty. I don't know what became of Eric the Red: he's either in the US, in jail or dead.

When we were making guitar cases Shep and Whitty used to argue who went upstairs to do the job. It was a glue thing.

Mick Wicklow: Orifices

Slim and I both remember Mick Wicklow – Lemmy's double – from the old biking days. Mick used to drink a lot: he used to vomit into his glass and drink it back. Typical biker's trick. There were never enough hours in the day for Mick. He had a gasket breaking business in Crewe and when he went bankrupt he went to London as a despatch rider. He just uproots and goes.

Mick lost his teeth in a motorcycle accident when he was sixteen so he had to wear false teeth. Never a good idea if you do a lot of throwing up. He once lost these teeth down the bog after a heavy drinking session and his wife had woken up wanting to know what was happening. Him coming in late and drunk was a bit of an issue and he didn't want her to know about the puked-up teeth and shout at him. But his teeth were down the bog and he'd flushed the bog! Imagine the scene: armed with the clear logic of the drunk he went into the night street, carefully pulled up the manhole cover, shushing himself every time it made a noise, peered into the black hole, staggered back a bit then fumbled about, found his teeth, staggered a bit more, shushed a bit more and put them in his mouth. His teeth still had bits of toilet tissue sticking to them. And God knows what else.

But his wife had gone back to sleep.

There's more where this came from: one day I was making love under a duvet in the room above the shop. Mick Wicklow came in and whipped the cover off. I was down to the short strokes. I grabbed him and thrust it in his ear. He went to the pub, proudly, with his hair sticking out like Biggles's scarf.

I think Mick was even more basic than Ozzie.

Anglesey Nude

There was certainly a lot going on – or rather coming off – in those Skunk Band days. I was once driving through Anglesey and couldn't help but notice that the girl in the passenger seat was gradually taking her clothes off. It was hard…to concentrate. The moment she was naked, the traffic began to slow down almost to a halt. Had they twigged what was going on? Actually the traffic was slowing because we had hit carnival time. Although tempted to upstage all the other acts put together, she slowly slid down the seat.

But it was touch and go in more ways than one.

If your girlfriends all seem to have the same tendency to disrobe your mind doesn't half become focused on it. One girl triumphed as a topless Winifred Atwell – a ludicrous idea in itself but adding extra rhythm to the proceedings – though at a private party, it has to be stressed. A couple of girls went publicly nude at a pub, to the great joy of the punters. Many of my girlfriends had sexy, erotic photographs taken of themselves, in some cases before they met me, in others after they had met me. Naturally I have thought a lot about this phenomenon! I came to the conclusion that although I enjoyed this nudity, I didn't necessarily inspire it in them. It existed in them irrespective of others and I certainly upheld their right to express themselves in any way they wished. Perhaps there was an element of this behaviour directed at me – to tame the beast, as they say, but this wasn't the whole picture by any means.

I've noticed that nudity doesn't make a person more sexy. Nor does clothing. If a person is sexually neutral or frigid nowt can be done until this changes. Sexuality is something within the person and clothes or lack of clothes can only enhance what is there already.

And isn't gross exhibitionism an intrusive annoyance?

I don't want girls to be nude to the point of hairlessness. I like girls to be natural. In the Fifties and Sixties body hair was more acceptable than it is now. Continental women didn't depilate and I liked to think that the most beautiful continental stars of the Fifties and Sixties: Sophia Loren and Gina Lollabrigida didn't. Not in my fantasies, anyway.

But nudity was very much the thing in the Sixties and Seventies. There was a trend for wet T-shirt competitions where everyone would end up without a T-shirt on at all. There were nightclubs where you hung your clothes by the door! I think one was called Club 49 – or was it 69? This started in New York and was aimed at the rich and famous: a nudist night club. At the other end of the scale there were teenage parties where we would advance from Postman's Knock to Postmistress's Knockers – then to Dustman's Knock which was a bit dirtier!

The Gig From Hell

Whilst in Wales, Whitty continued to play music for pleasure, supplementing his benefit with casual work, as he always had. In the end, the isolation and the terminal illness of his sister drove Whitty and Cathy back to Crewe and the Skunk Band entered its third phase. During his absence the music had changed quite a bit. I had placed more of my own stamp on it and in this second phase the set had a jazz, jug band and blues bias put to rock 'n' roll. It was less pop-oriented; I could set the old songs with more humour, in a manner that would appeal to bikers.

Whitty continued to go on benders which left him extremely depressed. One Sunday morning I was contacted in Moston by Shep who was then living in relative squalor above the shop with my dog Rafe. Pete, who had been staying with him, had slit his wrists in the bath. Leaping into my new car I soon left leafy deep-carpeted suburbia behind, not knowing what I would find at the end of my journey to Crewe.

I screeched up to the Nantwich Road premises and ran up the stairs two at a time to the seedy bathroom. There was Whitty still in the bath. Still drunk. Drunk and giggling in a blood-splattered bath, his arms held aloft by Shep who was also splattered. Quickly taking in the nightmare I assessed that the amount of blood lost was not enough to kill him though things looked bad. Fortunately he hadn't put any water in the bath – warm water would have drawn the blood out of him and he would have died. I know what they say about cries for help and this might well have been one rather than a real suicide attempt. Pete knew there was someone close at hand even though he did lock the door.

But I never have got on with the idea of suicide. It enrages me. I've seen too many people struggling for life to be impressed by anyone seeking death. "You selfish bastard – you've put every one of us in jeopardy!" I ranted whilst bandaging his wrists with rags. "You stupid selfish bastard!" – tying his wrists together above his head. "Drink this!" I fed him gallons of water – not something he was used to! It took about an hour for the bleeding – and the stupid drunken giggling – to stop completely. But I had no sympathy.

And he'd broken into the cases of wine I'd had delivered to the shop, the bastard.

Something else – something worse: his behaviour would have lead to involvement with the authorities: medics, police, people wanting to interview anyone involved in any way and family members having views to express. A terrible thought to us all in those days. That was why, when Shep kicked the door in and saw what he saw, he phoned me, not an ambulance and that is why we took the risk of not taking Pete to the hospital. We all knew that the police would find traces of party substances on the premises and the whole thing would all have been such a mither. When the crisis had passed we made jokes about Whitty needing to drink lots of Guinness. A bit ironic in the circumstances.

The bloodletting was not mentioned after that. Whitty and I never fell out. We loved one another but the rawhide he tied round his wrists didn't hide the scars.

There was a gig scheduled in Leeds – quite an important one at a big venue – and I had gone searching for Whitty. I found him at a friend's house; he'd already consumed a bottle of gin. I eventually got the van and the band and Whitty together in the same place, confiscated his drink and set off for Leeds. The van broke down between Knutsford and Manchester; we summoned the AA (the Automobile Association that is, not Alcoholics Anonymous!) and we got a relay to Leeds. The venue was in the red light district: strip clubs and prostitutes everywhere you looked. Under normal circumstances we wouldn't have got out of the van in bandit territory but we had a job to do and we were just about in time.

There it was: the size of two football pitches – the biggest pub you could imagine. I've never seen anything like it: a massive, massive hall. A great void. Yes – there might have been a hundred people there but it was still empty; the scale dwarfed everything.

There was a problem with the sound system: Shep was standing there at the desk shaking his head and throwing up his hands. We had cross talk: someone else can alter your sound and you have no control of it. All the wires in the multi-core go through from the mixing desk to the stage and if you get interference – spikes to the mains or strong radio interference – this can cause it. There was nothing we could do. It was one of the worst scenarios for a performer: the venue swallowing up the audience, no control over the equipment and no means of escape. And into the black hole of our impotence came Cider Sid filling the space with his scrawny alcoholic face, his teeth all over the place, plying Whitty with drink – something I was trying to ration. As if Whitty needed any more drink! If this was hell then Sid was a devil tempting someone who had enough demons to fight.

We were used to the banality of things going wrong. Sometimes it was part of the fun: dodgy vans, crap sound systems, lurid edginess, all belonged to the territory – as did the increasing cideriness. And we might have smiled through all that if it hadn't been for Cider Sid's tip of a flat where we had to crash out for the night until the cavalry could be summoned the next day. We drank ourselves to sleep.

The next day I arranged for Phil Doody to drive up my camper van so the ailing van could be towed. The lads in this van had no heating so they lit a camping stove to keep warm! It was symptomatic.

Although Whitty could stay dry for three months at a time he could also spend the whole of his wage packet on drink on a Friday night. His alcoholism and depression made him unreliable and unstable though his musical power was undiminished. Something had to give.

But happily not all out of town gigs were so awful; many resembled the hilarious times Slim had with his band, Barracuda.

A Load Of Balls

Being in my band Barracuda has been a combination of indignity and hilarity. Many of our venues were like The Wheeltappers and Shunters Social Club *and at one of these places the concert secretary gave us very, very precise instructions about what he expected of us. There was a heavy sense of occasion: he insisted on us playing as the curtains slowly opened. Well, the curtains began to open. Slowly. We were in full flow. It was all very dramatic…but the concert secretary was dithering. "And here we have… and we've had them before… they're good lads …it's…it's… let's have a good hand for…Barry and the… the… Cudas!"*

By this time the lads were rolling about on the floor.

Once we got going we played very, very loud and our hundred watt Marshall soon emptied the concert room. Remember: these were families in for the bingo who brought their own sandwiches in tin boxes. There were just two people left at the bar. The concert secretary stormed up – absolutely furious and with more instructions. We had to tone it down for the second set. The usual story.

We noticed after a while that the concert secretary was becoming less agitated. Then we realised that the concert hall was gradually filling up. But not with the sandwich-eating bingo fiends. What had happened was that the two remaining punters were students and they'd run across the road to fetch their mates. So it was all OK; rock 'n' roll had triumphed and we got paid.

We even got a bonus.

You get used to playing venues that might be unsuitable for your type of music and where the punters are there for reasons other than listening to your music. Arguments about volume are almost as common as arguments about money but sometimes it gets to you. One night Barracuda was in a typical bingo-dominated club. We had three spots and the evening was to finish on bingo. After the first spot we were told off for being too loud; we didn't alter it for the next spot and we were told off again. Dave Evans was getting pissed off with the attitude so I was surprised at the end of our third set when he didn't want to get straight off home. He told us all to hang about. So we went to the distant bar at the end of this vast room.

Everything went quiet. The bingo was about to start: eyes down for one hundred pounds! The machine was switched on but something was going wrong: balls were spewing all over the place and the bingo caller was sweating and totally confused trying to work out what was happening. More and more and more balls. A nightmare of balls! He had lost control and a hundred pounds was at stake. More and more balls! Everyone in the room became involved. People were on their hands and knees picking balls up and shouting things like, "I've got number twenty-seven; here's number three!" as if they could somehow sort it all out. It was chaos. Chaos.

On behalf of rock 'n' roll Dave had taken a terrible revenge.

Dave had taken the wire top off the bingo machine – the bit where the balls come out one by one. There was nothing to control them – the room was full of uncontrollable balls! In the meantime we were all standing at the bar trying to control our laughter but it was so ludicrous that in the end we could no more contain ourselves than the bingo machine could control its balls. The dreaded concert secretary realised we were responsible and told us we'd never be hired there again. Ever.

The band outlived the club. The club was demolished. Perhaps it couldn't survive the horror of a demented bingo machine.

Wayne Davies (Slim). **(10)**

The Skunk Band did tour widely in my teens and twenties but I didn't give myself completely to the tour van lifestyle. I had reasonable staff but I kept an eye on things at base camp because I had to do the trade-ins.

Transactions could be quite subtle: often involving hundreds of pounds, part exchange and a thorough knowledge of the value of the instruments involved. It was my responsibility and only I could make those decisions. I've always had something and I didn't want to squander it. By the age of thirty-two I had done enough touring; I didn't want the sort of hassle we had at Leeds.

Sleeping Bags

My grandfather used to say that the most important thing in life was a good pair of boots but I say, especially when on tour, that a good sleeping bag is the most important.

During my years on the road with Tower Struck Down: six in a van and staying in Travelodges throughout the country, we often had to live off the fat of the land. The maximum for a room was three people. One of the band preferred to sleep in the van anyway so that left five of us: two too many. So two were concealed in sleeping bags which were dragged in. Thus, only one room had to be paid for.

Whilst touring in the West Country sleeping bags were called into use again – to collect potatoes or corn. Tower Struck Down toured for three months in middle Europe. During the first leg of the tour, in Hungary, there was a hiccup – gigs not confirmed – and the band were at a loose end in Budapest. I went for a pee in a car park and noticed a large patch, about fifty yards square, of cannabis plants. The band picked the lot and concealed it in…a sleeping bag.

John Darlington. (11)

Hello Rockin' Brothers

The Leeds gig marked the end of the third phase of the Skunk Band. The something that had to give, gave: in the early Eighties Whitty made the important decision to go to Australia to see his family and to go walkabout. I received two affectionate, open-hearted letters from him. He was able to see his kids, see something of that vast country and play some music to support himself. The letters vibrate with interest and wit and life. They are full of detailed affection for his family there and his mates back home: Gwen and Edna who ran The Pig on Nantwich Road; Denzil – an old black guy who told tales of mustard on horses' backsides to make them run faster; Mick and Snowy the bikers who owned the bike shop in Hope Street. The second letter reveals his continuing success with the ladies and the fact that he has his drinking under some control. Australia was good for him and he has obviously absorbed some of the speech patterns and language. These are the letters of a man who believes in a future, who is happy to be who he is, where he is, having the friends he has. It's easy to understand why everyone loved Pete.

Hello Rockin Brothers,

How the hell are ya! I thought I'd better send you a report about my doings in the tropics.

Well it's not a bad old place really, if you can put up with the sand and flies. I tell ya there's insects here you'd have nightmares about! But I've got myself a place to live and I'm working with "Cov" putting up advertising signs which is pretty good because it means we get around a bit.

I think I did the right thing to stay over here even though it means I'm illegal (my visa ran out over 3 months ago!). It was good being with the kids at Christmas in Sydney but I've heard a lot about Western Australia from "Cov" and so I flew over here in February. I like it a lot more here than Sydney. It's more like I expected Australia to be: gold mines, sheep stations, kangaroos, etc. The kids came over here on the bus (3,000 mls) with Pat and they stayed for a week or so. We went down the Swan river to Fremantle and I did a bit of fishing with Raph. We had a great time; they're fine kids.

Perth is a brand new city all stainless steel and glass I like it but I prefer to go into Fremantle (10 miles away). You'd like Fremantle Pete. It's a lot like Plymouth, some great old pubs and big harbour.

I've got meself a guitar ($100 – £75). It's an Ibanez acoustic, nothing special but it plays well. I met up with a guy called John. He's from Yorkshire and he plays guitar so we're hoping to get an act together and play the bars. The pubs (hotels or taverns the Aussies call 'em) shut at 10.30 pm unless they have live music, which most of them do, then they stay open till 12 pm. So it's a healthy (is that the right word?) music scene. There are some good players over here, anything from jazz to C & W. Amplification is quite cheap here too, especially if *it's made in Japan as Australia has some sort of trading deal with the "Nips".*

Anyway, enough of this waffling. How are things with you Pete? Is the shop doing O.K? Is Lyn pregnant? Has Ralph eaten anyone lately? Tommy Kerley told me that Mick Wicklow married Alison. I s'pose that was inevitable, good luck to 'em I say.

Have you sold "Pequa" yet or you still there (now & then)? I'd like to hear from you as we've known each other a **long** *time and it would be a motherfuckin shame if we didn't keep in touch so* ***write*** *you barstad!*

Anyway regards to the following people
Give Shep: – some chewy
" Bip: – the rent
*" Lyn: – *!!* (twice)*
" Denzil: – a joint
give Mike Slaughter: – a visit
" Des: – an album
" Linda: – a smile
" Tom: – a drink
" Gary and Zoe: – my address
" Cathy: – my address and a kiss
" Gwen and Edna: – my undying love
" Snowy and Trev: – a yarn
" Dee: – anything
" Epiphone: – a strum
Good Luck to yous all,
Pete Whit.

P.S When you write, address the letter to, "Peter Kelly" as I've had to change my monica to avoid getting pulled by the law! (12)

Hello Pete,

How are ya.

I'm lyin' in me bed, bollixed after a hard workin day. I've been painting and decorating a house for a Portuguese/South African lady who insists on makin me eat all kinds of strange foods every ½ hour or so. I've been on this job for three days and I feel like I've eaten my way through a delicatessen! Anyroadup it was good to hear from you and I hope that "The Beano" was had in Cornwall (didn't see a little old man called Gascoigne did ya?). Been rattlin out a few tunes here and there – it seems 2,000 watts and a '57 Les Paul sounds fuckin dinkum; 'nough to send the Sheilas tropo! (sorry).

I'm still ruining the odd song or two about the place. There's one good thing about playing here. They don't hold you to a particular style; so long as it sounds half-right you're O.K. The worst thing that can happen is some "old swag'" askin you to sing something like, "Sweet Nell from Wogga Wogga"!! I did do a couple of gigs with this guy called John (from Yorkshire) but his wife really had the hots for me (fucknosewhy) and it got embarrassing me playing guitar with him one night, and her playing naughties the next; I had to bottle out!

Anyway, I plan to move around a bit this summer (about November) and I hope to go to the southwest coast maybe Albany or Esperance. I've heard it's beautiful country, very green, with lots of old whaling towns.

Must have been a choker about the anonymous phone call. I don't know why people do such things. Do they think it's going to improve anyone's life? Linda was probably quite content until the phone rang...I reckon it's the V.A.T man!

Anyway I'd better sign off and get some "kip." Remember "Old skunks never die they just stink away."

All the best Pete; love to Lynne and Ralph and everyone.

Pete Whitt.
P.S. What happened to Cathy, is she still in Crewe?
Write soon.
P.P.S I only drink ½ as much as I did, but I work twice as hard. (13)

Pete was in Australia for twelve months and was about to return to England when he died of a heart attack. Ironically, he had given up drinking, though he was still a smoker and he never looked after himself properly. Pete Whittingham was thirty-nine when he died in 1985 and I was thirty-six. If you lose one half of a particular partnership, you can't replace it. The same thing had happened with my sporting partner, Keith Brammer two years previously. The riding stopped. The music stopped.

I was invited to go to Australia but I declined, being more interested in the respect of life than the tribute of death. Everyone who knew Whitty was shocked and upset by the tragic waste. I received a letter from John Billington in New Zealand. It is very touching to notice that

John has copied Pete's style of writing about his friends. This feeling that I was a good friend to Pete Whittingham has a poignant echo in the letter, written in the form of a poem, which I received from Mr and Mrs Whittingham.

Dear Pete,

I got the news about Pete from Alice. What a fucking shame, it seemed like he'd sorted things out a bit for himself, seen the kids, realised where he stood with Pat and seen something of the world, so I suppose he had achieved a lot of what he needed. I find it really difficult to believe I won't walk into your shop to find you two sitting on amps, drinking Scotch and skunking it up. Alice told me he died of a heart attack, do you know anything else?

...How goes it Skunk in Crewe – are you playing? If you have any tapes of yourself I would love to have a copy to let people know what the Skunk band was about, also if you have got any of Whit's music I would really appreciate it. You know what I felt about that man and I would really like a tangible memory of him, I miss him. If you can find anything I'll refund the postage etc.

Give my love to people we know. As Whitty said:
Give Lynn sweet dreams
Shep a twelve bar
Mick the sound of a Norton
Jonty a bacon butty
Linda a rare bird
And yourself the knowledge you were a good friend to Pete, probably his best friend and that you kept him sane when everything else fell out of the window.

Thinking of You
JB **(14)**

Dear Peter Johnson,
A friend in need is a friend indeed,
That is what they say.
What better tribute could you give,
Or proof of your friendship true.
Believe us Pete, we his Parents,
Are really proud, that we know you.

Peter spoke of you so warmly,
Your friendship was so sincere.
Not just friendly handshakes,
But mutual help through many years.
And now, your final gesture,
Sums up your feelings, Lad,
For the Son we loved so very much,
One of the best any Parents could have.
God Bless you Lad,

Ivy and Joe Whittingham. **(15)**

For all his problems, Whitty's musical prowess hadn't declined. We'd played and sung when we'd been drunk and it had been fine. As long as I could get to him before he had a drink and then control what he had, things went OK. But it was rather edgy; I'm not the worrying kind but on a personal level I did worry about his self-destructive tendencies. The possibility of appearing on *The Old Grey Whistle Test* was round about the time of the notorious Leeds gig but the luck didn't happen and Whitty couldn't have been relied on at all. Of all the variables, I suppose he was the main one.

Every woman was in love with Whitty. Tall and good-looking, he had a regal, charismatic air about him; even when he was drunk he walked very tall. Linda's father said of him: "He always looks the same whether he's standing up or sitting down – like he's got a rod up his back." Whitty wasn't fazed by being in trouble, or in a formal situation. Once when he was in the dock for a minor drugs offence he said to the magistrate, "I am a fool. I've done a foolish thing." We all fell about: we recognised the lines from a Loudon Wainwright song. The magistrate thought it was an eloquent statement of remorse. He didn't know the subtext.

Pete Whittingham had ***style****.*

Whitty's death was a terrible blow to me. I had lost my friend, my musical brother. With regard to all important relationships I believe in total commitment – in going to the emotional edge without calculating the risks. All relationships are equally risky. The alarm bells don't ring for years.

I miss him.

After this death, I didn't play music for a while. Then I organized a charity gig to raise money to be put in trust for Pete's children. When the kids came of age they visited me in Crewe. I was morosely sitting in the Brunswick, having split up with a girlfriend, when two beautiful girls came up and kissed me.

These were Whitty's daughters. Later, Raphael, his son, came to England and played drums for me at The Limelight. I recall how like his father he was and how weird it all seemed.

I have a postcard from Whitty addressed to the Nantwich Road shop and another postcard addressed to the Edleston Road shop. Round the time he was away there was an economic downturn – during which I sold my Hanley shop and was forced out of my shop on Nantwich Road. I was on the edge of bankruptcy when I took the premises in Edleston Road. The going of Whitty and Brammer and the going of Nantwich Road were all of a piece and at the age of thirty-seven I entered a period of depression. I haven't recovered though I learned to live with it.

I was touched by this tribute I found on the website www.ogband.org. Adrian Peever, who wrote it, was a Crewe musician who went to live in Miami.

Snakey Jake has been a great influence on a lot of people in the thirty-plus years he's been providing gear and inspiration from his store, Custom Amplification, in Crewe, Cheshire. When I worra young snot-nosed brat passing his dark abode daily on my way to school, the barred confines, guarded in those days by an enormous German Shepherd lurking in the doorway, already fronted a place unlike any other in town. Of course, it wor all trees back then.

If you could get past the dog (for dog it was), you found yourself in a fragrant den hung with priceless pieces and piled high with speaker cabinets, on which there was always some biker or generally scary-looking character either reclining or trying out a vintage Gibson, or a National, or something equally far beyond my perpetually skint means. In those days I had to save up to buy my picks (hey, I still do!) but Pete was always as helpful as he could be, given that actually selling things never seemed to be on anyone's agenda. It hardly seemed a shop at all, more just a place where real musicians hung out.

Some of my earliest experiences hearing electric live music involved hearing Snakey Jake and the Dead Skunk Band, as Pete has generally called his bands. As I'd never heard any of the tunes he played I associated it all with him, though what I was hearing, I gradually discovered as time went by, was the music of Lowell George's Little Feat, of Ry Cooder, Loudon Wainwright III ("Dead Skunk in the Middle of the Road"), Hot Tuna, J.J. Cale, and a whole lot of other stuff I'd never have heard otherwise. Now that was what you call an education.

Snakey was the first slide player I'd ever seen, and his occasional acoustic sets with his great friend the late Pete Witt (billed as "Brahms and Liszt") showed me that there was more to the acoustic guitar than just bleeding-hearted singer-songwriters (though a few dozen more lessons in that department would have been even more useful!!). There was ragtime. There was hat-dancing.

Snakey and Pete even performed at Sandbach folk club more than once, though they were certainly not folkies, and that was the last time I saw Snakey play with Pete Witt, a great player who I'm sure Snakey has missed over the years.

In 1987, having often rented equipment off Pete, the Captain and I invited Snakey to Leeds for an evening, and to our delight he agreed, as long as we could lift his unassuming-looking 2x15 cabinet. Now the Captain is not a small person, and I thought this was no problem, but the cab in question contained speakers of such improbable mass that it nearly put both our backs out! However, a real one-off night of rare axe-wielding joy ensued at the Duck and Drake.

Snakey guested with us once more, at Crewe Oakley Centre in summer of '87, and the video recording of the evening remains notable for the way the sound breaks up entirely whenever the camera is pointed in Snakey's direction, giving the viewer something of the sense of being in one of those Maxell wind-tunnel ads.

Apparently he was in the US playing the Atlanta Blues Festival in 2000, and he doesn't play out very often. If you get a chance to see him, take it. A website, snakeyjake.com is also in the offing, I hear. Though there is apparently a commandment somewhere that all jakes must necessarily be snaky to at least a certain extent, this man is the real thing. Adrian Peever, 27th June 2001.

Just Seventeen

The shyest and most introverted of my girlfriends is associated with this period. She had a sultry earthy beauty: smouldering eyes and pre-Raphaelite hair. Public shots of her show a fresh-faced girl but more intimate photos show how good she looked and how comfortable she was in erotic clothes. She was affected by the photographer: the photos I took were more relaxed and more spontaneous than those taken by others. More trusting. In one photograph she is a cross between a biker chick and a hippie; another shows her in French mode with fishnets and a basque, no knickers, a snake armlet, a ribbon round her neck and a Hawaiian flower in her hair. There is a photograph of her wearing not much more than a Janis Joplin style woollen boa – clearly aware of the power of carefully placed accessories. For me the loveliest of the photographs belonging to this era shows both of us; it isn't posed but it has artistic integrity – something to do with the way the limbs are positioned – that makes you think it is.

When things went wrong with this relationship I became very wary of emotional involvement. One fun-loving girl I went out with combined directness with humour. She was very, very young and I had a mass of grey hair by then. When we arrived at Terry Butters gigs the band would be singing, "She was just seventeen" and we would dance. I knew not to get involved and hoped she would find a younger version of me but in the meantime we would have some uncomplicated fun. That was the theory, anyway. On one occasion Sweet Seventeen and I were visiting a classic car show and lying on the grass in the park having a drink. She was wearing a long dress and proceeded to tumble on top of me. "What will all these people think?" was my alarmed response. "Oh don't worry! They'll think I'm beating my dad up!"

In spite of moving on from me, this agile 'daughter' kept in touch. It would be fair to say that she always took the initiative but I enjoyed her company. She dropped by one Tuesday; I was having a very difficult time with my present partner and was glad of some no-strings simplicity. We went to a pub in Rode Heath and then for a walk across the fields. A few days after this enjoyable encounter I heard that she was honeymooning in Yugoslavia! A fortnight later Miss Seventeen came again to the shop and again invited me to the pub in Rode Heath. I ended up at her house and thought I'd better mention the husband. "Oh – he was too boring," was the response.

But that didn't stop her, in her mid twenties, marrying a heavy-drinking builder with an interest in guitars. I remember the two of them coming to the shop with photo albums of patios and garden walls, the whole thing seeming incongruous. Zoe, Andy Boote and I had attended their wretched wedding reception which teetered between disaster and farce: the bride had been drunk throughout the ceremony and there was no sign of anyone making a speech. Upset by this lapse in wedding etiquette I stood up and talked about the bride's partying ways, referring to the time she had 'dressed to thrill' in order to cheer me up when I was depressed and assuring the new husband that he was a fortunate man. I meant this with all lubricated sincerity but the bride's mother took exception and left the room. I think she had remembered the Winifred Atwell moment.

Three Piece

When Pete went to Australia the Skunk Band entered a fourth phase and had continued as a three piece band. I see that period as being fluid and more selective with regard to quality gigs. The fifth phase of the Skunk Band was less fluid and had a line-up of Moggsie, Melvyn, Andy Boote, myself and occasionally Des Parton.

Moggsie

Mark Bryan was thirteen when he first came in my shop and I took him on as the Saturday boy to clean things. He was a school contemporary of John Darlington and Andy Boote who used to send Moggsie into the shop to see what I had in; the others were obviously circumspect about my legendary grumpiness. Moggsie had been associated with the Nantwich Road shop, JD a little with the Nantwich Road shop and Andy only with Edleston Road, so Moggsie had some seniority over the other two. He had just lost his mother and paradoxically I became his surrogate father.

After leaving school he became an apprentice crane driver in Crewe

Works and was a bass player with the Skunk Band for quite a few years. I persuaded him to do a degree in Management Studies. One day he appeared in cap and gown with a bottle of champagne.

Every band has someone who keeps an eye on forthcoming gigs and collects programmes and posters. Moggsie was a walking diarist. I could ask him what had happened on any given date; he would think for a while and then tell me. Not only that, he could do the same for everyone he knew! Moggsie also had an excellent social sense: he would see to arrangements, was endlessly resourceful and paid attention to small details. He would discreetly place a chair for you before you knew you wanted one. His creative sense of occasion gave rise to cheese and wine or Stilton and port parties or, on a slack afternoon he would devise a culinary version of Russian Roulette involving tortilla chips and Encona Hot Pepper Sauce to make things interesting.

I remember Moggsie having two distinct lives that he ran quite harmoniously. He was always the gentleman but there was a bit of the rebel about him too. He had quite a high-powered wife and a circle of friends who went to posh restaurants but was equally at ease scumbagging it with the boys. He established the ritual of renouncing drink on January 1st every year and coming off the wagon with a flourish on April 7th – my birthday. Not that he was ever a heavy drinker, but it was one of his social occasions.

In 1996 Moggsie died suddenly of heart failure. He was thirty-six years old.

There is a video recording of Moggsie playing a charity gig with the Skunk Band at The Limelight, recorded in 1996: the year of his death. He is a cool, self-possessed man who just stands there and plays bass. Confidently. An excellent contrast to the more flamboyant styles of the other band members.

John Darlington

John Darlington comes from a musical family. His roots are Celtic: Welsh on his father's side and Irish on his mother's side and it's there in his music. John started playing twenty-five years ago and has appeared with Jools Holland, New Model Army, Tina Turner, Lindisfarne and Fairport

Convention. He toured with Tower Struck Down for many years, appearing at Glastonbury six consecutive years and touring in Ireland, the Czech Republic, Slovakia and Hungary. John and his brother Gareth are Chew The Roots: blues, country, boogie-woogie and Celtic rock.

John Darlington is an accomplished, versatile musician who fully exploits the potential of his guitar, at times making it sound like a fiddle. There is a flicker of restless concern preventing him from entirely immersing himself in his music. He is the one taking the on-stage responsibility but his apprehension is needless. Friday night's incarnation of Chew the Roots has three instruments: saxophone, guitar and fiddle with a backing beat. Whatever music is being played: Pogues, country, rock, jazz-blues, whimsical-humorous, blues, Hendrix, River Dance, folk, Dire Straits, whatever music is played, *the whole thing rocks and Gareth Darlington's fiddle – infectious – universal, dances over the top, Gareth himself standing there, grounded, unconcerned, solid as a rock, not separate from his music and without any other issue whilst he plays and responds to John's guitar. This sibling responsiveness is a potent force in music.*

Sandra Gibson. (16)

At the moment John is based in Cognac, France.

I played music in France with my brother Brendan for a while. He played acoustic guitar and I played electric guitar. He's a fantastic singer and he's written a couple of good songs. We did stuff by The Proclaimers, Thin Lizzie, Dire Straits, Irish stuff. We sang in harmony and had quite a cult following. He has this self-deprecating attitude sometimes. He said, "My brother is a guitarist who does joinery; I'm a joiner who does guitar playing."

But all my brothers are talented. Gareth is a world class fiddler and a fantastic guitarist; he's good on the mandolin and never gets up in the daytime. The tour bus will be waiting outside for him to get out of bed. Damien has international acclaim with the Australian Pink Floyd Show. He lives the kind of life where everything is taken care of for you, where gigs are packaged and all you have to do is walk on the stage. He lives from his music and although I wouldn't like to do his thing I respect him.

John Darlington. (17)

JD's latest group is the Champagne Charlies – named after the ritual of drinking champagne *comme aperitif* before each gig and he has become the most consistent musician in the Charente – an area as big as Cheshire – allegedly the only one making a musical living throughout the year.

John was an associate rather than a core member of the Skunk Band: the archetypal musician – into drink and drugs and sex! On one occasion, quite early on in my relationship with John, I received a phone call from his father: John was in hospital. Someone had spiked his Chinese food. Allegedly. Sceptical about this idea of John as the victim – more likely the instigator – I suspected magic mushrooms.

The Famous Incident Of The Magic Mushrooms

I was given the equivalent, in dried mushrooms, of ten good doses. I added the lot to my curry. On the way to a band rehearsal the mushrooms kicked in and, deciding I didn't want to rehearse, I stepped out of the car.

At 50 mph.

I fell on my face, went through a hawthorn hedge and slid into a wet cow pat. Terry Dwyer picked me up and took me to Leighton hospital.

John Darlington. (18)

When John started using heroin, I tried to dissuade him but to no avail. He claimed he was on heroin for two years but I think it was longer than that. The early years were spent dabbling but the last two years were more problematic.

Soup, Soap And Sun

The worst thing I did was the Eric Clapton thing: heroin takes away your manhood, your pride and makes you a victim. It leeches the spirit. Why did I get into it? Banging my head on a brick wall and not getting anywhere. With heroin your world is self-sufficient – you only need the drug; you replace all your problems with this all-encompassing one that gets you up very early to go and find the money. Fortunately I could make enough money with my music so I didn't need to turn to crime but it was a bit touch and go. I pawned my Stratocaster with Pete years ago. Owning a guitar was essential to my self-esteem and to my supply of heroin. On one occasion they were both in jeopardy; fortunately Pete was on hand with his quick mind.

When I was living on Nantwich Road I met a fellow Welshman – a fellow junkie – and let him stay at my flat for the night. In the morning my guitar was missing; Taff was missing. I went to Pete Johnson's shop to tell him the sorry story. He listened and then went behind the grand piano. "Is this what you want?" It was my guitar. Taff had taken it to the shop and tried to sell it to Pete, my best friend who, of course, had recognized it and wrestled it off him. And this is an example of why I love Pete.

When you're trying to get off heroin the biggest threat is people not wanting you to escape. My attitude is: you make it; you break it. So I went to France and stayed in a gite *with my parents. My mother thought I needed fresh air and soup. But what helped me more than anything was World Cup 2002. They tell you to combat depression by getting up to watch a soap so I watched the football and I lay in the sun. My main pain was not the heroin withdrawal – it was being two weeks with my family in a* gite*!*

John Darlington. (19)

As a musician John is very talented – a great player. If he hears a tune he can play it and when he puts himself into it, he's on fire. He's also very practical and a fully qualified electrician. He made Gareth's fiddle out of a coffee table and he's made guitars. When he needed an electric balalaika to play "Goulash" after a tour in Central Europe, he made one. He's a great jammer with a fabulous ear.

I met John when he was a very young teenager. The whole family became customers. At one point the family went to live in Dubai, where they ran a club called Snakey Jake and called their band by this name too. Back from the Middle East, they opened the Leisure Club in Edleston Road, Crewe and the Skunk Band played there on many occasions. One of Eugene's wakes was held there and so was my Fortieth Birthday Party, for which Jo had made a snake cake which I proudly held aloft like a waiter. And this was at the end of the night!

We had some amazing times. I remember after one of Eugene Van de Hoog's wakes – the one when he was actually dead – Pete was going through a bad patch. He was pissed and he had had another row with his girlfriend so he couldn't go back to her house. At that time I had the upstairs flat in the Edleston Road shop and I offered him hospitality. He declined and went to sleep behind the shop counter.

I was suddenly woken by a massive banging noise, like an explosion. I ran downstairs and I was banging to get into the shop – I thought Pete must be dead – but then he appeared at the door, bleary-eyed. "What's up?" Someone had only levered up a paving flag and chucked it through the window. Three guitars had been stolen. Pete hadn't heard a thing. After that bars were installed on the windows.

I believe Pete isn't aware of – doesn't know – the underbelly of crime and downright nastiness that exists; I think he's uncorrupted by things.

John Darlington. (20)

Andy Boote

Andy also came into the shop as a young teenager. He had a post-punk indie band which was quite successful and at first he and I had very little to say to one another, musically speaking. The idea that he and I could ever share the same stage was ridiculous. It was quite a while before common ground was established, partly because it seemed pointless to look for it. Neither of us did.

Warts And Winnets

Pete Johnson was quite a bit older than me. I had no way of knowing then that I would enter his boisterous world and end up playing in the Skunk Band, years later. I was well aware that Pete would dismiss my musical tastes as for "warts and winnets" but I remained a regular customer. One of the lads in my class – Moggsie – was a friend of Pete's. They had things in common, such as the loss of their mothers so Moggsie had status within this threatening world and would sometimes be in the shop when I went. This was reassuring.

My band The Train Set was signed to Playhard Records in Manchester set up by

Dave Haslam, a well-known Manchester DJ and Nathan McGough, son of the poet Roger McGough. We played local venues such as The Cheshire Cat and The Oakley Centre and further afield in Manchester, Liverpool and London – we played London loads of times. This was the post-punk era and our minds were passionate and stimulated as well as restless and frustrated. We wanted to get out of here to the real music scene, if you like. We hated the sense of stagnation in the Crewe scene; we didn't like people our age playing the same old pub rock...it's anachronistic. The commercial strand of post-punk music was represented by Duran Duran and Spandau Ballet but we favoured bands such as The Smiths, Joy Division, New Order and The Cure – the indie strand. It separated certain people into different camps. You were with the punks and this attitude or you weren't. You had to wear what you were. It was political: I got into it and sold anti-Nazi League literature. It was a stimulating, vibrant movement – a seminal moment – a revolution – a feeling that things had got to change. The music was fresh – it was yours...for a time.

The Train Set was a successful Eighties group, attaining Single of the Week in NME *and number 10 in the National Independent Single Charts with "She's Gone"(1988) and touring with The Happy Mondays and James.*

Andy Boote. (21)

Andy was just one of the many youngsters who came timidly into the shop; what eventually linked us was his mate Dave Evans wanting to learn the blues and Andy's growing interest in jazz. He realised that the line from jazz had origins in the blues and then we had something to talk about.

Common Ground

I continued as a customer for years; no particular recognition occurred until Pete met me in MFI and asked me how things were going with The Train Set. You can be sure Pete has never concealed his dislike for my music. I wasn't that keen on some of his music, either. Our musical differences appeared to be completely irreconcilable nor was there any desire in either of us to remedy this.

Common ground was to come through Dave Evans, another mate from school times whose musical tastes were more in line with Pete Johnson's. Dave would be off with bikers; I'd be off with my punks. I started teaching Dave Evans to play guitar: Beatles stuff – busking. Then he said he wanted to get into the blues. Through visiting the shop regularly, I knew of Pete Johnson's prowess as a blues player and admired his style unreservedly: I liked his finger picking style. I was impressed by his energetic party-style. Finger picking is usually associated with classical or folk. It's nice. Just nice. But Pete Johnson can have a party with it. I came to realise how well he could play because I had matured musically myself, so I was in a better position to judge. The other thing I thought was: what a nerve he's got! To sing so loud, outright in a shop to an audience of one! Potency. The experience of Pete singing to me stayed with me. He sounded like Leadbelly.

Admiration didn't make me want to play the music myself but I could recommend Pete to my friend Dave as a worthy teacher. Pupil and teacher had a lot in common besides the music – Dave enjoyed the riotous lifestyle. He was a keen, intuitive student and Dave loved it so much that he spent most of his time with Pete. This was the mid Eighties. He was a sponge for whatever he could get musically. There was never a guitar not being played and I sometimes joined them. Through Dave I got to know Pete better and I eventually started to go into the shop whether Dave was there or not, though there was still some reservation. It was the best laugh. They became best mates but I kept a distance because of the indie scene. I had to step out of it and be in an indie band. I was happy with it that way. I had the best of both worlds: I could leave my indie thing, go into that shop, shut the door – you were in another world.

I started to talk to Pete about the origins of jazz in the blues. Then we were away. We didn't become friends gradually; we became friends suddenly on the basis of a long-elusive common musical interest.

Andy Boote. (22)

When Andy eventually came to play for the Skunk Band I found an opportunity to make some fun out of his indie leanings. Andy was rather shy of the public gaze. He sang at parties and he went busking but never sang on stage. One night at The Limelight the Skunk Band was doing "Mamma Don't Allow" and Mamma wasn't allowing no indie music so I shoved some flowers in Andy's pocket and Andy had no option but to sing a Smiths' number. It's just a matter of confidence, really. He now fronts a successful rockabilly band called Vavoom! with such aplomb you'd never believe he was ever hesitant.

Vavoom!

"I wanted to combine the raw energy of punk with the distinctive Gretsch sound of Brian Setzer."

Andy Boote. (23)

Andy Boote is a serious musician who has built up considerable expertise. From his origins in indie music he went on to Charlie Christian and Django Reinhardt and was impressed by the very clever chords: chords that have been forgotten by today's musicians. Andy studied early jazz alongside rockabilly and blues and Vavoom! (started by him in 2001) has jazz and swing influences combined with the energy of early rock 'n' roll, the punk era of the Seventies and the Stray Cats music of the Eighties. Vavoom! -"Hot Rod Rock 'n' Roll and Rockabilly delivered on demonic drums, bangin' double bass and growlin' Gretsch guitar" – supported Bob Geldof at the 2002 Nantwich Jazz and Blues Festival and have toured with James and The Happy Mondays. (24)

Vavoom! At The Imperial

Vavoom!'s versatility and professionalism are impressive. They capture the strutting rhythms – essentially young, virile, Brylcreemed and male – of early rock 'n' roll. This pristine moment in pop music, created by Elvis, Gene Vincent and Eddie Cochran was soon to be obliterated by the disempowering economics of bubblegum rock.

Andy Boote's virtuoso guitar playing, movements and mudras are as authentic as any I've seen, incorporating momentary 'freeze-frames' into the choreography. The stage was literally and metaphorically too small a place for this dynamic band.

Sandra Gibson. (25)

A Minnow's Eye Left Of A Spliff

Dave Evans was a friend of Andy who lived across the road from my shop. I lived there with him for a while after I split up with my current girlfriend. Dave was interested in the country blues and I taught him to play guitar in exchange for a 4-pack of Special Brew for which he was happy to go busking.

Andy Boote and Dave Evans and I used to party together, one of our extended parties being a trip to France which also involved some bikers and a caravan site.

Calvados: an apple brandy produced in Normandy, isn't everyone's favourite drink but it was all I had on the long train journey from Paris to St.Tropez. It was vintage paraffin standard Calvados and my mates couldn't stomach it so I was on my own. By the time we reached the Med I felt very ill. Very, very ill. The lads found a disco on our caravan site and I don't know if it was the thump – thump – thump of the music or the thump – thump – thump of my head that sent me back to the caravan. The only alcohol there was two bottles of beer so I drank one and took the other to bed.

When the lads eventually returned from the disco they found me propped up in bed holding the last bottle in captivity. Fast asleep. Someone grabbed the bottle but my grip on it was so tight they had to give up. I was still fast asleep. I was lucky; some of these lads were bikers and they used to do daft things to people who were drunk. I could have ended up with half a beard, or minus an eyebrow, or covered in love bites or fully made up, or covered in paint – in fact anything that could have embarrassing repercussions the next day. But Dave Evans used to look after me so I was OK in spite of having commandeered the last bottle of ale.

Busking Or A Blowjob?

Knowing Pete led to some interesting places. If you were his friend you ended up in some amazing situations: horse-riding at Whitmore, yachts off Anglesey, open doors all over the place. The holiday in St Tropez is a good example of this. Pete offered to lend people money to finance the trip but it was always a grown-up transaction. The deal was that the recipient had to be straight about the amount needed and then not mither Pete about it afterwards. The money was to be repaid out of the proceeds of busking and there was an interesting forfeit. Anyone defaulting would give Pete a blowjob. I'm still uncertain whether Pete would actually have insisted on this and it illustrates another facet of his personality. Everyone knew he was capable of extreme – outrageous even – behaviour. He has an air of danger or a dark side or grumpiness which shows itself in mild or extreme forms. He could threaten with a meat cleaver for his band money or he could deliver fairly devastating one-liners for preciousness in behaviour. On one occasion in the shop a young musician was giving a virtuoso guitar performance that bordered on the over-zealous. "Do you know any tunes?" was the put-down. I think Pete's attitude is related to the apprenticeship idea. He would wind us up in an older bloke way – get others laughing at us. It toughens you up – like in the Johnny Cash song, "A Boy Named Sue". I remember an interesting appearance to mind having eaten magic mushrooms. Pete became a silver-backed gorilla and Dave Evans a monkey apprentice.

Another aspect of being with Pete Johnson was that there were going to be bizarre, edgy moments and plenty of laughs – often at Pete's expense. Pete sat down somewhere in France – it must have been St Tropez – looking dishevelled as people sleeping on the beach do, and, thinking he was down and out, someone gave him a packet of fig biscuits and a box of matches. Of course, the tramp story has since been retold a lot and the charitable donation has been exaggerated. A similar thing occurred when Pete was sitting waiting for me and Dave to finish our busking. A compassionate Manuel lookalike slipped a huge pizza to him edgewise through some bars from a basement kitchen. Another time, Pete was also busking and we drew a crowd which alarmed the local restaurateur to the extent that he used tear gas.

Loyalty has always been an important element in Pete's friendships and whilst on holiday with me and Dave, he did have the opportunity to sleep in a caravan with some biker friends but he chose to sleep on the beach with us and I've cherished this gesture.

Andy Boote. (26)

There's a photograph taken at Sacre Coeur with us boys sitting on the steps, a visit distinguished by the fact that tear gas played a part. Dave and Booty were busking; one broke a string and the other didn't feel competent to carry on because he didn't sing so I took up the other guitar to help out with the funds. It was all a bit hand to mouth: busking, drinking, eating… There were about sixty people gathered round listening. We were outside a café and the management were anxious about us affecting trade so CS gas was used to disperse the crowd. I knew straight away what it was because it had already happened to me once during that visit at a disco in St. Tropez. So I got away as quick as I could. You don't smell a bad egg twice.

On the way back from St Tropez two of us four lads were broke and couldn't afford the train fare. Dave and Andy were lurking in the toilets, avoiding the ticket man, as the train sped north towards Paris. It's interesting how people behave in situations such as this. When the dreaded inspector arrived the third mate wimped out and grassed them up: "They're in there, mate." Why did he do that?

All I was concerned about was being put off the train at Marseilles. You'd heard such tales about the place and I felt scared.

Dave Evans. (27)

Once Dave and I decided to forego tobacco. If you had a smoke without cannabis in it you had to apply a forfeit, such as eating a whole jar of my hot pickled onions.

But the daftness was interspersed with music; many a night at two or three I could be heard beating time for Dave to get his phrasing right. I'd taken my blues collection over to his flat and he was quite a grafter. I recently came across a tape amateurishly recorded at this time in the Eighties: a time capsule recorded solo under the influence of booze, dope and magic mushrooms. Zoe has edited out all the swearing so that she could play it to other people but the budgie singing away in the background still accompanies me.

Oh – that *tape! The fucking budgie sounds better than Pete!*

Dave Evans. (28)

It's a very informal and unplanned performance where I just play song after song to demonstrate the music to help Dave: the only audience I envisaged for this particular collection. What strikes me is how my singing, playing and repertoire have changed since then: the pitch has deepened and my voice is stronger, more resonant and more confident. I've noticed changes in other singers too: both Mississippi John Hurt and Son House sound slower, less jaunty but also more thought-provoking in later years. My playing style has become less twiddly and more refined. Whereas I used to do some folk and some modern songs from Dylan as well as blues, nowadays I concentrate on blues because I think my voice suits this *genre* better than any other.

Hearing tapes of my performances some people think that there is more than one instrument playing but it is all down to me and the little Gibson. One person 'heard' a harmonising voice. I can only suggest that the guitar, played in a certain way, is a little orchestra.

Another time capsule, probably recorded at The Limelight, shows the more public side of my playing. This is the partying, loud rock version of Vaudeville that proves so infectious. Listening to the tape I am conscious of the mistakes but in the context it didn't matter too much. It was the party that mattered and the band involved the audience in a ball. You had to be there to appreciate it, really. It was a spirited, humorous, spontaneous, rocking performance and all the songs had this slant, either because they were chosen for this or because we treated them like this.

The time came for my *protégé* to overcome his stage fright, so I took him to the Sandbach Folk Club where I always had a supportive audience. I seated Dave behind me and told him to scrub away and join in with the harmonies if he felt like it. After three songs I introduced Dave to the audience: "You might wonder why I've brought this friend of mine with me. This is Dave 'King' Evans and he's going to sing one of my favourite songs, 'I Wanna Be Like You.'" With that, I left the stage and left him to it. He was just gobsmacked. But it was OK. He looked just like a primate when he sang that song.

In the end, having served his musical apprenticeship with me, Dave's favourite thing was white country blues which he came across through some other route and to which he introduced me. This musical phenomenon was concurrent with the music of the black bluesmen – a little bit more bouncy and humorous. Dave's band, Swamp Donkey reflects this taste for the white blues.

Like many of my musical friends, Dave left town. His surveying job took him to Belgium and he eventually settled in Bath.

Des Parton

My relationship with Des Parton began in 1971 – I was twenty-two and he was twenty-five – and spans the decades since. I had a residency at a Congleton pub, playing solo once a week and several lads from Stoke asked if they could play with me, not realising the number of chords in the tunes. The only one that could keep up with what I was doing was the only one that didn't consider himself as a guitarist and that was Des. To this day, he's still nervous about playing with me. Thus began an enduring friendship.

Des is a singer-songwriter and record producer from Newcastle-under-Lyme. He is proficient on several instruments including saxophone, penny whistle, mandolin, guitar, keyboard and harmonica: all played on stage and in recording situations. During the Congleton pub days, Des was trying to get himself established as a songwriter. He had worked for Social Services for a while but they had refused him his two weeks' holiday time off to tour in Germany with his band. He tidied his desk, walked out and went to Hamburg where he worked on and off from the late Sixties till the mid Seventies.

He's never had to clock on since.

Like me, Des shows an interest in biography; with me it's instruments and songs; with him it's bands.

Smiling Hard

In Hamburg, me and the band were working long shifts of about eight hours – though this was not continuous playing – in clubs such as The Top Ten and The Star Club. It would be something like one hour on and one hour off if there were two bands. If there was only one band it was forty-five minutes on and fifteen minutes off. This could go on from 7.00 pm until 4.00 am.

The young musicians in Hamburg loved the city and many lived there for a while, including some from my band. It had that combination of glamour and debauchery so beloved of creative people. In this creative, lively city musicians received, through a rigorous schedule, a baptism into the world of being a professional musician, where they would hone their skills. Among the English musicians was Ritchie Blackmore from Deep Purple who, with the other band members, used to come and jam on stage with me and the lads. The same with Billy Preston – an American musician.

It was at this time that I met Smiling Hard – the best band around. It was this band's keyboard player, Spike, together with some men who played brass instruments, who later joined Dexys Midnight Runners and after that, Queen (post Freddie Mercury). It has been alleged that Spike used to spend time in the little room underneath the drum riser where he played secretly. It was the done thing sometimes to augment during a show. Some bands have extra players hidden away in other places; it's the way it is. As Pete sometimes says, "Some people spend their lives in boxes."

Gary Glitter's band formed in Hamburg after one of the little studio sessions that were going on all over the place. He originally played under the name of Paul Raven. Studios would often phone clubs for musicians to go and join in with recording. I had the chance of being in on the recording of the successful pop single Cinderella-Rockefeller but I'm now glad I wasn't. Boney M. also used to live in Hamburg.

Hamburg still attracts musicians; a Stoke band: The Climax Blues Band plays there quite often. It is interesting to know that Hamburg continued to be a Mecca for aspiring musicians long after the Beatles left.

Des Parton. (29)

Worked To Death

Once you did Hamburg you were naturally in a network of professional musicians but although Hamburg could be a gateway, you served a harsh, dangerous apprenticeship. You were worked to death – sometimes literally – Des once had a gun pulled on him when he asked to be paid. He was living in a world of gangsters and prostitutes, drugs and low life. Pushers are instantly recognizable – they hover around musicians. The big men are invisible.

Whilst in Germany his band split up for financial reasons so Des returned to the UK and concentrated on writing songs. He would hitch down to London with a cassette of songs and knock on doors. It was Tony Hatch's door that let him in, partly he feels, because of the Potteries connection. Jackie Trent came from Chesterton, her brother worked there in an administrative role and there were several others who came from the area. Tony Hatch liked his songs.

A Music Lesson With Tony Hatch: "Can You Hear The Quarter Notes?"

Tony used to push me, musically. I'd had no formal musical training and I loved receiving musical tuition from him. Tony would play notes on the piano and say, "Can you hear the quarter notes?" "No." He would play again. "Can you hear the quarter notes?" "No." He would play the notes again. "Can you hear the quarter notes?" "Yes." And I could! I had acquired something. With piano notation from one note to another is a jump; with a cello or a violin or a trombone one note slides to another; it slurs between one note and the next. Like a slide guitar.

People ask me how long I was with Tony Hatch. I never really left. We're still friends – I saw him about eighteen months ago. When I do any writing I always go down to Tony's office. I've been contacted by the BBC: Tony Hatch will soon be seventy.

Des Parton. (30)

Not Mr. Livingstone

Through knowing Des and frequently visiting London I met various people. One night in The Speakeasy – the club with the swivelling bookcase entrance in High Street – a bloke was admiring my girlfriend in the gritty gloom. Des introduced me to him. It was Tony Hatch. I didn't mind – people were always staring at Penny. Another time I went down to London to see Des during the period he was working in Leicester Square, fronting the Tony Evans Big Band with Tina Charles. I knocked on the door of Tony Hatch's office at Marble Arch, the door opened and I said to the man, "I know you, don't I? You're Tony Hayes." Hayes was the manager of Sweet Sensation. "No. I'm Tony Hatch," was the reply. Close but no cigar, as they say. He was on TV all the time but I'm so hopeless at recognizing people. Tony Hatch is special: a very, very clever musician.

Sweet Sensation

Des wrote songs for the Manchester group Sweet Sensation in the mid

Seventies. Sweet Sensation had a British Top Twenty number one hit and a US Top Twenty hit with "Sad Sweet Dreamer" in 1974. (31) Before their appearance on *Top of the Pops,* Des brought the group to the shop, where I kitted them out with equipment, on the strength of my friendship with him. "Purely By Coincidence" was also in the UK Top Twenty. Des arranged and co-produced both hits with Tony Hatch. The cover version of Stevie Wonder's "Isn't She Lovely?" (1977) was also co-produced with Tony Hatch. There was a problem: after a few days in the studio with the time paid for and passing and the backing tracks done, the lead singer was unable to deliver the precise vocal nuances Des and Tony were looking for. It was suggested that Des should demonstrate what was needed in the song. So he did. Later, Tony Hatch decided that these vocals would stand. It wasn't what Des intended and he was only paid as a session musician. But Des – David – Parton had a Top Ten hit single with Stevie Wonder's song, the B side containing one of his own songs. It was in the UK singles charts for nine weeks and reached number four. Stevie Wonder himself never actually released his song as a single.

Sweet Sensation went into obscurity. Marcel, the lead singer was only fifteen years old when he recorded "Sad Sweet Dreamer." He was always the little spark in the band – the Michael Jackson – a first class singer who could have been a world class performer.

Des Parton. (32)

Leroy Smith, Sweet Sensation's keyboard player, whose death was announced in the *Manchester Evening News,* 2nd February 2009, was described as one of the first British black pop stars. Terry Christian (33) has expressed his annoyance that Sweet Sensation, originally discovered by the talent show *New Faces,* were mismanaged. Instead of exploiting their teenage appeal, the group were playing to middle of the road "chicken in a basket" audiences. Thus they have never been recognized as they deserved in histories of black British music.

During the interview in which I was talking about Des' career I picked something up randomly from a drawer. It was the necklace – ethnic beads threaded on leather – that Des wore when he appeared on *Top of the Pops.* And as we looked at the necklace, the phone rang. It was Des.

The Cyril Dagworth Players

After his success, Des reassembled the original Stoke band as the Cyril Dagworth Players: a band best experienced live, in my opinion. I designed and built a PA system for them and this was the band Des had always dreamed of. The Dagworths appeared at many venues, including London's famous Marquee and could have made it big but the backing went elsewhere.

We went to one another's gigs when we could and there was mutual admiration both professionally and socially. We occasionally played together, but not often. Whereas Des wanted to run a professional band and make a living out of pop music, I made a living from my business which also gave me freedom and opportunity to perform my blues music.

Snuff, Sledge And Jameson's

The things Des and I have in common are a love of music, a love of drinking and a love of partying – which must include playing music. When someone asked Des how we managed to contact one another musically, he explained, "The periphery of my musical tastes approaches the periphery of his – for example we both admire Spike Jones and His City Slickers." We also share an interest in walking and the need to escape from our mithered lives into silence or lunacy or a combination of both. We've sat in silence for hours; we've had the odd two or three day bender; we've debated English comedy, poetry, politics, music…On one occasion we found a snuff shop in Longton – just the whole thing was snuff – you've no idea the varieties of snuff!

The lunacy of finding a snuff shop!

We bought some. Later on, in a pub in Longton, we were trying it out when the police arrived. Someone thought we were snorting cocaine.

We had many an edgy escapade. Lunch time at the corner bar at the Royal Hotel, Crewe: the place filled up with Irish rugby fans en route to a World Cup game in Scotland, drinking and generally having a beano, but not a problem. In my experience rugby fans, unlike soccer fans, are never a problem. We were laughing and joking with them and it was a good atmosphere. Enter Sledge, a solid nineteen stone black man: bouncer *extraordinaire*, watching and becoming increasingly uneasy about potential mayhem on his patch. I was also keeping an eye on things; he had no need to worry but he came storming over and started to drag one of the fans out of the bar. I interceded. I got hold of Sledge's arm – not aggressively – and was prepared to take him on. He was over the top in his reaction. "He's not doing anything wrong," I said, "let him go." Well, Sledge did let him go. Sighs of relief all round. "We never actually thought we'd find an Englishman who'd speak up for us," one of the Irishmen said. When the rugby fans left we found a bag they had forgotten. It contained two bottles of Jameson's. Fair wages! Well, we couldn't follow them to Scotland with it, could we?

Des and I have had many an argument for daft reasons – often alcohol fuelled – and Des has stormed off and walked all the way home to Newcastle. It's just stupidity – a lovers' tiff. We fell out in America because I didn't phone Zoe. We've been in some ludicrous situations and survived because I can trust his reactions and he mine. When we were on a boat Des fell in the canal, peeing. While the other two blokes discussed the situation I was at the back of the boat looking for him and prepared to jump in. Des was there in his insulated woolly bear suit doing the breast stroke. "It's all right once you're in," he said, cheerfully.

Although we have played music together our friendship was the key issue. Through all the ups and downs, the comings and goings, the changes, the stagnation, the bizarre events, Des has been the constant. He has always regarded me as the musically dominant one even though he's made more money than me and had greater accolade.

Climax Blues Band

On one of our frequent London trips in the Seventies, Des and I were just walking along when a taxi slowed up. The window was wound down: inside was the Climax Blues Band singing, "Isn't She Lovely," to which Des replied, "Couldn't Get it Right," each singing the other's current hit. A nice convergence.

Both Des and I have musical connections with this band, which, like Des, had served the Hamburg apprenticeship. Climax toured in the UK, in Europe and America and released eighteen albums. The original line-up included Colin Cooper who founded the band in the Sixties. He was musically knowledgeable with more of a jazz background than I had but the blues he played was a bit urban and recent to my ear. It wasn't hard enough – too polished. A bit cabaret for my taste. Derek Holt was the bass player who eventually left the band to run a pub in Stafford. John Coughley, the drummer, occasionally played with the Skunk Band. Climax Blues Band's excellent guitarist Pete Aycock caused a split when he left the band. There was an interlude at this point during which Colin Cooper kept the name of the band and there was a possibility of me and Colin forming a duo. Nothing came of it; the musical differences were too great and we were temperamentally too alike for it to work. However, during this time I was able to suggest Les Hunt as a guitarist for Colin's band. So Climax then consisted of Colin Cooper, Les Hunt and George Glover (keyboards) and Crow (drums) from Des' band for a while.

Des and Colin Cooper used to do this thing where they would put a record on and the other would have to guess the provenance. When Colin heard a recording of me he put it in the Thirties.

I'm unclear about the present line-up of the Climax Blues Band but I think Les and George are still there. They are all good and successful musicians.

Colin Cooper unfortunately died in 2008.

Something To Do With Wimbledon Fortnight

Like the Skunk Band, the Dagworths were on the brink of larger success on a number of occasions. For my band *The Old Grey Whistle Test* had been a possibility, through contacts and friends. But the competition was strong and contacts could never surmount the other complicating factors such as the talented front man going for three-month benders. Des Parton's band was in a stronger position: backed by Tony Hatch, his recording of "Isn't She Lovely" stayed in the charts longer than simultaneous hits by Roger Daltrey and others. Yet it never reached number one and this was psychologically important in the world of pop music. I recall that Wimbledon Fortnight had been a factor in some way. In spite of his connection with Tony Hatch, the big money went on another very accomplished band: The Police.

I don't feel any trace of bitterness about missed opportunities. In between all this celebrity stuff I had to make a living and my practical nature always had the last word. My main pleasure in music is and always has been what I play on my own.

Jam Nights

Being able to meet and listen to other musicians and having the chance to perform informally without the anxiety of having to be successful is important in the life of a musician. It's a good way for new bands to build up confidence and you can also get drunk. I organised jam nights at the Cheshire Cheese at Gresty, The Royal Hotel on Nantwich Road, Crewe, the Leisure Club in Edleston Road, Crewe and The Limelight, Hightown, Crewe. Jam nights have a shelf life then they fold only to reappear with renewed hope somewhere else. The difference between a jam night and an acoustic night is that in jamming the music is allowed to go and flow and musicians often mingle, whereas acoustic nights are arranged round discrete acts in sequence.

The Start

The Crewe music scene has always been fairly buoyant. I'm a drummer. I played for eight years in a local cover band: Beam until February 2010 with bassist Neil Beech and lead guitarist Glyn Sutton. We went all over the North West and this gave me the confidence I needed. Glyn Sutton and I also teamed up with singer-songwriter-guitarist Chloe Chadwick in late 2007, playing her original material and some covers. She left us after a twelve month stint together; I was gutted by that. I'm now in a band called The Start formed in October 2009. Neil Beech has a new cover band: Foulplay.

I came originally from Wythenshawe to Crewe in 1986. When I asked about the music scene I was directed to the Leisure Club Jam Night, where I became long-term friends with Plum, who worked in the shop with Pete Johnson. He was absolutely committed to live music and introduced a jam night at The Albion in Mill Street which later became The Office, and that's where my band Beam was born. The Albion had a long history of live music: Pete Johnson and Pete Whittingham started off there in the Sixties.

I remember listening to Keith Marriott and Damien Darlington – both top flight players in my view – at the Leisure Club with Plum on bass. Keith Marriott nearly blew me away. Another night I saw John Darlington and another time I met Melvyn, Pete Johnson's drummer – an inspiration. I also met Pete's bass player, Moggsie: a nice bloke – quiet – and he did a bit of drumming. He encouraged me.

Plum was the sound engineer when The Limelight opened. He did it for the first six years or so and I did the lights for twelve months, with Plum on the sound desk. That was my inspiration to play drums: watching all the bands that came through The Limelight.

I didn't start gigging till I was thirty-three and I'm still enjoying it. My latest band is The Start – that's what the Crewe scene gave me as a musician. People who've made the big time still have their roots in this area. I was chatting to Damien Darlington at the Haslington Cosy Club a couple of weeks ago. He formed The Australian Pink Floyd in the early Nineties and travels all over the world playing to thousands of people. He's touring England at the moment but looking forward to going back to the States – they play up to 9,000 a time there. I asked him if it ever fazed him and he said yes at first but not any more – he's used to it.

Andy Smith. (34)

Keith Marriott
"But I guess I let my playing do the talking for me." (35)

Keith Marriot first started coming to the shop when he was about twelve – a contemporary of Andy Boote and John Darlington. He was always reserved – he didn't quite fit with what he was. With other musicians it was more excessive: music, sex and substances. Keith was less hedonistic: he liked girls; he liked a drink but not to excess.

He's a fantastic electric guitarist – one of the few that has a style of his own and he's played with a lot of people. He just stands there and does it. His bad back stopped him taking a job with the Australian Pink Floyd. He's a bit self-effacing but his performance confidence has improved over the years and performance is what it's all about. His latest band is Headband: "We play Rock n Blues with a twist of funk and we try to be a little bit different".

Raphael

One of the last jam nights I did at The Limelight was with Whitty's son Raphael on drums. It was just like having Whitty there. It was a full-on Skunk Band that night: Moggsie was still alive; Bootie was there; the chemistry was there. There was a variety of time signatures but Raphael didn't put a beat wrong: Moggsie, who could also play drums, would indicate what was to come by tapping his foot. Raphael playing with the Skunk Band was amazing and emotional.

Clive Gregson: Any Trouble

Some musicians were peripheral to the Skunk Band but had a brief part in the story. Clive Gregson, who lived in the flat at the back of the butcher's four doors away was one such person. This would be the late Seventies, early Eighties. Inevitably he visited the shop, as all musicians did. My connection with Clive Gregson began when the two of us set up a folk club at the Royal Hotel. Like many of the musicians I've met, I came across him just before he became successful. He did John Martyn stuff and had been involved in the folk scene with a number of competent local musicians. They decided to enter the pop field as Any Trouble. Their style resembled Elvis Costello.

Any Trouble went on the circuit as a good touring band and received acclaim. They did five albums and hundreds of gigs before breaking up in 1984. Clive was the singer-songwriter and also a good guitarist – certainly in the folk music world. He eventually became a solo artist: a wise move since it's the songwriter who makes the money. If a band goes out touring then a respectable wage is possible but all the royalties go to the songwriter.

Stevie Wonder benefited far more than Des for "Isn't She Lovely?" Des has written songs and jingles and provided himself with enough money to live on: more money than he could have made performing.

Clive Gregson's musical partnership with Christine Collister was described by *Rolling Stone* as "the state of the art in British folk-rock" and he has become a worldwide performer, songwriter, session musician and record producer. His songs have been recorded by Nanci Griffith (the originator of the genre known as folkabilly), Kim Carnes, Fairport Convention, Claire Martin, Norma Waterson and Smokie.

Great Outdoors: The Black Run

I continued to pursue sporting activities side by side with my business and musical career. I am a very keen skier and always choose the most demanding run: the black run. I came to realise that this applied to my music too.

I enjoyed the off-piste opportunities as much as the sport. Snow is very stimulating. I remember a mountain escapade with the Head Buyer from a famous store: we literally fell for one another in the snow. The ingredients for the coupling were all present: a party mood with singing and dancing in a local inn – me being the chief musician; guiding the lady along the piste, through the conifers; both falling in the cold snow feeling each other's body heat; more partying and then, ever the gentleman, insisting on escorting the stylish young woman to her hotel, sending off the German rival en route and somehow, because of the lateness of the hour, the problem of keys and the Head Buyer's plain friend, ending up in my bed together, where the fortunate woman experienced her first orgasm. So she said.

One of my horse-riding companions with whom I had a long-term relationship liked making love outdoors – mainly at her instigation. She used to go out without knickers. I remember a few compromising situations where you had to stay very still for a while. Imagine a bench on a disused railway line and a fat bloke with a bag of cans lumbering past. Then a woman in a turquoise jogging suit. Then after a short while some kids shoving one another. All going past. Then someone else in expensive trainers. Then someone on a bike. Then another jogger with sweatbands. Then someone with a sniffing dog. This amounted to a lot of starting and stopping. I don't know how we got there. The dogs were the worst interruptions.

Tom Jackson: Tour Manager

Round about my fortieth birthday I kick-started my solo career, appearing as Pete "Snakey Jake" Johnson. The Skunk Band still did the occasional gig for charity.

Tom Jackson, an ex-singer with Clive Gregson's band, offered to manage me, organising gigs in Chester at Alexander's Jazz Theatre, in London at the Twelve Bar Club, at the Trades Club in Hebden Bridge, and at a place near the Scottish border. There was a week spent in Nottingham and gigs in Derby, Huddersfield and Lichfield. He did it all for love. He loved the music; he loved my virtuosity. This lasted about a year and both of us enjoyed the experiences but, socially and musically nourishing as it had been, there was no future in this because it was impossible to make any money in this league of venues and I had to cover time spent away from the shop, when the takings would inevitably be down.

There had been the customary wrangling over money. Being an entertainer, unless you are very famous, is still a low status profession. You usually have to wait for your money; sometimes it's dependent on the size of the audience and there's often vagueness about the amount – but never in my mind! For example, I started on £60-£70 at the Jazz Theatre in Chester, with the promise of more money if I was a success. One night the management let in a bus load of foreign tourists and Tom asked for more money. He was refused because the tourists had not been charged! So Tom, an ex-miner and a big union man, put an end to the arrangement and things came to a natural end. Not long after, I remade my relationship with Zoe.

Tobacco Tins And Hot Rods

Round about the time when every town had an Irish themed pub with pretend nicotine on the ceilings and wooden farm implements on the walls, I had a very brief career as a purveyor of Irish songs. Shortly after the charity gig at The Limelight (*circa* 1994) an agent phoned me.

"I hear you're out of retirement. I can fill your diary."

"What with?"

"Irish music."

"I'm not interested."

"It's £200 a night."

So I phoned Terry Fox: a good all-rounder, who sang, played fiddle and penny whistle – all the Celtic stuff – and Fluff, an excellent violin player who later joined the reformed Incredible String Band. I had done Irish songs in folk clubs so I wasn't working in the dark.

We did about eight gigs and hated it. The venues were awful and we didn't really like the music. Neither did the punters! Really, the people wanted karaoke. At one dockside pub in Liverpool all the tables had tobacco tins on. No problem with that until you realized that the lids had been decorated with spent matches. This is something they do in jail to pass the time.

Some of the best gigs come spontaneously or unexpectedly. One I particularly remember was upstairs at the Civic Hall, Nantwich about 1996. Loraine Baker (ex Boat Band and now with Baker's Fabulous Boys) was on double bass and Fluff was on fiddle. Andy Boote was playing acoustic guitar and I was playing electric guitar quietly. It was like an acoustic Skunk Band. There were various aspects: country rock from me, jazz from Andy and Celtic roots from Fluff. It just flowed.

I enjoyed performing with Jo Ann Kelly. She was an excellent slide guitarist and she didn't half belt it out in her acoustic delta style. She was influenced by Memphis Minnie, Charley Patton, Bessie Smith and Sister Rosetta Tharpe. Jo Ann in turn influenced other female blues singers. She jammed with Canned Heat but declined the invitation to join the band, forming instead The Blues Band in 1979 with her brother Dave Kelly, Paul Jones – ex Manfred Mann – and the original Fleetwood Mac bassist Bob Brunning.

Gary B. Goode and the Hot Rods were the resident band at Crewe's mirror-balled Majestic Ballroom in the Sixties. They supported all the famous bands but the reason I admired them was because Keith Haines, my musical guru on the school bus, played for them. The kid who watched them then didn't expect ever to play with them.

Fast forward thirty-odd years. Gary B. Goode and the Hot Rods did a couple of reunions for charity then decided to do one for themselves. Keith is committed to his own musical interests and will only play rock 'n' roll for charity, so they asked me to play guitar in place of him and this opportunity made me realise what strength Keith contributed to the band.

Dressing Room Talk: Fleetwood Mac

Talking about stories that span the decades I supported Peter Green at Bar Cuba in Macclesfield round about 2004. He was the founder of Fleetwood Mac who left in 1970 and an excellent blues-rock guitarist – admired by Eric Clapton and Jimmy Page. BB King said of him: "He has the sweetest tone I ever heard; he was the only one who gave me the cold sweats." (36) BB King once asked Fleetwood Mac to play "Albatross" and then they invited him up to play with them. I was struck by the number of hits Peter Green had written as song after song was played: "Black Magic Woman", "Man Of The World", "The Green Manalishi" as well as "Albatross".

I went to his dressing room afterwards; the band members were all younger than Peter Green, as was his biographer. "Do you want a drink?" Peter asked. "Is the Pope a Catholic?" I replied. "Where's the Jack Daniels?" asked Peter Green, who wasn't drinking. "Say when." "Next week," I answered. Everyone laughed and the conversation flowed. Peter Green, who had sat in the audience, said he enjoyed my set. "You've seen it before in Manchester in the Sixties," I replied. I had supported Fleetwood Mac at Alvaston Hall, Nantwich and at Manchester whilst I was at university. I went on to talk about a dressing room conversation I'd had with Jeremy Spencer, who had been playing fairly basic in E. I had shown him some open tuning techniques associated with the blues that not many people knew about at the time. There was a spark of recognition at this point and everyone agreed that I had triggered something in Peter Green's memory but I don't know what. As singer-songwriter and front man of Fleetwood Mac, extreme reaction to drugs had rendered him mentally incapable of remembering much of his earlier career and he was grateful to me for helping to restore something.

The second phase of Fleetwood Mac – the *Rumours* era – initiated by drummer Mick Fleetwood, is the Fleetwood Mac everyone knows but

Peter Green is remarkable. Sadly enough, there were fewer people there to see him than to see me on that occasion.

The following week the biographer came to my shop: he had a Dobro to sell and wanted to know if I had any more Peter Green stories.

A Degree of Confrontation: Sound Systems, Kisses and Cleavers

Parallel with the musical fecundity of the Skunk Band, my business was supplying sound systems for internationally famous bands all over England and Europe.

Endangered Puddings

There's a constant struggle to get correct information before a gig and payment after a gig. I had organized a sound system for a band at The George at Burslem. I'd been reassured that they were not a punk band but when I arrived with the equipment I found they were, indeed, a punk band and therefore the sound system was not adequate for their needs. At the end of the gig their manager Michael Dempsey was reluctant to pay. The argument took place in a kitchen and, incensed by the injustice of the situation and the fact that I had been misled, I picked up a meat cleaver and hauled it at the wooden work bench, close enough to the manager to make my point. He paid up.

In a similar vein I had two gigs booked in local Crewe and district hotels one New Year's Eve. The second venue wanted me there just before the midnight festivities so it was a tight schedule. I finished the first gig and went to see the manager for my fee. The manager was arrogant and disrespectful: "Oh, I'm far too busy to deal with that now!" The exchange was taking place – once again – in the kitchen and I seized my moment – and a gravy boat. "How many of these puddings do you have spare?" I asked, waving the gravy boat in a menacing way. Then, to underline my point I poured gravy over one of the puddings awaiting delivery to table. He paid up.

Displacing your anger into an object is a harmless way of making a threatening point.

It's still happening. Only recently, at a local folk festival there was an agreement that I should receive £150 for two sessions on consecutive nights. When the time came for payment there was a managerial vagueness about the fee. "£100, wasn't it?" Fortunately, Zoe's memory is extremely good and no meat cleaver was necessary. They paid up.

Just Another Town Along The Way

Sometimes, though, it was all too petty to bother with and I sublimated my anger in humour. I once supported The Edgar Broughton Band at the Bridge Street Arts Centre in Newcastle-under-Lyme in the Eighties. The audience was sparse and when Edgar Broughton, who had some acoustic numbers in his repertoire, heard me, he went and hid. At the end, when I went for my £75, the management only wanted to give me £35: the usual excuse – poor attendance. Furious, I threw it back at them and stormed off.

Des picked it up.

I called the resulting tape: *Live, Under Lyme and Underpaid.*

The Adverts

But, going back to the Burslem gig: so impressed were these punks that they invited me to tour with them and be their sound engineer. The band in question were The Adverts and I met them just before they became famous. I did the sound systems for all their live performances. Gaye Advert played the bass, TV Smith was the singer-songwriter and Lorry Driver was the drummer. I remember the awful row they made and the pogoing and the glaucous waterfall of spit after every song and me and Des sitting experiencing this next generation of music with some bemusement.

This group was formed in 1976 and within three months they were on tour with The Damned. "Looking through Gary Gilmore's Eyes" was the hit they had in August 1977. It's on *Mojo* magazine's list of best punk singles. A suitably macabre subject: Gary Gilmore was on Death Row and insisting on the death penalty for himself. This song referred to the wishes of the murderer to donate his eyes to medical science. What gruesome scenes had they witnessed? The song created just the sort of controversy an up and coming punk group needed.

Inappropriate Thrift

Gaye was the bass player but we had to tune it up for her. Al Dean said to her, "These strings are knackered."
"But I only bought them last week!"
"Yes but you bought them second hand!"

Slim (Wayne Davies). (37)

The Adverts were a well-regarded group; in addition to The Damned they supported Generation X, Slaughter and the Dogs and The Jam. When Annie Nightingale took over as host of *The Old Grey Whistle Test* in 1978, The Adverts opened her first show. "At last: the 1978 Show!" said TV Smith – probably in reference to the Whistle Test's failure so far to embrace punk. They did four sessions for John Peel on Radio One: two in 1977, one in 1978 and one in 1979 by which year it was all over. The Adverts split up after the death of their manager Mike Dempsey.

Some punk bands were good; some diabolically bad but they all had raw energy. The Sex Pistols and The Boomtown Rats had talent and an eye for the main chance. The only way you can make a punk band sound good is to make it sound as bad as possible. You produce a wall of non-melodic sound and you pin the audience against the back wall with the blast. If you put a coat or a plastic glass on those speakers the vibration would send it two or three feet but these mad audiences would come to the front and put their heads inside the bass speaker cabinets!

No-one in The Adverts could play but TV Smith who wrote some great songs including "Looking Through Gary Gilmore's Eyes" now appears on Radio

Four. His recent work is Dylanesque and I feel glad he is still out there doing it.

Waterfalls Of Spit

With punk events you were a little bit on your guard. They were all crazy – the audience as well. They all used to rush to the back of the hall then rush forward and crush one another. Things were always edgy. Buzzcocks had a very strange following. The Adverts – OK, Generation X – OK but the Buzzcocks – a bit wild. They used to encourage the audience to spit. It was like waterfalls everywhere. The cables had to be dried out with rags – fortunately there was no AIDS then – before we put them into the van.

Wayne Davies (Slim). (38)

On The Road

Being constantly on the road, either doing gigs or doing sound systems we would meet up with other bands at transport cafes at unsocial hours. There were all sorts: people destined to become famous and some already well-known; averagely good bands and flavour-of-the-month bands; all on the road and tired and hungry. But no tribute bands in those days! You can tell a musician if you are a musician: it shows in dress, hair length, general aura, extreme fatigue and a few seconds of conversation. We would often end up talking about cooking or vintage cars or the architecture of a city, rather than about music. It's the opposite of what you would expect. Little needs to be said about gigs because everyone has experienced mismatched audiences and technical horrors so unless there's a really funny or terrible or sexy story there's nothing to add. This is why Des and I don't find Billy Connolly's stories interesting: that sense of humour is in the back of every band's transit van cruising down the motorways of Britain.

Basic Requests And Poor Timekeeping

I was involved in setting up sound systems for some high-profile bands. At that time Pete had a big PA – he'd designed it and we used to hire the sound system out. That was the punk era – there were lots of them – and they needed a big PA to make lots of noise. One of these bands had an outrageous girl: wild and liberated. She used to say things like, "Have you got some gaffer tape? I've just come on."

One night, at Barbarella's – or it might have been The Longhouse – in Birmingham, this band had been due to go on fifteen minutes ago; everything was all set but Miss Gaffer Tape was nowhere to be seen. I looked in all the possible places for her and I looked again. Things were getting desperate – the crowd was yelling and stamping and the only possible place she could be was the toilet. I knocked on the door.

"I'm having a shag and I'm not coming out till I've finished."

She was another quarter of an hour.

Wayne Davies (Slim). **(39)**

Hit Me With Your Rhythm Stick

I don't know a musician that hasn't got respect for Ian Dury and the Blockheads, whatever their taste in music. Dury was an artist (he studied under Peter Blake at the Royal College of Art) and a storyteller: his songs were vivid, witty stories told by an artist. He was aligned with the punk movement but his original band, Kilburn and the Highroads, was a very well thought of small band, not labelled as anything but good. Dury was also a polio victim and his drummer had only one leg; the whole band was characterised by courage and style, even in death. At his funeral the flowers were arranged to spell DUREX and he had a glass-sided Victorian coach with white horses.

I met Ian Dury in transit and I admired his funny and sad storytelling songs. His music was in the rock genre, original and technically sound and you could hear the vocals. I liked the way they were done in an English dialect and rhyming slang, reminding me of the obscurities in some blues lyrics. He was asked to write the libretto for *Cats* but refused because he hated Lloyd Webber's music and I applaud him for that.

Des' band supported Kilburn and the High Roads and I liked the Dagworth's songs for the same reason: "Brixham Harbour" has a nice Englishness.

Whores And Weed In Knightsbridge

During this period of my life, I was quite well off. My association with Mike Dempsey, the manager of The Adverts, took me to some interesting places and he was my main source of contacts in those days. Dempsey had a great penthouse in Knightsbridge – very posh and built on various levels – and we were invited there. This would be about 1977. Well, we pulled up in our van and went through a cordon of press photographers and policemen. We thought they must be there because of The Adverts but it turned out to be another reason.

A prostitute was being evicted.

It was a big news story – she'd been having an affair with a well-known MP. Anyway once in the flat Mike offered me a very meagre amount of weed in a tin. "Wait a minute," I said and I went through the cordon again, collected a carrier bag from the vehicle and went back in the flat. The world's press was not interested in me and my mission. Good job. The carrier bag was full of weed: my slice of a harvest I had helped gather in! I distributed it.

These good times only came to an end when my connection with Michael Dempsey was severed by his death, which inevitably curtailed my business.

The Three Degrees: 1976 or 1977

The lads phoned me. "Everything we're doing's wrong according to this man. He wants echo on this and that but he doesn't have a stage sheet!" The manager of The Three Degrees was hassling the lads about the sound system. They were right to be upset: a set list with requirements set out at the side for special things like echo was essential. This manager was being unreasonable. I got into my 3 litre Volvo – a very impressive model complete with all the refinements – and drove over to The Heavy Steam Machine in Hanley.

The manager was a small slim black man in a salmon pink suit. I threatened him: "You're the wrong size to shout at my lads like that!

There's only me shouts at my guys. Right lads: load up. Take the gear out." Pink Suit stormed off to the Three Degrees' dressing room, panicking and mouthing off and ridiculous. "Right lads – carry on." The lads carried on with their job as if nothing had happened.

The show went on and all went well. Afterwards the girls came and each and every one kissed me: "The best sound we've had all Europe." They might as well have said it was the best sex in Europe, so tremendously pleased was I to have my work recognized. A rare occurrence in the business.

The Three Degrees were attractive, sexy ladies; more than that: they had star quality. Unmistakeable.

A fortnight later I received a similar phone call from the same venue: more trouble. Exasperated, I stormed over to Hanley and flung open the doors. It was dark inside: only the stage was lit and on the stage was the biggest man in the world. His arms were bigger than my legs. He was as big as Texas – complete with hat. I just looked up at him. "Do what you like," I said. Then there was laughter. It was a wind-up. A very creative wind-up.

Give Me Sunshine

You get used to prima donnas when you're in show business so it's good to meet entertainers who behave well, as the Three Degrees did. Unlike their manager.

I used to provide the sound system for corporate entertainment at a stately home near Stafford. A posh setup. KC and the Sunshine Band were performing. This was a nine piece band but I had only provided two microphones. I apologised and was about to call it off so they could make other arrangements. "Does it work?" someone asked of the sound system. "Certainly. Of course it works." "Then we'll work round it."

Then followed what I would describe as a perfect night. They were probably better not having what I should have taken – brass instruments are loud anyway and it sounded great: just like a live acoustic band. I'm always bowled over by professionalism in musicians. The Drifters were similarly professional: a consummate cabaret act, perfectly polite and a great band. I did the sound for them at The Heavy Steam Machine round about 1977.

Homeward Bound, I Wish I Was

Like being a musician, being a sound engineer or a roadie meant getting used to a mobile life spent largely on Britain's motorways. It could be fun and it was not unusual to meet Rod Stewart at the services but it was exhausting and stressful as well.

Partly as a result of the connection with The Adverts, Custom Amplification built up a reputation for providing good sound systems for punk groups. Accordingly, I provided the PA for high-profile groups such as the Sex Pistols – they were just punks! – and The Boomtown Rats. I didn't always go with the sound engineers. Sometimes I was not needed at all and at other times, for special things, I went separately. Al Dean and Shep usually went in a large Mercedes 608D van, with a couple of others. Such heavy and expensive material needed guarding at all times so I hired out stuff on condition that Shep went with it. I had confidence in my sound engineers: they knew and understood how it all worked.

This life had none of the romance often associated with travelling. Asked if I had done gigs in Belfast or Dublin, I once denied it only to be reminded that I had played both cities with my band and solo, and I had also done sound systems in these places. Yet no city distinguishes itself from any other if you're focussed on motorway routes, venues, hotel rooms and relentlessly moving on. There simply isn't time or energy to allow the mind to imbibe a sense of place. Imbibe something else, perhaps.

Shep

Shep had been introduced to my shop through Pete Whittingham. He'd been sleeping rough on a park bench and looked like a tramp. One day I locked him in the premises and threatened not to let him out till he'd had a bath. After that he stayed at the shop and started to work for me. Shep went on to tour with Bob Geldof and was briefly to be seen on the Live Aid Concert, adjusting a microphone stand. According to him the Live Aid technicians had T shirts made: "Fuck the world – feed the crew" but were banned from wearing them. Although this is a humorous, possibly apocryphal story, it does highlight the fact that this profession, although it touches the lives of the rich, talented and famous, is not prestigious in spite of being crucial.

Shep toured the world with performers such as ELO, Joan Armatrading, Ozzy Osbourne and Ginger Baker. I met Ginger Baker briefly. A total eccentric. Shep remembers seeing him heading for the hills with two very rich young ladies and a big bag of coke. Shep was with Alex Harvey when he had a massive heart attack on a dock in Belgium. The second heart attack killed him in the ambulance on the way to the hospital in Zeebrugge. It was the day before his forty-seventh birthday and he had been performing with his new band, Electric Cowboys. I never claimed the money for the sound system.

Shep has returned to Crewe and worked as the sound engineer at The Limelight until recently.

The Comedians

Custom Amplification did the sound systems for Bernard Manning and Ken Dodd.

Part of Manning's act at Rolls Royce Club was to make the microphone sound as if it was working intermittently. Then he would give the sound engineers a good 'telling off'. I knew he would do this so I was prepared. When he got to this part of the act I shut the out front sound down and left the monitors on. So Bernard could hear it through the monitors and the audience couldn't hear it at all. Bernard was complaining that the sound system was going wrong – "but only through the monitors, Bernard," I said. The comedian laughed at this reversal of his joke.

With Bernard Manning what you see is what you get and it's the same with Ken Dodd: a true professional and a nice man. I remember him sending an envelope with money in for the lads to have a drink.

The Rolling Stones

I met the Rolling Stones at a party somewhere in London, some time in the Eighties. I remember the exclusivity of the event: how you had to have someone to take you and how generous the hospitality was once you had made it into the venue. I found with them as with other performers that if you treated them in an ordinary way you had a good time with them. You could just get drunk and powder your nose: if someone empties a line of coke in front of you, you tend to join in, or else they won't ask you again!

I've thought about the drugs scene that celebrities are involved in. I wasn't into drugs until I was about thirty but drug-related belonging is not the only option. It's not *my* only option anyway. There's another way of being part of things: if it takes someone to bring a party to life by dancing or singing – that's me. They love you for it and they ask you again.

Political Shoes

Not all of my brushes with celebrity have been through the world of entertainment, unless of course you include politicians in this world. We visited the Scilly Isles: there are five altogether and you can visit each one by boat taxi. Walking along the high street on the main island, St. Agnes, was a man with a Labrador, a mac, a pipe and a wife. He just said, "Good morning," pipe in the corner of his mouth. It was our Prime Minister, Harold Wilson.

We visited Tresco: lovely gardens with wild budgies flying about, birds that would eat off your plate and ships' figureheads all over the place. Later on, we went to the only pub on the island and someone was playing guitar, quite averagely. It didn't take many pints for me to borrow it.

"Don't break any strings!"

"I've got a whole shop full at home. If I do I'll put a guitar on the end of it."

The songs went down well. I went for a pee. Harold Wilson came and stood next to me. I was that shocked I part turned round and splashed his shoes! Harold Wilson was my father's hero; he liked the idea that class barriers were being brought down. They certainly were! The PM complimented me on my guitar playing, though not my aim. In retrospect the most amazing thing was that there were no photographers and no security men. Today's prime ministers couldn't go for an egalitarian pee.

My combined activities in music and sport put me in contact with the famous and the notorious. I discovered that they were the same as me and even prime ministers piss.

More Endings

Though death loitered in corners as we partied and shagged and bent our minds to avoid its gaze, that death letter always caught you unawares. You pick up the phone expecting to talk about amps and microphones and mither or the best route to a gig and someone's saying,

"There's no easy way to tell you, Pete...."

The deaths in the Skunk Band years have tended to be sudden and therefore more shocking than the previous deaths in my family. Pete Whittingham, Keith Brammer, Moggsie and Plum all died suddenly. My best friend and musical brother, my sports companion, my surrogate son and my one-time business partner: all suddenly gone.

Alcohol was to claim a beautiful girlfriend and Des Parton's guitarist Ron. My friendship with eccentric entertainer Eugene was conducted partly in bars and partly in the cancer ward. There's a fine line between a party and a wake.

Notes: Section Two

(1) John Darlington, interviewed by Sandra Gibson 3rd January 2007.

(2) Andy Boote, interviewed by Sandra Gibson 4th September 2006.

(3) Wayne Davies (Slim), interviewed by Sandra Gibson 30th January 2007.

(4) Andy Smith, from a conversation at Custom Amplification, 2006.

(5) Phil Doody, from a conversation at Custom Amplification 19th March 2009.

(6) Zoe Johnson, interviewed by Sandra Gibson 26th April 2007.

(7) John Darlington, interviewed by Sandra Gibson 3rd January 2007.

(8) Zoe Johnson, interviewed by Sandra Gibson 26th April 2007.

(9) Wayne Davies (Slim), interviewed by Sandra Gibson 30th January 2007.

(10) Ibid.

(11) John Darlington, interviewed by Sandra Gibson 3rd January 2007.

(12) Letter sent by Pete Whittingham from Perth, Australia in May 1984.

(13) Letter sent by Pete Whittingham from Perth, Australia, 21st August 1984.

(14) From a letter sent from New Zealand by John Billington shortly after Pete Whittingham's death.

(15) Letter sent by Pete Whittingham's parents to Pete Johnson, 5th February 1985.

(16) Performance by Chew The Roots at The Imperial, Crewe, 29th December 2006, reviewed by Sandra Gibson.

(17) John Darlington, interviewed by Sandra Gibson 3rd January 2007.

(18) Ibid.

(19) Ibid.

(20) Ibid.

(21) Andy Boote, interviewed by Sandra Gibson 4th September 2006.

(22) Ibid.

(23) Website: www.vavoom.altpro.net.

(24) Ibid.

(25) Performance by Vavoom! at The Imperial, Crewe, reviewed by Sandra Gibson, 2006.

(26) Andy Boote, interviewed by Sandra Gibson 4th September 2006.

(27) Dave Evans, Shady Oak, Beeston, 9th May 2009.

(28) Ibid.

(29) Des Parton, interviewed by Sandra Gibson, May 2006.

(30) Ibid.

(31) M&M Music, i.e. Tony Hatch and Jackie Trent.

(32) Des Parton, interviewed by Sandra Gibson May 2006.

(33) Manchester Evening News, 3rd February 2009.

(34) Andy Smith, from an e-mail sent to Sandra Gibson 9th February 2010.

(35) Keith Marriott on myspace.

(36) BB King quote from Wikipedia.

(37) Wayne Davies (Slim), interviewed by Sandra Gibson 30th January 2007.

(38) Ibid.

(39) Ibid.

SECTION THREE

Where The Moonon Crosses The Yellow Dog: The Country Blues

For all the partying of my rock 'n' roll life, my passion has been the country blues and I have kept faith with this since the age of thirteen. No matter where my journeys in less-than-reliable vehicles took me, the constant soundtrack to everything was the blues. It has been my rock.

The closest I got to having a religion.

Bully For Me

An Unfair Match

The blues embraced me at the threshold of my teens. My needs for comfort, self-expression, stimulation and exploration of technique were fulfilled by the blues. The blues galvanised my sense of justice.

Like all kids in a northern industrial town I had spent my childhood on the streets: doing errands; measuring the time by dandelion clocks; absorbing the tribal laws; guarding the bonfire stuff; registering those who wouldn't give you your ball back; aware of those slightly exotic types in bright dressing gowns rumoured to be ex-opera stars and those shadowy presences our parents told us not to speak to.

When I was nine, three lads cornered me, bent on giving me a pasting. An unfair match. I spotted my chance: one of the lads put his shopping bag down. I grabbed it, swung it round and round my head and sent it clattering, crashing and smashing all across the road. Pretty spectacular. The boys were in tears – they'd be in trouble at home for this. Surviving against the odds has always been instinctive for me and I have extended this into fighting on behalf of others in a similar situation.

The Land Of The Free
"Every time I go downtown
Somebody's kickin' my hite around." (1)

My study of slavery and the blues revealed an epic story of exploitation and oppression: from street bullying to the sanctioning of lynch law. Everything the Southern black had been through was abhorrent and it was still happening. I was aware of this before Martin Luther King's Civil Rights Movement entered my consciousness. Segregation and discrimination against black people in the Land of the Free, especially in the South, had created an impoverishing apartheid long after slavery had been abolished. The overruling of the remaining Jim Crow Laws and the ratification of the Voting Rights Act took place as late as the mid Sixties. All this is so recent and so fresh in the memory. A white Nina Simone fan posted this comment on YouTube: "We had a cross burning in our front yard because a multi-racial band was playing touch football when neighbours were driving by". (2)

Indignation reinforced my appreciation of the blues. I felt compassion for the plight of the black people of America and admiration for the way they combined raw emotion with supreme musicianship in responding to life's big issues – often with humour. Meeting so many of the old blues singers during the Sixties confirmed my respect. I wanted to resist bullying on their behalf. Feeling their songs deserved to be heard by a wider audience, I've done my best to communicate this.

The country blues has always been my main thing and by the country blues I mean music originating in the Southern states of America from the conditions of the black people living there. The rawness and realness I found in some of the music was a true expression of the black experience, as far as I was concerned. The poor quality of some of the recordings gives it a distant, plaintive sound that I have always responded to. My repertoire also includes music not labelled as country blues but interpreted in the spirit of the *genre*. And the *genre* does have a wide scope and a big heart: light and shade, subtlety and harshness, humour and sadness, farce and tragedy, love and passion and bawdiness.

The Origin, Scope And Development Of The Country Blues

The Blues Did Not Originate In Africa

The country blues was first published in 1912 and first recorded in the Twenties: long after the blues had been established as an oral form. Some archivists have claimed it had its origins in Africa but as a musician I would refute this. People singing what came to be known as the blues wouldn't have heard African rhythms. They weren't even recorded – where would they hear them? I think that the African influence in the blues is minimal, if it exists at all, because the oppressor always commits cultural genocide on the oppressed. The slaves brought to America had to be stripped of any sense of identity other than that of being owned. Families were split up; they weren't allowed to gather in large groups; they were worked to death. Oh yes – their culture was beaten out of them one way or another. Not even rhythm was allowed: there were religious reservations about dance and rhythm and black people were not permitted to play drums because communication of any kind had to be suppressed in the interests of political control.

No: I don't accept that the blues came from Africa – not even the rhythms. A primitive quality is in the music because of the way the Southern blacks lived: subsisting in rural poverty and playing raw-edged versions of what was available in the prevailing culture: mainly European music. Thirty years after I made this claim, some prominent musicians have made similar statements.

They would have had access to sea shanties – especially the first generation of slaves – work songs, white hillbilly music, folk songs from Europe and gospel from white folks' hymns. If you study the provenance of songs you can find the same song being reinterpreted as it travels from one culture to another. We think of "St. James Infirmary Blues" as a blues from New Orleans, originally called "Gambler's Blues" but it's probably based on an eighteenth century English ballad: "The Unfortunate Rake". The melody to "Streets Of Laredo" comes from the same song. "The Gallis Pole" is strongly associated with Leadbelly but it's from a traditional eighteenth century American song.

The Devil's Music

The only place where numbers of black people were allowed to gather was the church and for some this was a comfort and an expressive outlet. Mississippi Fred McDowell spoke of the origins of the blues in what was called a "reel" and how singing this represented a turning away from religion. This was why the blues became the devil's music for some.

The Blue Came From The Reel

Now what you – what we call the blues now? At dat time you know what dey called 'em? A reel. Tha's what the blues come from, a reel...

Now you don' know what a reel is, do you? Okay. Aright is jus' like a r- uh... Old people raised you when I was coming on. You go to church, you- you- you call yourself confess t' 'ligion. Okay. Well everybody had got confidence in you, y'understan', dat you, you really done confe[ss]. Well you turn around? From the church song and start singin' 'at- well see, didn' call it a blues then, you call that a reel, you understan'. Well that – the reel came from – the blue came from the reel. They change it, just to say blues…

Fred McDowell. (3)

Fortunately musicians found ways to get round the embargo on drumming: tapping on the guitar body, stamping the feet, using the voice and guitar strings rhythmically as well as for melody. This strand found later expression in the music of Bo Diddley and ultimately in rap, where the voice was stripped of melody and became an instrument of rhythm.

A Lighter Shade Of Blue

The blues has always been associated with the black musician. For reasons of common heritage, white performers also sang the blues but we praise them in proportion to the 'blackness' in their voice. I have a tape called *A Lighter Shade of Blue: White Country Blues 1926-38* which shows that the white singers recorded concurrently with the black blues players. Clayton McMichen performs "Prohibition Blues" complete with yodelling. Black musicians only occasionally yodel; white ones do a lot. Whites tend to sing the blues more clean, yet Larry Hensley's rendition of "Match Box Blues" sounds very 'black'. Generally speaking the white blues was more controlled and more sophisticated than black blues, which is more exuberant, less inhibited and happier in tone.

Because music transcends barriers there would have been musical fraternisation between blacks and whites from the beginning. Musical passion and poverty and whisky would draw people together at barbecues and medicine shows. Then again black and white musicians would meet at recording studios during the Twenties and Thirties. I don't think familiarity with the country blues just came from listening to the radio – many were too poor to own one. Perhaps, as Frank Walker (4) said, it had something to do with proximity:

Right Close

...on the outskirts of a city like Atlanta, you had your colored section, and then you had your white...right close to each other. They passed each other every day, and a little of the spiritualistic type of singing of the colored people worked over into the white hillbilly, and a little of the white hillbilly worked over into what the colored people did.

Black and white music wasn't parallel; it was integrative.

Black and white musicians mixed in jazz bands too. Jazz guitarist Chet Krolewicz was the only white player in a black band; "I wanted to play with the best," he said. In order to do this he shared with them the inferior facilities "for coloreds". (5) A black performer in a white band would be screened off. This is sickening of course but if you're a good musician you do have a kind of passport; social class and race isn't a bar if people recognize and respect you as a musician. Thelonious Monk met Baroness Pannonica de Koenigswarter, a member of the Rothschild family in Paris in 1954. She became a lifelong friend and patron of both Monk and Charlie Parker, hosting jam sessions in her New York suite, putting up with racist taunts about being a "nigger-lover" and getting in trouble with the law over her *protégé's* possession of drugs. *The New York Times*, reporting her death in 1988 stated that she "offered sustenance and care to many musicians who needed help". (6)

But this is all a world away from the controlled mixing that actually reinforced apartheid at Harlem's Cotton Club. Even the name was patronizing. The performers were black; the audience drawn from the white social elite. I think about this when I sing my version of "Stormy Weather", composed by Harold Arlen for the 1933 *Cotton Club Review.*

Joog, Honky Tonk And Medicine Show

The country blues goes back a long way in recording terms. The women were the pioneers. The first blues record was Mamie Smith's "Crazy Blues" recorded in 1920. Ma Rainey, Clara Smith, Rosa Henderson, Lucille Bogan and Bessie Smith made their recording debuts in 1923. The first jug bands were recorded in 1924 and in 1925/1926 Blind Lemon Jefferson, Bo Weavil Jackson and Blind Blake all recorded. In 1927 it was Blind Willie McTell and Barbecue Bob followed by Leroy Carr and Scrapper Blackwell in 1928. Their "How Long, How Long Blues" was the most successful blues hit of the year. One of my heroes: Mississippi John Hurt was also recording in Memphis in 1928. Charley Patton made his first recording in 1929 and another of my heroes: Son House recorded in 1930. 1933 saw the first Leadbelly recordings for the Library of Congress followed by his first commercial recordings for A.R.C. in 1935. Robert Johnson didn't record till 1936 – two years before he died aged 27. (7)

But before that the music would be played live all over the South. Juke joints – *joog* meant rowdy or disorderly – also called barrel houses, were established at rural crossroads near plantations, sawmills and turpentine camps for the rural work force. Operated by black people for black people, they sold alcohol and provided music such as ragtime and boogie-woogie in the late 1880s and in the 1890s then later, the blues. The guitar would be widely available in the 1890s. There would be dancing and gambling; these were wild places.

Medicine shows were the original "word from our sponsor" combining entertainment: music, magic, flea circuses, jokes, freak shows and storytelling with the sale of dubious remedies. Many black musicians travelled with them to make a living or because the itinerant life suited them. Honky-tonks were the urban version of juke joints but the name also became associated with a type of music related to classic blues in tonal structure but with a stepped-up tempo. These performances were essentially small scale and intimate affairs. The most basic venue for playing music was the street corner and some places became legendary.

The original audience for most country music would be limited to a small number of people from the local area. The use of acoustic instruments would limit the size of audience. A more sinister reason was that groups of black people became targets for the Ku Klux Klan.

Reckless Disposition

The itinerant life of the blues singer was often their only means of survival or it supplemented a meagre income. For a disabled person it would be one of the few things they could do. That's why there were so many blind musicians: Blind Lemon Jefferson, Blind Willie Johnson, Blind Boy Fuller, Blind Blake, Reverend Gary Davis, Blind Willie McTell, Sonny Terry, Brownie McGhee, Sleepy John Estes – all handicapped by more than their skin colour. Being on the move would suit those in flight from the law or from their family responsibilities or from a broken relationship: recurrent song themes. There's always a train whistle blowing. Although some blues artists achieved fame and wealth, on the whole it wasn't a job for the upwardly mobile; it lacked respectability and certainly didn't have the blessing of the church, and no matter what your skill and fame you couldn't share a hotel, restaurant or drinking fountain with your white band-mates. On the plus side, though, the movement of musicians from place to place would facilitate cross-fertilization of musical ideas.

You have to remember that the blues gurus in the black and white photos were mostly very young men when they were recorded. They sang protest songs about poverty and the domination of the white man: the punk of its day – though the political comment, like the sexual innuendo, could be obscured by the language. This music originally had a separate classification as "race music" and very few white people listened to it. I've performed it for decades – much longer than many of the original musicians who died young and before they had the opportunity or the pressure to adapt, dilute or refine it for a white audience. And although the early and often violent deaths of these musicians are regrettable, their rawness remains uncompromised.

The Oral Tradition

"Two plus two son of a bitch is four." When their small son started mixing his tables with inappropriate American slang, my friends asked his teacher about it. She told them the children were taught to say, "Two plus two, *the sum of which* is four." This story illustrates the strengths and the weaknesses of the oral tradition. What you lose in accuracy you gain in novelty; what you gain in liveliness of language you lose in clarity! Like Chinese Whispers, you never know what will become of the original phrase and this is what I treasure about the country blues: its secrecy and obscurity; its capacity for change and reinterpretation as it passes from one musician to another and from one region to another.

People are surprised that I have learnt the lyrics without seeing them written down. It was a question of listening time and time and time again – but then I worried about wearing out my records! In his introduction to Leadbelly's *Library of Congress Recordings,* Lawrence Cohn mentions the difficulties involved in deciphering Leadbelly's: "broad, thick Texas-Louisiana accent which was punctuated by poor placement of microphone and artist in many instances and the inferior quality of the surviving disc". (8) Sometimes the microphone is being moved between guitar and singer and parts of songs are missing because the artist carried on singing whilst the disc was being turned over.

But I've enjoyed puzzling over the songs and interpreting them for my audiences. The phrasing is not easy to follow and the language is often unfamiliar; sometimes it's a question of musical balance or pronunciation. Then there are words and phrases that are code or patois for controversial content. It's like learning another language and a whole new set of references. For example in the line "Goin' where the Moonon crosses the Yellow Dog" you've got to know that "Yellow Dog" is not a hound but the blues nickname for the Yazoo and Mississippi Valley Railway, "dog" meaning a local or branch line. I have always interpreted "Moonon" as a poetic description of the long straight rail track, gleaming in the moonlight, which intersected the Yellow Dog. This is only my interpretation; people have written whole theses on the subject of WC Handy's "Yellow Dog Blues".

Sexual references are relatively easy to decipher. You'd have to be innocent to think Blind Boy Fuller's "I Want Some Of Your Pie" is about confectionary. There's more where that came from: "Let me put my banana in your fruit basket, then I'll be satisfied", or "We gonna churn, churn, churn until the butter come" (9) and "If you were a dresser I would pull open your drawers" (10) are all fairly clear! But Mississippi John Hurt's "I'm Satisfied" is more challenging and it took me ages to interpret it. There was of course a Vaudevillian tradition in suggestive songs which got our own Marie Lloyd in trouble. Other songs are shockingly direct: "Show Me What You've Got" by Kansas City Kitty and Georgia Tom is an unambiguous, sexy and teasing song about a raunchy financial transaction. "My Man O' War" by Lizzie Miles refers to anal sex and you can't get more straightforward – and confident – than Lucille Bogan's, "I've got something 'tween my legs'll make a dead man come" from "Shave 'em Dry". Blues singers often made such recordings for the sound engineers' personal listening. (11)

Moonshine and sex were often the only release from the drudgery of life and a line such as "make me a pallet on the floor" is as much about a place to rest your body as it is about sex.

Gwine Dig A Hole To Put The Devil In

I wish to refute the allegation that the blues is 'domestic' when compared with the 'political' folk music of people like Woody Guthrie, Bob Dylan and Pete Seeger. From casual street-level to institutional level, discrimination against black people was pervasive, abusive and frequently fatal. People could be lynched for the slightest thing. In his excellent book about Blind Willie McTell: *Hand Me My Travelin' Shoes,* Michael Gray refers to the lynching of Mary Turner in Lowndes County in 1918 for making "unwise remarks". If you were black you had to watch your words. In this context it was all the more courageous of a musician to be covertly or overtly political. The expression of the suffering of discrimination and poverty is a political act anyway. In his recordings for the Library of Congress, Leadbelly explains that in the line "Gwine dig a hole to put de devil in" (12) the devil is the white boss. Leadbelly's "Bourgeois Blues" is a condemnation of day-to-day discrimination: "Me and Miss Martha standing upstairs. / The white man says don't want no niggers up there". It's interesting that black performers often used the white man's terms for them but in claiming the name they were subverting the power. Leadbelly's reference to the "Scottsboro Boys" in the Library of Congress recording is more directly political:

Now I'll tell you about in Alabama, must be Jim Crow. If a white woman says something, it must be so, and she can say something about a colored person, if it's a thousand colored men, they kill all of 'em just for that one woman; if she ain't tellin' the truth it don't make any difference.

In "Milk Cow Blues" – a Kokomo Arnold song – the loss of a woman is likened to the loss of a milk cow. Perhaps not very flattering to the modern woman and only understood in the rural context of a cow being a wealth-creating asset. You have to get beyond the sexy earthiness to see the economic point.

A world away from mainstream popular music, the blues faced life's harshness. Blind Willie McTell's "Reckless Disposition" is about a relationship that has reached crisis point because of a hard-drinking woman. Look at the hinterland of violence and despair in blues lyrics:

To keep her quiet I knocked her teeth out her mouth. (13)

Cocaine for horses an' not for men/Doctors say it'll kill you but dey don' say when/An' ho, ho, baby take a whiff on me. (14)

When you think she's in your kitchen, cookin', she's got a stranger by the hand. (15)

Rather have my head in alcohol, my body on some railroad track/than have that black bee bite me in my back. (16)

The 1910 jazz classic "Shine" with lyrics by Cecil Mack is a humorous song about a shoe-shine boy. This exuberant song, Vaudevillian in mood, slightly cocky, slightly defiant and life-embracing – you can imagine someone tap-dancing to the rhythmic guitar in my version – is an early black pride song. There are versions by Ella Fitzgerald, Louis Armstrong and Ry Cooder. If I play "Shine" then it's what you call a jazz turnaround: easy if you've studied a bit of jazz but if all you know is pop then it's a whole new set of different chord progressions.

During my third trip to Georgia I remember feeling apprehensive about doing the hundred-year-old lyrics because of audience reaction to what might be considered politically incorrect phrases:

...Oh chocolate drop, that's me
'Cause my hair is curly
Just because my teeth are pearly
Just because I always wear a smile
'Like to dress up in the latest style
'Cause I'm glad I'm livin'
Takes troubles all with a smile
Just because my color shade
Is different maybe
That's why they call me "Shine".

The reaction was generous. It was generous I think because I managed to convey that irrepressible pride.

People And Places

The pinning down of places, events and famous people gives a certain atmosphere to a song. Knowing that "Parchman Farm" is a penitentiary and that "St. James Infirmary Blues" is about a morgue sets the scene and sets the tone. "On the corner of Peach Tree and Vine": a legendary busking spot in Atlanta where Blind Willie McTell allegedly played, occurs in a few songs. I've actually played at Fat Matt's which is situated there; it felt momentous. To widen his appeal, Leadbelly sang songs about contemporary events such as the Titanic and the Hindenburg disaster, about political leaders such as Franklin D. Roosevelt and Hitler, and about celebrities such as Jean Harlow and Howard Hughes. "Sweet Home Chicago" (17) marks the economic migration of black people – "Ain't gonna dig no more potatoes/Pull no more corn"(18) – from the rural South to the industrial North.

For a non-American blues musician certain place names are exotic-sounding and poetic or just significant. I always enjoy singing the alliterative line, "I've been from Tucson to Tucumcari Tehachapi to Tonapah" in Little Feat's "Willin'" but it's very disappointing to find that the Chattanooga Choo Choo no longer runs and that there is otherwise nothing memorable about Chattanooga except the famous big band song popularized by Glenn Miller.

Ownership

The question of the ownership of these early songs is obscure. Originality was claimed but usually not substantiated. Robert Johnson, for instance, has been credited with songs that predated his career: stuff that had been recorded ten years previously, with only one line being different! Blind Willie McTell reworked songs by Sippie Wallace, Bessie Smith and Ivy Smith to produce "Statesboro Blues". (19) W.C. Handy, an important popularizer of the blues, claimed hundreds but in reality most of these songs and tunes were handed around. As folk songs they belong to everyone.

Blues Compilation

As well as identifying emotionally and politically with the early black musicians I've also admired their mastery of musical techniques that look so simple to the uninitiated. The country blues is surprisingly varied in mood and complexity and there's such a wide range of feeling too, from the profound spiritual primitivism in Blind Willie Johnson to Blind Blake's music full of laughter and Skip James on the edge of a weird place. They could make a guitar sound like a piano; they could make a guitar sound like two guitars; they could make a harmonica sound like a train. They didn't need drums: they could stamp the earth and pound the side of their guitar. They didn't need other voices – they could answer themselves, converse with the audience or with their guitar. They could create a stage full of characters and set them off into action. Some blues music like Robert Petway's "Catfish Blues" takes you into rhythm; some, like "Down 'n' Out Blues", into melody with all possible variations in between.

Without realizing it at the time I was exposed early on to all the main strands in country blues music. It was as if the spirit of the blues had created a comprehensive compilation for me: the reverberating spectacle of slide in the convulsive blues of Son House, the melodic complexity of finger-picking in Mississippi John Hurt, gospel influences through Sister Rosetta Tharpe, showy, party-time professionalism from boogie-woogie pianist Roosevelt Sykes and the expression of raw suffering in John Estes. Then the bridge-makers: Jimmy Witherspoon shouting his blues/big band cross-over numbers, Sonny Terry and Brownie McGhee entering mainstream popular culture and John Lee Hooker providing the cross-over between blues and rhythm and blues. The music ranged from the earthy and domestic to the religious and existential with many a laugh in between.

Experiencing The Blues

See I have got up out of bed an' played the thing. Played the blues? When I got satisfied, I put it down, wen' on and went to bed an' went to sleep. You see, it was off my mind.

Mississippi Fred McDowell. (20)

After my mother died. I found it an uplifting thing to sing the blues. At a certain level it's just a relaxation; at another it's meditation or even medication. I still lose myself for hours in a normal working day just doing fun things on a guitar. It only takes a spark to light the fire: I can be holding a conversation and be playing and not know I'm doing it. Once the memory bank hits on something it's another hundred songs.

Georges Adins, who went to meet John Estes in 1962, wrote:

His voice cries and moans – his singing has the ring of actual reality and deep truth…filled with intense anguish, a fierce sorrow…He is unhappy and unfortunate and has nothing else but his voice and his guitar to tell us about the desolation and loneliness which a blind man feels. (21)

This is the experiential view of the blues: a feeling expressed as a musical soliloquy rather than a specific form of music. Blues is described in other ways too. People talk about its origins in ragtime, early jazz, religious songs, minstrel, popular, folk and so on and its characteristics and functions: pentatonic melody, typical chord progression, call and response. Call and response songs were an important influence in the development of the blues. These old work songs in which someone would sing and all the other workers would sing a response, gave a rhythm to the work as well as bonding the workers. "Old Alabama" – a prison song recorded at Parchman in 1947 – (22) gives a very powerful impression of call and response punctuated with what sounds like the fall of the whip. The percussion is actually listed as "axe strokes".

You hear echoes of this dialogue in the songs of Blind Willie Johnson. His wife Angeline sang a rather feeble answer-back on his 1930 recording of "John The Revelator". In "Nobody's Fault But Mine" the plaintive melodic guitar answers the harsh voice and in "Dark Was The Night" Johnson sings and responds as if comforting himself. Charley Patton's dramatic, rhythmic rendition of "Down The Dirty Road" (1929) has the singing voice answered by spoken words.

It's all very well to know about these songs but when you realize the implications of their origin in the toil of a whole people, it adds emotional impact.

No Longer The Country Blues

You know a musical *genre* is relevant when it spreads prolifically. The country blues spread throughout the South and also to cities in the South and in the North. There are blues known as Memphis, Detroit, Chicago, Texas, Piedmont, Louisiana, Western, East Coast, Swamp, New Orleans, Delta, Kansas City, Atlanta and St Louis. Each region developed its own flavour. By the Twenties, with mechanisation on farms, there would be unemployment and social upheaval as rural workers moved to the faster pace of life in the North – its urban tensions exacerbated by this influx.

When the country blues moved from the cotton states where the majority of black people lived to the mass manufacturing cities such as Chicago and Detroit, it changed and a lot of the features of the early blues music were forgotten. Both the country blues and the urban blues are based on the twelve bar structure but the former is more characterized by melodic structures, whereas the latter is more closely associated with twelve bar blues, as is most of slide music. People regard the twelve bar blues "I woke up this morning" strand as being the definitive blues and this is what led to rhythm and blues in the Fifties.

I would put the urban blues as starting in the Thirties. If you change the climate, the pace, the technology and the economy this is reflected in the music. Once things move on the music evolves. There was a social and economic demand for more and bigger venues to accommodate large audiences; in response to this the resonator guitar – which had a short reign between the wars – was developed to give greater volume in large spaces. For the same reason blues shouters such as Jimmy Witherspoon came into being. The intimacy of acoustic guitar playing was coming to an end. If you're working in a band, it doesn't take long to know what the audience likes; you respond with the beat they favour. You might modify the emphasis in quite subtle ways but it's cumulative.

It's no longer the country blues. How can it be? This is Chicago. This is New York. This is Detroit.

This is how music changes – in response to the audience – which in turn reflects the society from which it comes and this is how the original forms can be lost. Some people feel regret for this and yearn for a lost golden age which may or may not have existed. When all's said and done, although we should take the music seriously, we shouldn't be too solemn about it. Like all popular music the country blues was of the moment. Perhaps what we should really mourn are those musicians who didn't get the chance to record or whose recording perished. Who knows what has been lost? The precariousness of musical treasure is well illustrated in the story of Blind Willie McTell's last session tape. Ed Rhodes, a white guy who ran record stores in Atlanta in the Fifties, persuaded McTell, then in his sixties and busking in parking lots, to do some recording. This amateur recording was the only tape not to perish when Rhodes discarded his tapes and sold his recording equipment. Strangely enough, the photo of the young McTell we all know survived obscurity in a bin outside the premises of an avant-garde magazine. These precious things survived by the skin of someone's instinct. (23)

In 1936 Charlie Christian used a jazz guitar with an electric pick-up. The resonator's days were numbered but wouldn't come to an end till the electric guitar came into widespread use. Meanwhile, progress in guitar technology was halted by World War Two which focused all engineering efforts onto the war effort. This happened with Rickenbacker, Gibson and National. Although the solid body electric guitar was developed in the early Forties by Les Paul and popularized in the late Thirties and early Forties by T-Bone Walker, it wasn't until after the war that manufacture of the electric guitar began to supersede all other types in the world of pop and blues. By the late Fifties every teenager wanted one.

Me? I wanted a resonator.

I do mourn the golden age of country blues. In a world where it is an anachronism, the hardest thing is to educate other musicians that it has a distinctive quality and is not just a pedantic or a pedestrian beat; that it has range and subtlety and makes large demands on the performer to exploit as fully as possible the use of voice and acoustic guitar. Unfortunately this is largely unknown or forgotten. Twelve bar 'dumpty-dumpty' music as associated with the urban blues is probably the worst thing that ever happened to the blues: so much of it is banal crap. That goes for all popular music after the Fifties while I'm on the subject. The original blues has been so watered down that it's lost its potency. It's been corrupted by commercialization and severed from its roots. I'm not just talking about black performers. Jim Reeves singing at the Carnegie Hall had balls. His other music was saccharine country pop.

But it sold records.

Yet the early blues singers had so much more to offer. Take a fairly random example: Scrapper Blackwell. People tend to talk more about his musical partner Leroy Carr yet what he could do acoustically was subtle and sophisticated. His guitar playing was influenced by the more varied inversions and chord progressions demonstrated by Leroy Carr's piano-playing. Using both acoustic and jazz conventions, you get nice little jazzy inversions then the next moment he's playing what a rock star would play – decades before it happened! One of the albums I inherited from Bert Bellamy: *Mr. Scrapper's Blues,* (24) the cover showing him playing an economy Kay guitar, has a couple of instrumentals which display his virtuosity and attitude. He keeps them abstract by calling them by the key in which they are played, and explores the possibilities from bass runs to lyrical passages high on the treble strings, or he will use a staccato strum for dramatic effect so that a musical doodle becomes a classic little jewel. "'A' Blues" has an interesting jazz inversion in D9 in it. I am totally impressed by this musician.

The Country Blues And Europe

In the Sixties the country blues had a rebirth in Britain and Europe but as in America the interest came largely from white, educated people. Possibly because black people associated the blues with their oppressed past, their musical interest gravitated towards the glamorous pop music and role models produced by Tamla Motown. But you could still hear that train a-comin' in the music of Jimi Hendrix, especially in his acoustic tracks and it whistles relentlessly through "Voodoo Child". And the rhythm that survived slavery finds its most potent expression in rap.

Modern Blues And America

If you're into modern blues it is much better done in the United States than anywhere else. The Chicago blues is fast, rhythmically strong, emphasizing beat rather than melody and focusing on group performance. Today's white blues performers play a more complex style than the black country blues players did, the exceptions being Blind Blake, Kokomo Arnold and Lonnie Johnson. When I performed at The Annual Labor Day Blues Festival in Georgia in 2000 there was a tremendous variety of music under the umbrella of blues. Des and I and The Producers were doing the country blues but the other people – there were more than a hundred performers altogether – were playing a wide range of music.

One of the musicians: Beverly "Guitar" Watkins names Sister Rosetta Tharpe as an early influence and has had a long career as a blues musician. She describes her musical affinity: "I like that real Lightnin' Hopkins lowdown blues…I would call that hard classic blues, you know…railroad smokin' blues!" (25) She and Francine Reed both performed what I would call modern blues. They represented what the blues in Georgia has become: it has authenticity, is less twelve bar in essence and has more of a raw edge than Chicago blues.

Singers And Songs

Many Versions

Lil Son Jackson – a Texas country bluesman – became famous just after the war. His sound was acceptable to white audiences and he also updated and adapted country blues forms and themes to his own use. I came to identify with him because that's what I did. "Lay Down My Old Guitar" – one of his earliest recordings – is the number in my repertoire. I was impressed by his finger picking which reminds me of John Hurt, though he's usually compared with Lightnin' Hopkins.

I've used pop songs such as Little Feat's "Willin'" and turned them into country blues, or then again into rock or a jug band style for the Skunk Band to play. I've taken jazz classics such as "Stormy Weather" and given it a country blues slide effect. This happens in music all the time, of course: Lonnie Donegan took country blues music and turned it into pop – he recorded "Rock Island Line" in 1955. The Rooftop Singers' cheerful pop song, "Walk Right In" (1962) was done originally by Gus

Cannon's Jug Stompers. I have a 1963 Collectors' Issue: a "Strictly Limited Edition" of the music of Gus Cannon recorded in 1926 which includes their version of "Walk Right In". Incidentally, the folk trio's Sixties hit boosted royalties for Gus Cannon who had recently pawned his banjo to pay bills!

Because the country blues music was collectively owned, there would be several versions of the songs from the earliest recordings in the twenties till the present day. Take Blind Willie Johnson's music, for example. "Nobody's Fault But Mine" was covered by Led Zeppelin; Eric Clapton did "Motherless Children"; Bob Dylan was influenced by "Jesus Make Up My Dying Bed" in his song, "In My Time Of Dying". You only have to look at the web site Spotify to get some idea of the countless versions of blues songs in existence.

Listening to the early blues, noticing alterations and all the technical nuances has helped me develop my own versions. Absorbing the style of the musicians I admire means I can also play in the fashion of, say, Louis Armstrong or Blind Blake. This can be quite useful when you're showing people techniques: you can demonstrate the differences to make a point. I can play a version of "St James Infirmary Blues" that shows its folk roots or I can evoke Louis Armstrong's jazz-oriented interpretation in my blues style.

I'm fascinated by the biographies of songs and guitars.

Black Ace

"Black Ace Blues" was originally released in the late Thirties by Babe Karo Lemon Turner – impressive name – and it became so popular that he took the name Black Ace. He played a National steel guitar on his lap, using slide – one of very few bluesmen to use this technique. The others were Kokomo Arnold and Turner's mentor Oscar "Buddy" Woods. Like many performers he lived in obscurity for a while until Chris Strachwitz of Arhoolie Records sought him out and recorded him in 1960. Critics seem to agree that Turner has been underrated, partly because his output was lean and also because it was difficult to categorise his style, which Scott Cooper described as "Hawaii meets the Delta". (26)

I came across "Black Ace Blues" on the album, *Texas in the 30s, 1935-38. The Complete Recording of Carl Davis Dallas Jamboree Jug Band, Black Ace, Kitty Gray and her Wampus Cats.* I liked the tune; I liked the story and I could see its dramatic potential. I don't regard this song as Babe Karo Lemon Turner's best number: his version is a bit thin and two-dimensional and lacking in resonance, even though he has two guitars on the disc. My treatment of the song is more full-bodied. His "You Gonna Need my Help Some Day" is a more traditional blues number and more successful in my view.

"Black Ace Blues" is a song about male confidence and potency: "I'm the boss card in your hand" and it's one of the most popular numbers I do on twelve string with slide. You can't do a successful version of a song about confidence unless you can make your voice as potent as your guitar. The guitar doesn't compensate for vocal inadequacies: it shows them up.

John Lee Hooker

By working to my strengths, accepting that John Lee's way was not my way and having confidence in my own interpretation, I also found I could do quite a lot with John Lee Hooker's song "Groundhog". His rendition is slow and sexy with a bluesy guitar and a slowly ticking rhythmic fuse. He does "Dimples" in the same way: slowly and taking a lot of effort with the timing which doesn't suit my style at all. For me, "Groundhog" is a song you want to hit with, so I take the original influence and give it a white rock manner. John Lee's slower version would be done with a little combo filling in all the gaps and Hooker playing simple guitar. The thing that works for him is a lazy slow feel – a pace that's not natural for me. In my version I use slide for verve and texture. "Groundhog" is a song about territorial aggression so I want to give it a feral edge. My guitar rumbles away, at times like a growl, increasing in pace to emphasize the aggression whilst I vocalize scorn and menace. You have to use what you've got and my voice – between a tenor and a baritone – is double the volume of anybody I've played with. With long hard nails and strong fingers I can maximize guitar sound and fill all the spaces with threat. John Lee creates tension from slowness; I create tension by using slide and by upping the tempo.

Like BB King, whom I saw when he supported Fleetwood Mac at the Manchester Free Trade Hall in 1969, John Lee Hooker has amazing presence. He's a scene-stealer: low brown half-spoken vocal style; slow effortless playing – his big hands doing sexual things up and down the neck of his guitar. I went to a Bruce Springsteen concert about twenty years ago in Manchester and John Lee Hooker appeared with him. "Boom Boom" was the number and John Lee did one verse. He's sitting down and as soon as he sings, "Boom boom boom boom," he demolishes everything Springsteen has done in the song. He's coming from stillness; his power comes from stillness and Springsteen's efforts in that song are wiped out.

Effortlessly

Effortlessly but not lazily. Yet Springsteen was pushing volume out, using energy and yes – it was powerful but not compared with John Lee. John Lee Hooker did it from his own natural draw. There's such power in his vocal restraint; he's the essence of cool and for him performance is an expression of his own sexuality.

Mississippi John Hurt

Unlike songs such as "Black Ace" and "Groundhog", Mississippi John Hurt's songs don't lend themselves to any interference! You can't do a Pete Johnson version of a John Hurt song because everything he does is complete. You either play it like that or leave it alone. He has a distinctive three finger technique like no other musician and a fluid and syncopated style. His guitar playing seems effortless but it's actually complex and his gentle voice fits the intimate setting in which he would have played. I have immense respect for this musician, whom I never met though I do have a treasured record of his Newport Folk Festival (July 1963) performance which came from Bert Bellamy's collection. I copied his style of finger picking and liked his songs, which have been described as "old time music" – coming from a folk source that produced both blues and country music. There is no 'modern' blues influence in his styles and it has been suggested that he is the musical link between the nineteenth and twentieth centuries. Hurt's music has been admired by white musicians as well as black musicians. There's a story that a pupil played a John Hurt record for the classical guitarist Andres Segovia. Segovia wondered who the second guitarist was.

There was no second guitarist.

"I'm Satisfied" is a song about sexual joy originally recorded in the late Twenties. Then John Hurt disappeared until rediscovered in the Sixties. The lyrics in this song are interesting for their sexual innuendo. You can't always hear them and because of the way they're pronounced, the *double entendre* is not always apparent. Phrases such as "total load" and "total-on shaker from my navel down" certainly stimulate the imagination. The relaxed and tuneful style contrasts with the earthy sexual confidence.

John Hurt's short song "Pay Day" has a restrained, minor feel with complicated rhythms and is again from an earlier tradition. It's about stealing in order to survive and about the transience of relationships. It's hard to understand the lack of economic power experienced by people still, in effect, owned by the plantations. The subject doesn't have a dog to help him catch rabbits so he steals food and now he in turn is hunted by hounds. The lyrics speak of survival at a level unfamiliar in Western society:

Pay Day

Well, I did all I can do and I can't get along with you
I'm goin' to take you to your Mama, Pay Day
Pay Day, Pay Day
I'm goin' to take you to your Mama, Pay Day.

Well, a rabbit come along and I ain't go no rabbit dog
And I hate to see that rabbit get away
Get away, get away
Oh, I hate to see that rabbit get away.

Well, just about a week ago, I stole a ham of meat
I'm gon' keep my skillet greasy if I can
If I can, if I can
I'm gon' keep my skillet greasy if I can.

Well, the hounds are on my track, a knapsack on my back
I'm gon' make it to my shanty, 'fore day
'fore day, 'fore day
Oh, I'm gon' make it to my shanty, 'fore day.

"Louis Collins" (1928) is a lament about the violent death of a pimp and as with all Hurt's songs there's only one way to do this understated song: his way. The trademark finger picking makes it sound as if there are two guitars. Again, the bleak subject matter and mournful tune shock. The finality of "laid him six foot under the clay" isn't alleviated by the reference to angels. It's compassionate but not sentimental – a song which upholds the individual's right to be mourned, whatever the background.

Son House

When the man hit the downbeat on his National steel-bodied guitar and you saw his eyes disappear into the back of his head, you knew you were going to hear some blues.

Cub Koda.

John Hurt sings about life's harshness in a melodic, contained way. All the energy is in his skilful hands. You can't say this of Son House – he engages his whole body. "The blues possessed him like a lowdown shaking chill" – to quote Bob Groom. (27) Some of his performances were allegedly terrifying in intensity. At the height of his powers he was billed as the "Father Of Folk Blues" and legend has it that he wouldn't give Robert Johnson lessons because he didn't think him a worthy pupil! He also said Johnson was "no good until something happened" – a reference to the pact with the devil he allegedly made. People have referred to this with regard to Charlie Parker and Louis Armstrong as well. So why is this myth so widespread amongst creative people? I think it must mean that a good musician goes into a sort of wilderness and gets in touch with another musical dimension through the power of technical practice, and through the power of mind and spirit so that there is no distinction between the music and the musician performing it. Technical expertise does matter, but only if it's so ingrained that you don't have to think about it and only if it's contained by passion. Or it contains the passion.

Son House's performances were certainly passionate. His most famous number is a song of traditional provenance, "Death Letter". Lyrically bleak and feverish with intensity, it has a sense of clamouring urgency and I have tried to capture this energy in my own version of the song, using slide. Son House performed it on a metal-bodied National resonator guitar using a copper slide. He often altered the tempo and lyrics for different performances, sometimes playing it twice in one set and some versions could last fifteen minutes.

The fact that Son House let me play his guitar and that the song meant a lot to me because of my mother's death, made it an important choice for my repertoire. The emotion and power are his; the emotion and power are mine as well. In my version some of the vocal phrasing and some of the words are changed. I wanted to create my own interpretation. Or it might have been that I wasn't good enough to do it like the original. But I certainly wanted to play it just as Robert Johnson, who reworked it as "Walking Blues" and many others did. When I listen to Son House on a 1960s recording again, I hear things – new things – that I might add on to my version or to another song altogether.

Francis "Scrapper" Blackwell

I feel close to some musicians because of a sense of technical compatibility. Scrapper Blackwell, a performer from the inter-war years who played piano as well as guitar, is an undervalued but consummate blues player in my view. *Wikipedia* describes him as "an exceptional acoustic single-note picker in the Piedmont and Chicago blues style" and as veering towards jazz. I respond to him partly because he plays from a pianist's point of view as well as a guitarist's point of view, and I found this accessible because I had been taught piano. There's this element in Leadbelly too: the walking bass lines, heavy strings and low tunings give a sound resembling a piano.

There's another reason for my interest in Scrapper Blackwell. He had an extremely colourful and precarious background: he came from a very large and musical family and was involved in bootlegging in the Twenties. A combination of Cherokee and Negro, he was never going to have an easy time and I was impressed by his determination to be a musician and by him being an instinctive blues player: "when I did went to playin' the real blues, I was gone too, just gone…the minute I saw the string, I hit it. And when I hit it, it was the right string. But I couldn't tell you today how I ever started playing." (28) He made his first guitar from cigar boxes, wood and wire, taught himself to play, became an itinerant musician and eventually teamed up with pianist Leroy Carr in the late Twenties. Their 1928 Vocalion hit "How Long How Long Blues" was the biggest blues hit of the year but it's his version of "Down And Out Blues": a song written by Jim Cox in the 1920s and popularized by Bessie Smith that most appealed to me. In spite of the depression in the lyrics there is a nice jaunty, jazzy Chaplinesque quality that I have absorbed for my version of this song. You can't keep a good man down! Scrapper Blackwell does what a conventional acoustic player doesn't usually do: he repeats the chord structure on barre chords.

Blackwell's is the finest version of this song I've ever heard. This premonition of the Great Depression in an era of frantic hedonism is one of those songs: once you've mastered it, you can play anything. It has minors, diminished chords, melody and feeling with some cross-over jazz and blues. There are thousands of songs using the same four chords but this song uses much more. There are lots of chords. It's like the musical equivalent of that exercise they used to do in typing schools: "the quick brown fox jumps over the lazy dog" – which uses every letter in the English language. Count the chords: C, E, A, D minor, A, D 7th, C sharp 7th, D 7th, F, F diminished, C, A, D7th, G. I make that nine; there are only eight notes in a scale. There's also a jazz turnaround in it and you can get an embellishment on that.

The jazzy and clear vocals in Scrapper's version of "Down And Out

Blues", the depth and resonance of the voice, together with the skilled guitar playing do indeed produce "a little orchestra", such is his virtuosity. Yet it's just him and a guitar or piano. That's all.

When I play this I use all my fingers and my thumb. Scrapper Blackwell uses mainly the thumb and one finger – with stunning results. Grossman will tell you to use two fingers and a thumb. At the time I was learning the songs I presumed that all fingers would be used to produce those sounds; I was ignorant of how they were produced. Only contemporaries such as Keb Mo, whose blues style combines modern elements with influences from Son House and Robert Johnson, use this way of playing.

I've stuck to Blackwell's melody and guitar playing but have never been able to produce the intensity in his voice, despite the fact that I have a 'black' voice. Next to Scrapper Blackwell I sound like a pop singer. He lives his story; he is that man. He has the ultimate weary blues voice in this song. Being black was a bastard.

"Down And Out Blues" became the theme song of an era. Used to having the back seat of the car piled high with money in the partying times with Leroy Carr, Blackwell went into obscurity when Carr died. He was rediscovered in the late Fifties and recorded for the Prestige/Bluesville label in 1962 but was unfortunately shot and killed during a mugging in an Indianapolis alley – another violent end and a crime that has never been solved.

Blind Blake
"Here's somethin' gonna make you feel good!"

My other heroes of technique are Blind Blake and Kokomo Arnold. If I was on a desert island I would try to master Blind Blake's "Rope Stretching Blues". Like Scrapper Blackwell, his piano-playing influences his guitar-playing: he plays from notation, not from chord boxes using the guitar neck as keyboard, but handling it conventionally. "Rope Stretching Blues" has all the innuendos that he can make: musical jokes, out of context links and he laughs and talks over the top – totally relaxed. His linear style repeats a little but changes, moves on – just skips along, extending the phrases. In places the guitar work in this song is reminiscent of the piano accompaniment to the dramas of the silent screen. You can't get a more dramatic situation than a man waiting to hang!

My version of "Early This Morning" is influenced by Blind Blake. I had to change it quite a lot because nobody can play like him! You listen but you can't work out the chords. He's one of the most skilful artists I've ever heard and Steve James described his instrumentals as "hypermetabolic". (29)

Blake was one of the pioneering musicians in Chicago. I have an album: *Blind Blake's Blues in Chicago* in the Classic Jazz Masters series, which I had to search the length and breadth of the country to find in the Sixties. Many such albums were limited editions. There is plenty to impress. Leola B. Wilson sings on some of the tracks, as does Bertha Henderson; Blind Blake on vocals, guitar and piano constantly surprises by emphatic rhythmic change. The use of rattle bones adds a new dimension of texture, rhythm and jollity: like tap-dancing faster and faster. How incongruous the xylophone sounds, giving an air of surprise and mystery. Surely it's deliberately out of tune? But I don't think it is; things were just so relaxed.

Andy Boote had the tablature to "Blind Blake's Rag". I asked him to work it out and show me what was actually being played so I could make corrections to my rendition. He came back to me: "Don't bother. You sound a lot closer to it than the tablature. Stick to doing it by ear."

I also love Fats Domino for this quality of conviviality – the way he can play while he's laughing. "Feet's Too Big" is impressive for its techniques too and hearing this makes me flip through the entire catalogue. I do a version of "Ain't Misbehavin" for my own private pleasure in which I use different chords. Fats, like Blind Blake, has a bounce of fun I want to get. So I use the piano chords.

It's worth remembering that the blues had this aspect of life-celebrating humour. "Let's Have A Party" by Kitty Grey and the Wampus Cats is another favourite of mine. She's a great piano player and daft storyteller in clever lyrics. Her "I Can't Dance I Got Ants In My Pants" has an infectious humour and liveliness in the piano and voice. It's resourceful partying music which shows the cross-over points between blues and pop as the Leadbelly Woolworth's album did. Similarly jazz and blues meet in Louis Armstrong's "Don't Get Around Much Any More" – a number he did with Duke Ellington on *Together Again*. A lot of jazz enthusiasts would find this too 'popular' but it's good quality music.

If I sit and chill I can imagine each song and each musician. I can't play all the instruments but I can understand what each one is doing musically, especially harmony; Louis' harmonies are stunning. Melody is simple: it's the harmonies that make the whole thing. You can either hear the swing or you can't; you can only explain it by conducting but there's no guarantee. I suggested to a very accomplished guitarist that I should conduct him in order to demonstrate the swing: he was offended. But he didn't feel it in his heart, you see. With my guitar I can live Louis. The trumpet harmonies in his version of "St. James' Infirmary Blues" are incredibly haunting. In a minor key. In some versions it's a simple folk tune but the way I play it is the Louis Armstrong way: with a jazz feel. I take it from a three chord song to six chords and I put some harmonies on top of the tune like jazz musicians and classical composers do. The basic tune is extended by harmonies and when I play my version I can hear his trumpet. This is artistic freedom.

Even songs that are about having the blues, like "Down And Out Blues" can have an underlying melodic optimism. In "Know Just How I Feel" I like the cacophony of verses: there are about twelve verses from which I pick and mix. I change them every time I play the song: individual words or whole verses like the old bluesmen did. This song has a minor feel to it with a descending cadence in: "I feel like an engine/ Ain't got no drivin' wheel". There is optimism for the future in the guitar picking although a blue feeling in the melody for the present circumstances.

Blind Blake was gone by the end of his thirties. His dates are vague (circa 1893 – circa 1933); there's only one photograph and the cause of death is not established, though Reverend Gary Davis said he had heard Blind Blake was killed by a streetcar. In the black argot of the times, "a blake is a man of tough, unrelenting character" (30) and rumour has it he was a blind wrestler. Like many of these deaths – Blind Lemon Jefferson, Robert Johnson, Scrapper Blackwell – the matter remains unresolved and therefore open to lurid speculation. The death of a black man was not treated in the same way as the death of a white man, sad to say. Would Leadbelly have escaped the gallows if the man he killed had been white? But I celebrate Blind Blake's joyful expertise and paid homage by cutting my Georgia CD in four hours.

Recording engineer: Can you do a dozen in an hour?
Blind Blake: I can do as many as you want, boss!

All in one take. (31)

Kokomo Arnold

Kokomo Arnold, also named Gitfiddle Jim, is the only other musician who comes near Blind Blake. A left-handed player: he played his guitar flat. No-one has surpassed Kokomo on National slide. It's as if you've got guitarist, bass player and rhythm section all at once and don't forget – on top of that these guys sing and laugh! "Busy Bootin", an earlier version of the Sixties hit, "Keep A-Knockin' But You Can't Come In" is one of the Kokomo Arnold songs I do. Lots of people have done versions of this and I also play it rock 'n' roll style.

What I can't understand is how Kokomo can play jazz chords on an open-tuned guitar. He plays slide but the chord structures are the same as an ordinary guitarist would play. Yet getting 7ths and minors is quite difficult on slide unless you're tuned to these but then you can't do majors. I've long puzzled over Kokomo's supreme guitar skill and found it impossible to do what he did. Because of my desire to preserve my precious records I deprived myself of an important piece of information! In order that I wouldn't damage them by playing them too much or by being clumsy with the stylus, I used to record them onto tape or cassettes. To learn the songs I would play these instead of the records over and over and over. But in doing this I often neglected to read record covers and sleeve notes. So – it's only recently that I've discovered that what I thought Kokomo was achieving with one guitar was actually being achieved by two guitars. This doesn't make him less amazing, though! He accompanied himself on most of his recordings nevertheless.

But to think that for many years I had been trying to get this effect with only one guitar!

This story illustrates the difficulty a musician has when he tries to study long-dead musicians from the pre-video age. They were often not filmed or archives were carelessly lost. Seeing them play would clarify some things because there has been no-one to ask about their techniques.

There was very little country blues influence in folk circles; none of the folk greats I met knew and it took the Stones and Eric Clapton to raise its profile.

Ry Cooder made the same point with regard to Blind Willie Johnson whose "incomparable sense of timing and tone" he admired. He puzzled about him like I did about Blind Blake and Kokomo Arnold and concluded that Johnson doesn't play chords – he didn't put in extra chords. The listener perceives chords nevertheless. Often with music it's what you leave out that makes it special. You can put on a monophonic harmony with slide – that's what Blind Willie Johnson does, maintaining his rhythm with open chord. With him you get a haunting vocal and guitar line that in places don't quite fit but the whole thing is a statement in music of his spiritual certainty. I agree with Ry Cooder that his guitar playing is unique – you can't copy it – though I think his description of him as "an interplanetary world musician" is a bit over the top. Cooder described "Dark Was The Night" as the "most transcendent piece in all American music". (32) It inspired his soundtrack for *Paris Texas.* Eric Clapton thought Johnson's slide playing was supreme. I would say he was a black guy singing songs and accompanying himself in a fairly basic way: the only way he knew how. Hence the simplicity of the structure.

But many musicians and commentators have been in awe of this musician and he is a one-off. Johnson's "Dark Was The Night" was on an album sent off into space in Voyager I in 1977.

So he was interplanetary after all.

"The Twelves" is one of Kokomo's songs that I would try to learn on my fictitious desert island. It's virtually the same song as "The Dirty Dozens" recorded by boogie-woogie pianist Speckled Red. I don't know what it's about: it dances along at a relentless pace and it's so fast it's difficult to make any sense of it. It's incredible. I've heard many jazz bands do the same chords but I don't understand how he does it. Even if I saw it I might not understand.

The Dozens is a verbal abusing match – part of the oral tradition – in which two people try to out-do one another in increasingly extreme and mentally agile put-downs. This has become an important element in the development of hip-hop. But the term probably has its origins in the slave trade when slaves who had been punished by dismemberment were sold "by the dozen". The biggest put-down.

Blind Blake and Kokomo Arnold are so far ahead of me it would be like trying to play football with Ronaldo. I'm about fit to change their strings; polish their guitars; carry their bags. Yet my experiences with the bluesmen I did meet were all positive; they were happy to demonstrate techniques and give encouragement.

Kokomo was found in the Sixties working in a car plant in Chicago. Unusually, he was not interested in resurrecting his musical career. "No you HAD me last time round," he said. Who knows? He might have lost his ability to play well – perhaps he hadn't touched his guitar in the intervening years because he was too busy bootlegging but I like to interpret his reaction as black pride.

As often happens in music, the master is more well-known through the popularity of his disciple, in this case, Robert Johnson. But I rate Kokomo above him, musically speaking, though I think Johnson comes close to John Estes as a lyricist. Johnson's lyrics are more modern, more accessible than those of some of his contemporaries and this could be one of the reasons he was admired by modern musicians such as Eric Clapton and Led Zeppelin. Many people think Johnson is the greatest blues player. I don't think they can have heard the others but he certainly made easier listening. Some of his verses were blagged from other musicians but that's what happened. Arnold's "Old Original Kokomo Blues" became Johnson's "Sweet Home Chicago" but Arnold had based his song on Scrapper Blackwell's "Kokomo Blues".

John Henry Barbee

"Dust My Broom" is one of those songs like "Kokomo Blues" and "Death Letter" that has a biography of its own and which raises the issues of technique and feeling and accessibility that have pre-occupied me all my life. There's an ongoing controversy about whether Robert Johnson or his contemporary Elmore James wrote it but I'm less concerned about that.

In my interpretation of "Dust My Broom" I've taken the feel and tried to express it from my heart. It's a song of acceptance: "I believe my time ain't long". "Dust my broom" means to leave for good. I've tried to reflect that in the stately rhythms and the dynamic of my slide playing. At the end of the day I'm a middle class white guy but this is what I tried to do. No-one is quite sure whose song it is but I regard John Henry Barbee's as the definitive version as far as technical expertise goes. However, the most famous interpretation of this song is by Elmore James. Like John Lee Hooker, James had limitations but this did not thwart his influence. Whereas Barbee cannot be faulted from a technical point of view, both John Lee Hooker and Elmore James play from the heart and that's what makes the difference. I still find it difficult to make up my mind between the technical excellence of Barbee and the heart of Elmore James and this has affected my musicianship in ways I can't measure. If the style I play is more technical it isn't because I chose that; it's just the way I've learnt, the way my style has evolved.

Heart wins, though.

And the story of John Henry Barbee is heart-breaking. Barbee had a singularly unfortunate life. Perhaps I should say a doubly unfortunate life. Thinking he had killed his girlfriend's lover, he disappeared from music – he had played with Sonny Boy Williamson – and was later found working as an ice cream vendor. His novel way of attracting customers was to play slide. He was told the good news that the man had not died so he agreed to tour Europe in the Sixties with people like Lightnin' Hopkins and Howlin' Wolf. Unfortunately, he fell ill and had to return to the States. Driving the Cadillac he had bought with his new wealth, he knocked someone down and killed him. This was in the Southern States. It seems the karma was just too strong. He died in jail ten days before his 59th birthday. I often recount his rather sad story, ending with, "That's how people get the blues."

Strange Fruit

Thousands of men and women were lynched throughout the South, the perpetrators so confidently above the law that the process became known as "lynch law".

Michael Gray. (33)

I've been drawn to some songs because they really encapsulated the lives of black people: disenfranchised and hounded by white prejudice, they often lived in fear and danger, longing for a freedom which was only possible in the afterlife. I'm not going back very far in historical terms: the last lynching took place as recently as 1981.

"Strange Fruit" is the ultimate gallows song. In 1937 Jewish school teacher Abel Meeropol saw a photograph of the lynching of Thomas Shipp and Abram Smith in 1930. He was so moved by this he wrote a song which he showed to Billie Holiday after a performance in New York. It was a hit in spite of establishment hostility and the difficulties of getting anybody to record it.

Strange Fruit. (1939)

Southern trees bear a strange fruit,
Blood on the leaves and blood at the root,
Black body swinging in the Southern breeze,
Strange fruit hanging from the poplar trees.

Pastoral scene of the gallant South,
The bulging eyes and the twisted mouth,
Scent of magnolia sweet and fresh,
And the sudden smell of burning flesh!

Here is a fruit for the crows to pluck,
For the rain to gather, for the wind to suck,
For the sun to rot, for a tree to drop,
Here is a strange and bitter crop.

If anything the horror is understated in these dark, tight lyrics. The deathly stillness of the hanged man a contrast to the terrible time of terror and pain: begging to be hanged, not burnt, that would precede it.

To express these events I thought it was important to emphasize my voice. For my performance of "Strange Fruit" I use a Guild guitar just suggesting the key, with the minimum amount of guitar work: discordant punctuation and occasional increases in volume for emotional emphasis. Although I learnt this song very early on in my career I haven't performed it that often in public: I become almost scared of my emotions because I feel that in singing this song I resurrect the suffering. I can smell it: I'm there.

If you want dexterity listen to a guitar playing; if you want feeling listen to a voice – not necessarily at its best. Billie Holiday does the definitive version of this stark song. From the heart. It doesn't matter that her performance suffered from years of alcohol and drugs: her last recordings include some of her best work and her voice is poignant not pathetic. I think she stopped being a performer and became herself: she and the suffering and the music are indistinguishable.

Billie Holiday ended her performances in a single spotlight, her eyes closed as if in prayer. The waiters stopped serving; the mood changed. Then she sang "Strange Fruit".

The importance of "Strange Fruit", twenty-five years before the Civil Rights Movement, was pointed out by Samuel Grafton of the *New York Post*: "If the anger of the exploited ever mounts high enough in the South, it now has its Marseillaise".

Meeropol's political compassion translated into another dramatic action. In 1957 he adopted the two sons of Ethel and Julius Rosenberg: executed for spying.

Oh Freedom
"The last friend, death," Olaudah Equiano (slave)

"Strange Fruit" is a protest song: an instrument of change; "Oh Freedom" is a song of acceptance. I first came across the song on a recording by Carl Sandburg, the American poet and folklorist. It is a song that conveys the longing to go home to the Lord and I try to sing this spiritual with the dignity and confidence that befits a song about faith. As a non-believer I wouldn't be able to perform this without becoming that rock-like faith.

The guitar is merely touched as underlining – as with "Strange Fruit", the voice is the dominant instrument here – and there is a falling cadence on the word "grave". The sentiment is one of acceptance and affirmation at the same time. Freedom in this song is associated with the liberation of death, not with politics. "Ain't goin' to worry Poor John's mind any more" it says on Sleepy John Estes' gravestone.

My anger at the plight of black people was increased by not believing in an afterlife for them. There was no "home to my Lord and be free" in my view.

Leadbelly

Leadbelly, whose music stopped me in my youthful tracks, became my all-round hero and shared the crown as king of the twelve string with Blind Willie McTell. His music resonated with the angry young man I was. He was a huge character: strong, libidinous, hard drinking, hard working, persuasively charming and violent. This zest for life is there in his music: the driving rhythm of the twelve string guitar – taken up in Texas where he also teamed up with Blind Lemon Jefferson – fading in and out. Then the voice – impressive and expressive, the high clear vocals counterbalancing the instrument. It has been said that his perfect tenor voice could have been trained for opera. Sometimes it's almost a speaking voice to emphasise the message and when he sings *a cappella*...

Then there's the sheer eclecticism in his repertoire: an approach the Skunk Band favoured. I have Leadbelly's *Library of Congress Recordings*. Serious listening. In essence it can't be called popular and some of it's about as accessible as opera or classical music. On the other hand, I also have his *Good Night Irene*: country blues directed at a white audience where some of the songs don't even sound 'black'. "When The Boys Were Out On The Prairie" sounds like all the other songs popularised as cowboy songs. "Roberta" is full of sensuous detail and powerful storytelling and the clarity of the vocals in "Telling John Hardy" is impressive. Lonnie Donegan did a version of this song and so did I. "Black Girl" – also known as "Where Did You Sleep Last Night?" – is a dramatic story with a haunting melody and a sense of dread. In my version I use Leadbelly's Texas waltz tempo because it makes a jaunty contrast to the macabre details. Other versions exist: by the Four Pennies in the Sixties and Kurt Cobain in the Nineties. (34) Cobain's guitar playing is more emphatic, the pace slowed down, building the vocals to a climactic ending. He pitches the song in E flat in order to sing an octave higher at the end of the song. These songs live on.

"In New Orleans" is a faster, upbeat version of what we came to know as "House Of The Rising Sun" when Eric Burdon did it in the Sixties. There's no comparison. Leadbelly's style: running bass lines on a twelve string is piano-like and complex. A Library of Congress number called "If It Wasn't For Dicky" similarly became a pop song as "Kisses Sweeter Than Wine". Leadbelly's song is darker – more sombre – and like "In New Orleans" very complex. I think that's why I don't play either of these!

So, although some of Leadbelly's music was alarming and inaccessible to a white audience some of it was approachable. This was in the Thirties and Forties, long before the Sixties explosion in folk music. The popular potential in Leadbelly's songs has been fully exploited. The usual thing happened: he didn't become a successful recording artist in his lifetime but his music was popularised by his disciples. Pete Seeger's Weavers had a big hit with "Goodnight Irene" just after his death and his repertoire has been interpreted by a wide range of performers since. Leadbelly's fast-paced version of "Gallis Pole" with its earth-thumping rhythms is a forerunner of folk rock.

Leadbelly attracted the political left. In New York he met Sonny Terry and Brownie McGhee, Pete Seeger and the as yet unknown Woody Guthrie who moved in with him and his wife, forming the hub of the folk movement for a while. Leadbelly sang about topical and political events and in this respect he was like Guthrie. I've always wanted to do a version of "Sacco's Letter To His Son" – on the Woody Guthrie album *Sacco & Vanzetti,* the music actually written and performed by Pete Seeger – because it combines the personal with the political. On the eve of his politically contrived execution, Niccola Sacco writes to his young son asking him to look after his mother and those round him. The words are very moving and this is reinforced by the fact that the writer will soon die; what he imagines his wife and son doing:

And when you want to distract her from the discouraging soleness
You take her for a long walk in the quiet countryside,
Gathering flowers here and there
And resting under the shade of trees, beside the music of the waters,

will be denied to him.

I find Seeger's version too contrived and too folkie so my interpretation would take it further towards the style of Woody Guthrie.

Being black and a musician, Leadbelly had double low status and his itinerant life would take him to wild places. His violence incarcerated him; his musical skill coupled with charm freed him. He allegedly sang his way out of jail twice! "If I had you Governor like you got me I'd wake up in the morning and set you free," was his famous plea to Governor Neff and there was another musical plea to Governor Allen years later. Apparently Leadbelly was due for parole and the Governor's decision was economic rather than appreciative but you shouldn't bother folks with the facts when a mythology is at stake. It is true that Leadbelly's music had entranced the Governors and inmates as well as John Lomax, whom he then persuaded to let him work as a recording assistant. Huddie Ledbetter was a powerful musician and a powerful human being.

Performance

"One monkey don't stop no show,"- Curley Weaver (35)

Performing solo is hard, lonely work. Basically you have to find the breath and energy to project the song to the audience whilst playing an instrument and being aware of all the ambient details. It's a survival situation. That you won't forget the words, break a string, lose your bottle, suffer a power- or heart- failure has to be taken for granted or you wouldn't get out of bed. On a more subtle level there's a continuous interaction with the audience – gauging whether to match the mood, modify the mood, challenge the mood, innovate… and with this in mind choosing the next song, mentally balancing the rest of the set list. And all this is happening against a background of constant, single-minded movement to the bar, the bogs, the smoking tent, check-shirted blokes playing darts, a scratchy-headed youth on simultaneous ringtones, underage kids gnawing one another's necks, United playing Chelsea, the epileptic jackpot machine, the landlady's husband hijacking the karaoke, a perspiring bloke announcing a taxi…it doesn't look promising if you'd planned a song requiring respectful attention, does it?

To a great extent, if you can't hack it you shouldn't be doing it but being a soloist does stretch you more than any other type of public performance. Being a soloist is being a front man without a band! Being a soloist requires charisma, confidence and commitment without the benefit of having your musical brothers there to make a joke whilst you retune your guitar or lose your grip.

You Have To Communicate With The *Music*

So how is it possible to do a song justice with so many variables? You can't if you're angry with the ringtones, or concerning yourself with double drop Ds, or chewing up your set list. I have developed a strategy – a philosophy if you like – with regard to performance. In order to communicate with the audience you have to communicate with *the music*. This is one of my core beliefs. I don't hold with the notion that music comes from the spheres – that's a bit esoteric. At the other end of the spectrum there are people with a knowledge-based approach to the blues: they collect records; they attend live performances; they do research; they know about the blues; they produce the equivalent of the perfect photograph of a song. This to me is pedantic; it lacks soul and I see our interests as being essentially different. To truly understand the blues you've got to be able feel it, to *be* it in order to play it. It's the difference between learning about and experiencing: it's about immersion – the best country blues musicians were immersed in the music for their own sake. It was part of their being – not essentially public. It's the same with me. For me to play it in front of an audience is a side-step – it's not why I do it. What anyone thinks is of no consequence; I do it for me though I do love an appreciative audience. For the sake of the music.

I didn't develop this approach consciously: it was instinctive and emotional though based on a firm foundation of technical expertise. And I don't always lose myself straight away – I'm nervous for the first two or three songs and this is an ego-centric condition. Once I've bypassed the ego I'm away and whatever I'm singing and playing, solo or in a band, I'm in the world of that song, evoking its time and place, losing my identity in the storytelling, like an actor.

This isn't to say that my versions of songs are the same as the originals; that isn't what I'm seeking. Music is of its own performer, its own time and its own place. It evolves. If you try to fix it you diminish it. What I do is an interpretation of what I've heard live and on record and what I can manage with my limited skills. I try to get the *essence.*

When I hear a song I like I work on it with my visual skills as well as my hearing. I create a picture rather than a series of notes: diving in and painting the whole atmospheric picture. I can see the notes and the potential development on the configuration of notes. I don't need to hum aloud and I don't learn it in little bits and then put it together. An inspiring image for me is a concert pianist holding the whole symphony in mind without touching a piano. And I play by ear – oh Des can analyze it and tell me where the diminished chords are – but what I do is largely intuitive, though based on a degree of expertise that allows me to forget about technique. A good musician doesn't walk on the stage thinking.

The paradox is that whilst recreating the past I can simultaneously inhabit the present. My granddaughter Maya sways to the music; rain drips off the microphone. There's a convivial scent of wet foliage, fried onions, oil and metal at the bikers' reunion as I launch into and find the world of Guthrie's *Dustbowl Ballads*.

Woody Guthrie's "Vigilante Man" is a song I've been performing since the late Sixties. My interpretation involves recreating a sense of brooding presence and desperate waiting. I have to be the vigilante and I have to be the relentless tension and those experiencing the tension. Combining my voice with the haunting layering power of slide, I can slow things down to capture the uncertain waiting. And the voice has to match the power of the instrument in order not to be diminished by it or the epic scale is lost. Compared with my version Guthrie's is faster – jolly almost. This seems incongruous to me; I wanted to create space – stillness even – for the iconic omnipresent stalker.

If I can achieve this I can involve the audience fully. As Bob Groom said of Son House: "When he performs it is a corporeal thing, audience and singer become as one." (36) And it isn't laboured or done with deliberation: Louis Armstrong created atmosphere just by smiling; Mississippi John Hurt through gentleness and John Lee just sang, "Boom, boom, boom, boom".

Guthrie's haunting songs are simple but he deals with the big issues and they get you emotionally. "Deportees", a song about illegal itinerant workers caught between local hostility, the vigilance of the authorities and exploitation by the employers, requires the same sense of scale as "Vigilante Man". I need to paint a broad canvas of human need and vulnerability, and on a personal level find the line between compassion and sentimentality as John Steinbeck did in novels such as *The Grapes of Wrath.* When I sing songs with a humanitarian message this is my fight on behalf of oppressed people. I'm honouring their individuality in the face of systems that take it away. "You won't be a name when you ride the great airplane/all they will call you will be deportees" – that's why I sing *a cappella* at one point.

And if I'm singing the songs of John Hurt, Son House, John Estes, Blind Willie McTell, Kokomo Arnold, Blind Blake... I hope I've communicated well enough with their musical world to be a conduit for a modern, largely white audience. My song might only hit one person and not make any quantifiable difference to the rest. The point is that it did make a difference to that one individual and that's the point of doing it.

Another song from the Depression era: the American folk standard "Good Morning, Mr. Railroad Man" needs to capture the American theme of riding the freight trains: an illegal and often dangerous way of life. It's still happening. Train sounds haunt the country blues; they are the accompaniment to dramatic escapes from the law and other bad situations, or they punctuate the beginning of a new life in the more prosperous North. Blind Boy Fuller and Sonny Terry's "Train Whistle Blues" is a good example of this soundtrack to the rural South.

What I've done in my arrangement of this song is emphasize the sense of the regulated world of the train timetable: "nine sixteen and two forty-four and twenty-five minutes to five" as a counterpoint to the anxious anticipation of the man smoking a cheap cigar and pulling his hat down waiting and checking, waiting and checking while he thinks about his wife who has left with another man. It's minutely observed and this gives it humanity.

This is a good song especially with the right chord structures. I try to get the whole melody line into the chord shapes: I'm walking from chord to chord, continually moving, never on a single chord. And set against this movement is a sense of melancholy inevitability in my guitar solo. Someone like Woody Guthrie would do this song with four chords. His emphasis would be on the message getting across, not on the guitar. Dave Evans would rely on the character in his voice to get more out of the song without being a great fingerpicker. The voice would compensate. Ry Cooder does clever things with minors where they wouldn't normally be. I just get the feel and I pour myself out.

Learning The Hard Way

Achieving the freedom of technique that enabled me to perform without concerning myself with it and lose myself in the way I have described, was a long hard road. I spent years trying to be free of my fingers before attempting to play the music to any level. For me it's four digits and six strings and I can play any of those strings with any of those digits – it's become a reflex. In listening to so much music from the Twenties and Thirties I discovered that the virtuosity of these country blues players often surpassed the modern musicians considered to be great. The more you listen and learn the more you get to know your place! But I wanted to play the music. I certainly wanted to play the music. So I persisted but I have never considered myself to be a good musician.

Like all the local kids I had been taught piano by Mrs. Coffin and this was to be helpful in my painstaking learning of blues guitar. Like many people I taught myself to play by listening to records and trying to duplicate the sounds, but some of those early recordings are terrible and probably nothing like the live performance. So I was copying something that was not true to the original but what could you do? Then I had to get the lyrics down and fit them to the music. It was slow work. But help was there from friends who could show you chords or from watching musicians and making notes. Aged fifteen I used to rush for the early school bus because Keith Haines would be on it and we would talk music. I'd ask him the chords to songs like "Georgia" then write them down. I took the basic chords and made a melody whilst keeping the bass line going. This was free-form finger picking.

Learning to play by listening had other unexpected limitations. Sometimes I found it impossible – let alone uncomfortable – to make the sounds I was hearing in the tuning. So when listening to Mississippi John Hurt I was often unable to get the proper key off the records because the guitar wasn't necessarily tuned to concert pitch. Also some of the older recordings – the older technology – could be running faster than they were played, which would sharpen the key. If they were running slower than they were played this would flatten the key. John Hurt's "Pay Day" can only be played in open D tuning. So open D was: D A D F# A D. When I'd worked out the Mississippi John Hurt stuff in D I always thought his guitar was a little high – not considering it could be a little low because he was in C tuning.

I don't possess an amazing ear: I think I just absorb the maths of it and come out with a personalized approximation, then work like mad at the dexterity. I sorted this stuff out by myself; no-one in my circle knew about this kind of tuning in the days when I was discovering it.

I once found myself in a tricky situation brought about by the constraints of a particular occasion and my lack of formal musical training. Fortunately my trial and error approach – which had landed me in this nightmare – also saved me from it. I was involved in a rock extravaganza to demonstrate Gordon-Smith guitars. This was in Manchester in the Eighties. Three famous rock musicians were also involved, including Jeff Beck, who found fame with the Yardbirds, the fast country rock picker Jerry Donohue, well known for being in Fairport Convention – I've forgotten the third guy – and me playing slide guitar. There was a good resident band and the idea was to insert us to play with them and demonstrate the guitars.

I arrived late because of dense fog and the other three didn't get there at all. People were panicking. I was pushed onstage into a situation more unknown than the fog without any time to ask anything or do anything: it was all down to me. "Oh don't worry – there's a guitar up there tuned for slide," someone told me. This was the guitar I was to demonstrate. Much to my dismay it had a locking tremolo system tuned to a chord: my pet hate. The thing about the locking tremolo system is that you can't retune it. The device is designed for heavy metal players whose guitar can easily go out of tune because of vibration: hence the locking device. The bad news is that you haven't got enough adjustment on a tuner without unlocking the whole thing with an Allen key.

The only musician to turn up in the fog, I'm standing there naked with a guitar and slide, not knowing what it's tuned to and stuck with it anyway, my reputation as one of the best slide guitarists on the line, with the responsibility of demonstrating the guitar to advantage. No pressure then. Fortunately no time to panic! The band strikes up and I need to know the key of the guitar so I let the band play and I'm thinking and trying my notes: that works…that works…that works…We're half way through the first verse; the audience is responding well to what I'm doing and I realize the guitar is tuned to E. I don't know whether this playing by numbers is a recognized thing but that's how I do it. I know when I'm in D or G tuning. If the guitar is in open G or open D I know how to get twelve bar and relative minors. I can find a relative minor: I know that's number nine. But I don't know notes: I only know numbers and this doesn't usually matter because either I'm playing for myself or others are fitting in with my playing.

But not on this occasion…

Until I got home and tuned my guitar to E I didn't realize I'd made such hard work out of something so easy. It had been in open E – basic – the first thing you learn is twelve bar in E. What I hadn't realized till then was that the mathematics of playing in E was exactly the same as playing in D. I needn't have struggled in the first few songs. It was easier in that tuning than in what I would have tuned myself, because I would have tuned to D or G. But the easiest way to play slide with a band is in E because it's the easiest configuration: there's no counting for me; I can find the notes intuitively and I don't need to think about it.

This foggy incident gives some insight into the limitations of my self-teaching!

But although my musical education was not structured I often find evidence of how hard I worked: scraps of paper with chord diagrams, written observations and comments on techniques used by other musicians, hard-won lyrics, self-critical notes on set lists and phone numbers everywhere. When I look at the scruffy, beer-stained, sellotape-edged lists of songs I think of the people who wrote on them besides me: Whitty, Andy, Dave… There's Plum's writing all in upper case as if to make it louder and all spelt correctly except "DEBBLE". Deliberate, I should think.

Dim. Repeats in 3rd.

Slide various inversions e.g. C7 shape 5.3 frets. Black Snake try odd rhythms. When runs take place think notes finish run on note corresponding to known note same with diff. fretting and string.

Down 'n Out.

C. E. A(?). Dm A. D. F. Dim. C~A (D9).

Dm to get other tones take Sub Dom~Am. On 5th same as all other chords.

(Run through treble with 3 fingers with Rockin Bass)

Down 'n' Out	*good, lazy vocal. Second solo?*
Shine	*bum solo 1st part guitar too strummy.*
Stormy Weather	*[sp*d]* illegible.
Loving You	*energy mistake 2nd verse scrappy solo.*
Roll 'em Easy	*reverbed guitar.*
Vigilante	*fucked up* solo.
Eug [?]	*voice thin.*
Groundhog	*voice thin horrible end* [word illegible]
Willin'	
So Long	
Louis Collins	

But for all my formal musical limitations there are certain originalities and sophistications in my work. I use blues scales: the bass notes are there as well. You get to know where all the safe notes are round every chord there is. If you change keys when piano playing it's not massively different but on a guitar it does sound quite different. A good pianist would be able to explain which keys sound right for which piece of music. Music is just maths – triads – three notes equally spaced on a piano. In the case of simple pop songs with basic simple chord structures, if you're playing it on a piano and you play a triad you're playing equally spaced notes (apart from sharps and flats getting in the way!) whereas on a guitar, because you're playing 5 – 6 strings for most chords, then the change from one to another is more apparent. It's why you can make a guitar sound so good with three chords. You can do three chord tricks. You couldn't do that on any other instrument. "Wild Thing" on a piano would sound awful. Take each pop song back to its basics and you find the differences between them are very slender. If you know twelve bars and pentatonic scale, you're a lead guitarist! You can play Mississippi John Hurt's "I'm Satisfied" with just three chords if you strum it: C, F, G. I can hear any pop tune, including folk, and work it out and play it. You could play any of those songs well in three months. The guitar is the only instrument you can achieve that with – hence its popularity with young people in a hurry.

I play melodies and bass lines along with the chord at the same time. The average electric guitarist plays block chords linked up with scales. I don't do that. It has nothing for me. In the main they use pentatonic scale and they'll get a riff out of that. It's quite crude: a series of single notes, a series of chords. The electric guitarist doesn't use the orchestral potential of the guitar as I do. Playing melody lines on top of base lines whilst playing chords, the right hand is liberated: any finger can pick any string at any time. You just pick the convenient melody. Conventionally, people are taught to allocate certain fingers to certain strings. I can create the melody out of a set of chords. Des will give me the chords and I will use that to place a melody over it. It's collaborative. The music stands up without vocals or other instruments. Everything you can play for a melody is a 'safe' note.

Some music does indeed demand a high level of technical flair, good timing and manual dexterity. I have a few numbers by Little Feat in my repertoire: I would describe their music as American swamp rock. It has a laid back feel: it still rocks but it's kind of lazy. "Willin'" is a modern song I used to sing with Whitty. It's not in strict tempo so needs sensitive timing. "Roll 'Em Easy" – also by Little Feat – requires a sense of containment and release. It's a love song I dedicate to every woman I ever loved and to the man who wrote it: Lowell T. George, a member of Frank Zappa's Mothers of Invention who founded Little Feat. He died in 1979. You have to get the balance right: containing the passion within the restraint of tenderness. I have gone for emotional focus over the variety of sound chosen by Little Feat. These songs are in my repertoire for two good reasons. They remind me of singing in harmony with Whitty, whose extremely good voice did justice to the melodies and they are also close to the sentiment and style of the Skunk Band. Creating a fusion of California rock, folk, rockabilly, blues, country, boogie, funk and jazz, Little Feat had the same eclectic approach to music as we did.

Speaking of technical challenges, I was impressed by The Grateful Dead song "Friend Of The Devil" which I heard at the Bickershaw Festival in Yorkshire in 1972. Jerry Garcia wrote the music and Robert Hunter wrote the lyrics. It has a folkie flavour. The lyrics are at variance with the melodic music and I liked the harmony guitar work which made me wonder if I could do the two guitar parts on one guitar. I also noticed it has the same tuning as "Bourgeois Town". "Friend Of The Devil" is an interesting challenge on two counts: you have to tune two strings down then deal with the problem that the lyrics are going in a different direction to the guitar, which is on the run. It's like rubbing the stomach whilst patting the head. Incidentally, it's hard to play on a twelve string. I have used this number when tutoring up and coming musicians.

Maximizing The Minimal

As a solo performer, whatever your level of expertise you have to exploit everything available to you with discrimination. Early blues singers made instruments with whatever was to hand. Jug bands were popular in the Twenties and Thirties, playing primitive party music on household articles such as washboards, jugs and tea chests. Some people even added mouthpieces to the jugs.

Fortunately I haven't had to recycle cigar boxes and bits of wire to serve my musical needs! I have choices. For example, my 1936 Gibson Blues King has a warm resonant depth, a slur, making it suitable for blues playing. If I want something precise and crisp like a piano for playing ragtime numbers then I use my 1923 Martin. For a loud blues sound I have a 1932 National style 0. My 1936 National Tricone, on the other hand, has a wonderful mellow tone suited to a jazz treatment or a Hawaiian sound.

There's a mystique surrounding the twelve string guitar. People think it's twice as difficult to play as the conventional guitar. This is too simplistic. It isn't twice as difficult – it's just the same as playing six string because each string is played in a pair. Not a great many people use the twelve string guitar but it has more overtones, more power than the conventional guitar. You've got notes you couldn't play on a six string: I can get notes that are an octave higher on a twelve string. The facility's there when you need it. But you have to use discrimination. There are times when I would choose a twelve string and times when I wouldn't – for the same song. It's a question of mood. You wouldn't ever use a twelve string with certain songs, though. It detracts from melodic tunes like "I'm Satisfied"- fluffs it up and makes it too cluttered. Few people use the twelve string on slide; it has its limitations, though if you listen to Leadbelly and Blind Willie McTell they adapt the instrument to suit what they're doing dramatically. Because the strings are in pairs and each of the paired strings is an octave apart (except for the first pair which is in unison) it's a lot easier to make a mistake when using a twelve string. Manual dexterity is required if you're picking out one string or if you're playing melodic slide. When using an electric Dobro I do use the strings separately for dramatic effect or vibrato effects. For example in "Stormy Weather" it gives accent and subtlety.

Demystifying the instrument with discrimination and skill, you can then exploit its capacity for greater volume, depth and resonance to advantage.

Many soloists include a range of instruments for interest and texture. A mandolin adds colour and variety to a set. It is an eight-stringed monophonic melodic instrument but I tend to like it as a rhythm instrument – like Des plays it. You need little fingers to play a mandolin but in US bluegrass music it's usually the biggest bloke who plays it – generally for top harmonies – and it looks comical.

Lap guitars are a curiosity: a keyboard rather than a guitar and visual as opposed to tactile. My view is that a singer should sing out to the audience, not down to a guitar but there's no problem if the lap guitarist doesn't sing.

But having musical wisdom and the appropriate instrument is only the beginning.

Performing alone you need power and ways to conserve energy. There's no-one to help you and it's no use having an inoffensive pop voice: you need immediate impact. You need to fill the room with sound. Because solo performance is so demanding and arduous it's important to be as economical with effort as possible. You have to go back to basic chords and getting melodies within chord shapes. If a musician was going to spend long periods on street corners then he needed strategies for maximising sound and impact. As Leadbelly said, "I never change chords; I just walk to the next one." If there was an easier way of producing the same sound he would take it; if he could use the guitar as a percussion instrument in order to add rhythmic texture, he would; if he could add variety by using his voice in different ways: moaning, humming, answering back to his guitar, spoken asides to the audience, he did. At the end of the day the impact of his performance would determine whether people threw coins in his hat, or bought him drinks in the juke joint.

Take, for example, Blind Willie McTell from Atlanta who played a twelve string guitar. I really rate some of his Last Session recordings. Among his numbers in my repertoire are "The Dying Crapshooter's Blues" and "Beedle Um Bum". I am also interested in his song "Reckless Disposition": a melodic and virile song full of relentless movement with interesting tuning – the same tuning as I use for "Friend Of The Devil" – a double drop D. His technique was very economical and was later taken up by some of the folkies. To understand what he did I needed another set of mathematics. For a start his bass note is lower than on my guitar. The natural thing to do is to take it down a note to make it deeper. You can get the note but not the melody line. So you take the first string down to D as well; then I've got my D chord with two fingers, my A chord with one finger – almost in an open tuning again – and my G chord is two fingers again. As well as getting economical chords finger-wise, bugger me I've got some spare fingers! What to do with them: well you do melody lines with spare digits. And just see how little the left hand is doing! You get economy of effort plus a different sound – ideal for someone standing on a street corner hoping to draw the punters. I repeat: why chase chords when you can walk to the next one?

With maximum skill and minimum effort the musician can add surprise. Voice and instrument can be varied and one technique is to have the vocals going faster than the instrument. Blind Willie McTell's "Statesboro' Blues" has vocals and guitar moving at different paces, the increasing pace creating tension. Blind Lemon Jefferson's "Matchbox Blues" is another example. In parts of this the guitar is going faster than the voice and at a different rhythm giving an exhilarating sense of movement. His "One Dime Blues" has the guitar rhythms doing a little jig when the subject is hot. In Robert Johnson's "Terraplane Blues" the guitar has life of its own irrespective of the voice. The same can be said for "Crossroads Blues": the guitar rhythms are not the same as the singing rhythms. The guitar is not just an accompaniment: it's a separate voice.

Now these were all good musicians and would know what they were doing so it would be intentional. It's surprising how few musicians have picked up on it. This dislocation of voice and guitar is there as musical punctuation: the musical equivalent of an exclamation mark, say, to add interest and definition. Another thing I've noticed is that there are very few musicians who know the value of the dramatic pause. This can maximise the effect of what is to come, creating a moment of tension and expectation, often followed by a musical surprise. A note is picked and it hovers, suspended, without the audience knowing what will happen next.

In a band the importance of a good, intuitive drummer cannot be over-stressed in this connection either. My drummer Melvyn could read my body language – specifically my elbows – and know how to respond:

when to wait, when to act. One of the few beat-based electronic exponents of the blues, BB King, certainly knows how to introduce drama. He's dynamite! A great exponent of contrast. There's a musical pause – you can hear a pin drop – then a wall of sound. It adds shape; it adds tension; it adds climax and resolution. It's the same in a joke or in a story; you have to get the pace right; you have to time the punchline or the effect is lost.

I'm aware that some guitar playing is deceptively simple. The untutored eye follows the left hand and discerns, for example, that there are just three chords to a particular song. But look what the right hand is doing: it's picking a tune, creating harmonies and this is how a song can be rendered more interesting, more layered: by picking rather than strumming. I can demonstrate this with a Little Feat number. If I strum the song as they do and then pick it as I do – the result is strikingly more complex.

Another way to add an element of surprise is to play a song in a different key. This can completely change the whole atmosphere of a song: from major to minor as Ella Fitzgerald sings. Some of the songs I do won't go into any other key: because I'm playing melody lines, only a certain chord shape will allow me to have those melody lines and bass lines. You can only really travel around that chord to get those melody and bass lines. Each different chord has its own atmosphere. A lot of the songs I do are in a different key from the original so I am creating a different feel from the original – something that suits me and my style of playing.

Of course, the modern electric guitarist has many ways to create variety and drama but I can't help but feel that some of these are cheap tricks having little to do with virtuosity – though effective and popular. One of the ways is to use distortion. Classic lead guitar solos are always distorted because musically speaking, people got louder and louder using the valve amp to saturation point to sustain notes longer. In the early days amps didn't have distortion. Distortion was taken further by electronics so that modern amplifiers do have it. Imagine someone playing saxophone: if there's a prolonged note in a melody and it's not a quiet passage then the player would play the sax louder and like a harmonica, it's on the edge of distortion. It'll only sustain as long as the breath will hold. With the electric guitar you can take a note to the edge of distortion and hold it there indefinitely. With a clean note there is instant decay; with a distorted note there is much slower decay. Playing a distorted guitar covers all sins, making it easy for anyone to get away with approximation.

Slides And Gitfiddles; Half Tones And Quarter Tones

For immediate impact, though, the solo blues musician can add a whole new dimension through slide: an extra tool that enables the guitarist to get a vast array of notes in a short space. You can play slide with any guitar as long as it is open-tuned. Slide had very basic origins. There is a transcript described as "old-fashioned Southern vernacular speech" in which Mississippi Fred McDowell, who slid a bottle neck on his finger, describes the early use of the slide:

An my type of blue? I play it with a bottleneck? I first got this style from a beef bone, y'understan' me. Rib wha' come out of a steak? My uncle, when I was a small boy in the country. He ground this bone down, and filed it with a file, and put "t" on his little fi[ae]nger. But I play't on my ri[ae]ng finger, y'understan'? and nis a-dis here bottleneck sound better'n the bone, cause you get more clar- clear sound outa it, [plays a chord] (37)

Slide is the nearest thing to the human voice. The advantage of the monophonic instrument is that you can use it to emulate the human voice and you haven't got the restrictions of frets. Voice and slide sound converge and diverge. There's an explosion of notes in a short space but you can only hear the amalgamation. Violins and slide whistles and trombones also have this quality. How many notes are there as the slide slides down with no fret? A lot of notes. But the ear doesn't discern them separately unless you have a very special gift. When you do it in slow motion it is possible to hear the separate notes. Whereas frets limit you to half tones, this limit goes with slide. You can use the fingers as a slide but this still separates the notes: nothing gets rid of frets like slide does. Ry Cooder says of slide: "When nothing but the bar or knife touches the string the guitar tends to ring more; it's released and open." I agree. (38)

Playing slide takes the rhythm guitar and chord basics of a tune and allows your guitar to be a violin. Monophonic harmony note is the melody to what I'm playing in the chord.

I like the continuity you get in a slide performance. Listen to "Amazing Grace" on slide: there are so many harmonies, you can imagine a choir whereas played with frets it sounds a bit Scottish. You can only do it on certain songs. It either sounds OK or it doesn't. Blind Willie Johnson uses one chord then a monophonic melody line, the chord droning, using the slide to produce the note. The man to listen to is Kokomo Arnold. He makes everyone else look as if they haven't got out of bed.

Mississippi John Hurt uses the slide to fret the note, as if he's using his finger. I do this and I use all the notes in between with slide and I also use my finger as slide.

A lot of people use slide as if they are playing an ordinary guitar whereas the real masters of it play melodies to anchor the whole thing. "Stormy Weather" and "Vagabond" have to be very precise whereas harsher songs such as "Black Ace" and "Dust My Broom" rely more on power, though there is still an anchoring of melody.

People often ask me to explain about slide guitar. A slide guitar is a gitfiddle: a combination of guitar and fiddle. It has no frets and is played flat or conventional with a slide or a bar resting on the strings. I have a 1947 Gibson Hawaiian guitar I traded for a copy of a National. Through one of those musical coincidences the very same week a 1938 Gibson Hawaiian guitar arrived through a friend, off the internet.

The weight of the slide is important. It should be heavy enough to create the required sound but not uncomfortable. Slides come in different weights and are usually made of metal. Original slides were fashioned from bottle necks or, more gruesomely, from hollow bones. I frequently demonstrate the purpose and method of using slide or bar by placing the guitar on my lap, producing a distinctive Hawaiian sound when the bar is used. Although it takes more effort, it is possible to get quarter tones and half tones by pressing the strings down.

Practice is one of the main factors in successful slide playing. The other is open tunings: strings are tuned so that a chord is achieved without fretting, or pressing any of the strings. With such a tuning other chords may be played by simply barring a fret or through the use of a slide.

Practice applies to all areas of course but aptitude must count too. There are some really good guitarists who can't play slide. When I first started playing guitar in the Sixties and met famous slide guitarist Mississippi Fred McDowell, he handed me his guitar and when I tried to play it I realised it was out of tune according to my way of playing. I didn't move the pegs but I started to distinguish which strings were out of tune and where they were out of tune. I was sorting out the mathematics. The first string was two frets lower, which in fact made it a D and going across the guitar I realised the next three strings were in tune – according to tradition. The fifth string was one note higher which made it a G. The sixth string was tuned on the same fret to the fifth string, which made it a D. So from the bass string (the thickest) it was D G D G B D. And that's how I first learnt about open stringing for slide playing. So by sitting and working it out and using the mathematics from my piano playing, a new world opened to me. This was open G tuning and this was the occasion when Roosevelt "The Honeydripper" Sykes said, hearing me: "Ain't bad for a pink!"

You've got an open chord; if you're playing slide you're already one finger down but you've got a completely open guitar to do the rhythm line, putting melody on top with slide. It's easy to play rock 'n' roll or blues with this tuning. Most rock 'n' roll is based round the twelve bar: first recorded in the Twenties. So open tuning without slide is rock 'n' roll. A lot of Rolling Stones music is open tuning; Keith Richard plays a lot in open G including "You Can't Always Get What You Want" and "Honky Tonk Women".

To continue the story. It didn't take me long to realise there were certain things I couldn't do in open G tuning. There were songs I couldn't play in that tuning because the notes wouldn't flow where the fingers could go. So I needed another set of tables: more mathematics. Because slide guitar demands open tuning it has to be tuned to a chord. This is why musicians have several instruments lined up, depending upon what songs they are doing. They can be tuned to D, G, E, C and so forth. They can also be tuned to minor chords.

To play slide guitar well, it's got to be picked. Electric players don't pick and a lot of people emulate them because that's all they've heard. In reality, because you've only got a bar on the finger of your left hand, your right hand becomes more important. To demonstrate this I usually play the opening part of "Black Ace" to show the right hand picking and the left hand sliding.

Damping provides another control. It is used to suppress quirky notes and overtones you don't want when playing slide. You just let your fingers fall across the strings. Some musicians use the palm of the hand. Some use the right hand but I find it easier to use the spare fingers of the left hand.

A solo guitarist is a one man band. To be convincing he has to hold the audience in the same way a play does: with skill, artistry, dexterity, surprise, timing, variety and a good story. Get one of these aspects wrong and the illusion goes, the atmosphere melts into drab reality.

Audience

Add one other person to your lone guitar doodling and things change. There's an increase in pressure, a shared experience and real or imagined expectations. Opinions – not necessarily unwelcome, negative, or unproductive – make it a performance; a dialogue rather than a monologue; a restriction rather than the freedom to explore, make mistakes and be unselfconscious. You have an audience.

In the early days of my musical collaboration with Whitty, it often happened that we were each other's audience and the audience watching us was not all that relevant. Our public performances were an extension of the private playing we did all the time in the shop.

At jam nights there's a blurring of performers and audience, of performance and rehearsal and a cross-fertilization of musical ideas which can be exciting. In the Cheshire Cheese days the Skunk Band would encourage new bands to get up, often providing some musical scaffolding so they wouldn't feel too exposed. Or jam night can be deadly: cliquey, self-indulgent and musically barren. Why don't they come clean and say they just want to fiddle with the equipment – and drink?

But there is always a need for jam nights – otherwise they wouldn't happen. I was involved in local jam nights at The Cheshire Cheese, The Leisure Club, The Limelight, The Royal and Square One. Jam nights in one particular venue have their moment, then there's a decline and then they sprout up elsewhere. Andy Smith reckons the heyday is about eighteen months but some go on longer than that. Why do people pay a lot of money to see performers then talk all the way through? I can understand this happening when the entertainment is not the only agenda – like in a pub – or when it is completely informal – like a jam night – but when the entertainment is the point of being there why hijack the space? It's disrespectful, unfair to the rest of the audience and a waste of money. It's up to the performer to grab the attention of course, but they have to be given a chance.

Generally speaking audiences in folk clubs are more respectful; the audience has made a conscious decision to listen. In the Sixties and early Seventies, people would listen and wait until the end of a song before going to the bar. Hard to believe, I know. But many in the audience would be waiting for their turn to perform so this protocol was in everyone's interest.

But even more formal situations like competitions are not immune. In 1989 I was competing with four bands in a big Birmingham pub at the Banks' Best of Blues Competition. The four bands were all doing rhythm and blues numbers. I stuck my neck out during my solo set. I had no problem competing with the bands but I drew a line at the in-house competition. "It's difficult to compete with piped music. Unless you turn it off, I won't continue and I doubt whether anyone else will be able to, either." They turned it off, grudgingly. I don't know if I sabotaged my chances. I didn't care.

It was strange to find that I was the wrong audience on one occasion. Reputation is double-edged. Sometimes being well known in a district does you no good. People take you for granted; you don't get the recognition. Familiarity breeds contempt they say, or indifference. Sometimes reputation can induce fear in others. Once I was sitting in The Barbridge after a meal and a band started to set up. "You won't be sitting there, will you?" a girl said. "Only I've seen you perform at Square One and I'd be too nervous if you were sitting there watching me." So that was me, a performer, being what someone imagined would be a critical audience: one she didn't really want! So I left, of course. It was a sort of compliment when I think about it.

If you're in a band the best venue is an intimate setting with 150-250 people in the audience and a space for dancing. If you're partying on stage, they'll join in. As a performer, you're the first person to party; you can't have a barrier because you having no barriers is the only way you can get the audience to let theirs down. It's getting that first half dozen to dance that matters. In the old days you could rely on all the girls immediately going onto the floor with their handbags. I've seen some bizarre examples of people letting down their barriers. On one occasion there were couples waltzing at the same time that bikers were doing a "wanky dog" dance. A song like "Goodnight Irene" can get people up and waltzing even though it's being performed by a very loud band.

Doing a festival is totally different: you've got to lure an audience into your particular gig by giving it ten on ten and keeping at it. The scale is too big at festivals – you don't notice individuals. When I did the Labor Day Festival in Georgia I didn't notice anyone in particular except for a mass of black people responding to my rendition of "Shine". This might have been selective attention due to my anxiety about their reaction.

Many of the big names I've met have said they love to do the local pub, if they can. I see their point. If I'm playing in a small bar I can pick out the interesting characters and best-looking girls. You can make eye contact in a small venue but if you can't see anybody, you can't connect in this way. You just do your best and hope for the best.

There are tricky moments on stage: drunks shouting raucous stuff, people wanting to sing out of tune with the band, demands for impossible songs and de-briefed girls climbing on the stage weeping with passion. These were the good nights. It's a risk you take if the barriers are down. There was no point anyone trying to sing at my microphone, anyway, because my voice is so loud, but you go along with it to a certain extent because it can be funny and it can be incorporated into the action.

But you always keep control.

At the right moment you thank the sideburned man with barcoded hair and ask the audience to applaud. His performance has turned him from a mean drunk to a happy, maudlin' drunk but you don't want his intoxicated meandering to detract from the band's pace. I've always had enough stage presence to deal with anything and I knew I could throw people off stage if necessary. I've never been in any physical danger on stage partly, I think, because I have what it takes to be a good front man: you've had good practice if you also do solo work.

The front man has a complex role. He is the bridge between the audience and the band and its music, but also part of the performance and part of the organization. He has to take control of the space. He's the one who communicates with the audience – a buffer between the band and the audience, holding things together, giving the band space to get organised or adjust the equipment.

In terms of the technology of playing music we invariably got the sound system right. After all it was my job! We rarely had any technical problems so I didn't have to cover for that.

The front man is also a conductor: the band members will watch his body language in order to know what happens next. It's professionally important to know when a song is going to end – some old blues songs have many and varied verses. Sometimes I would bring a song to a sudden end if it wasn't going well with the audience. The easiest way to indicate this is to step back from the microphone. The front man is also a continuity man and compere. He represents the ethos of the band and he carries the band's information, telling the audience anecdotes about the band members and about the songs, introducing solos, filling in gaps while people organise themselves for the next number, keeping the audience happy. Humour is the best ploy: some stand-up comedians began as musicians. The front man is the public face of the band so he has to do a good job.

Some front men, like Bruce Springsteen and John Lee Hooker use the power of sex appeal; others like Dylan are enigmatic and keep the audience in awe and guessing. But I keep going back to BB King. He certainly has the supreme power of good timing: the manipulation of sound and silence. He's the best front man I've ever seen: a mountain of a man who plays with economy of effort and sings like a gospel singer. When he did "Put the Hammer Down" he started off talking, like in a cabaret act then went powerfully into the punch line: "PUT THE HAMMER DOWN!" It was dynamite.

Did you know a male spider can seduce a female spider by playing a tune on her web?

A front man can only be successful if he has power and as power is the best aphrodisiac all powerful front men are sexy: it comes with the territory. If you don't have initial confidence you can't get up there. Confidence is rewarded and this feeds back to increase charisma. "When he plays slide it makes me cream my knickers," said one new bride at a concert I did.

In the Skunk Band things were a bit unusual: both Whitty and I were extrovert; the rest of the band just got on with it. Can you have two front men? Definitely. It worked with me and Whitty because we were such good friends. Our harmonies expressed our friendship.

The rapport between musicians can create a good atmosphere onstage; if there is tension then this can be negative but it can also be positive in the sense that edginess can create exciting music, as Andy Smith of Beam said recently.

Adrenalin

Beam played all over the North West doing a mixed bag of Eighties and Nineties stuff with some T Rex and a couple of originals. It's just a bit of fun. I can always find a bit of energy for it. There's always a bit of adrenalin there whether it's six people or sixty people and feedback from an audience is a great feeling. If the band has a fall-out it can give you a bit of extra edge as well.

Andy Smith. (39)

Our most responsive audience was at a bikers' do at Warmingham Village Hall in the early Eighties. Bikers used to come and watch me and

Brammer race so there was a certain amount of respect and common interest. This gig was a send-off for two biker brothers going to Australia. Bikers always dance straight away. Straight away. They soon joined in with the band to be part of the spectacle and soon there was throttle and back wheel spinning and spinning the bike on its own axis: doing a "doughnut" which made a black circular mark. This all took place within the meat and potato pie supper and beetle drive space of the village hall! Whitty was singing "Born To Be Wild" but he sang "born to drink mild". I think the original words were more appropriate on this occasion.

But it's a mistake to be more intimidated by bikers than by musicians. For sheer wild abandon musicians are more anarchic than bikers – in my experience anyway. I'm speaking here of the type of musician just above the semi-pro level who would have thrown caution to the wind even to get there in the first place. Musicians with a day job don't have the luxury of abandon!

You always remember your worst audience. For me it has to be a tiny bar in Georgia – the second or third gig on my first visit to America. It was actually due to shut the next day. Imagine the atmosphere: shit wine, shit coffee, a couple of rednecks and a girl pestering us about kinky sex. Tom was tempted to linger over lingerie but I was more streetwise and sensed a scam. I was more concerned about our gear. Our musical gear.

I rarely feel angry with an audience; it's my decision if I agree to play in a rowdy bar. At a more formal level I have felt angry with promoters over the years. They're the ones who make the decision to put you in an unsuitable venue when it's their job to be discriminating. A recent solo gig I was engaged to do in the Potteries was cancelled because the proprietor felt he could not guarantee the civilized behaviour of the audience for my type of music, though to be fair Andy Boote's Vavoom! got a very good reception there. I don't mind that. He was right to intervene.

I do wish audiences generally would be more respectful, I suppose; I consider what I do as an art form. A conductor doesn't have to put up with people talking all the way through a symphony. One ringtone and he halts the performance!

Why I Hate Recording

Essentially Live

I've played all over the place and halfway across the planet. It hasn't been the sort of music that's been popularised by anybody. If a CD sells five hundred copies, why bother with doing CDs? But there are other reasons for my reluctance to record: as a means of communicating recording is an indirect way. There is a technological process between the performer and the audience in which the voice, the instrument and the listener are separated. Modern recording techniques make it possible to interfere with the performance in such a way that the recorded version bears no resemblance to the live event and I feel uneasy about that.

The country blues was essentially a live performance and that's how I feel about it still. Yet although I saw some of the musicians live, I am grateful that it was recorded, otherwise I wouldn't have any idea of how the rest sounded. Of course, the early blues singers were recorded in the Twenties and Thirties using the recording technology of the time, giving a mere approximation of the actual sound so this has to be borne in mind. It's better than nothing and when I think of what has been lost through carelessness or simply not being recorded at all...

There's a lot to interest you: things like changes in voices when you compare recordings done in the Twenties and Thirties with those re-recorded, upon re-discovery, in the Sixties and stories about early recording studios which give an insight into the state of the art at the same time that they illustrate social attitudes.

Corner Loading

For example, Ry Cooder (40) raised the issue of Robert Johnson recording his songs facing the corner walls. It was alleged by some that this was because he was in awe of what was happening but there is a more likely explanation. The amplification created by the corner and the plaster was conducive to amplifying the mid range. It was called corner loading. It's not likely that he sat facing the corner because he was shy or overwhelmed. Researchers who came to this conclusion were not necessarily musicians and would therefore not give the behaviour a musical explanation. It's possible he sat like that because he felt more comfortable, or the recording people might have suggested it. If you sing in an empty house or at the bottom of the stairs or in a bathroom you get reverberation off the walls. That's what Robert Johnson was doing in the corner; he would have noticed different acoustic effects.

Vinyl Versus CD

I started my record collection when I was thirteen years old. I would choose vinyl over CDs any time. I play vinyl records on a record deck that floats and I'm able to hear individual instruments and vocals much better than on the CD version. I do have a trained ear. The music simply doesn't sound as good on CD or using digital amps and modern speakers. When music is mixed down in a studio, the best equipment is always used, as well as some cheaper speakers more akin to what the average person would use. The sounds produced are aimed at those particular frequencies. You get a mathematically contrived sound, according to my way of thinking. Notes can be slid up and down or eliminated altogether.

On the other hand, if you listen to my old jazz records you can hear the individual instruments. Take, for example, recordings by McKinney's Cotton Pickers – from the late Twenties, early Thirties. They were often done in only one take. Each musician would have cushions tied to their feet so that when it was their turn to approach the microphone, they wouldn't make a noise! I do a version of one of the numbers on this album. "Beedle Um Bum" was also done by Blind Willie McTell and I learnt my version mostly from this, though I do it based on several versions so that it's my own version. The album notes are historically significant because they are in French. That's because black musicians were more readily accepted in France than in the US. According to the sleeve notes, McKinney's Cotton Pickers were rated as highly as Fletcher Henderson and Duke Ellington in their day.

In The Studio

A recent recording I did in a local studio illustrated perfectly the reasons I am uneasy about recording and the things that can prevent me losing myself in the music. Fortunately I didn't have to worry about the thousand knobs – that really would sap my artistic integrity. Nor did I have to concern myself with the stridency of urban sounds but there were plenty of other things to go wrong! Although the owner, Jason Woolley (41) is a friend who has always wanted to play with the Skunk Band and whose job takes him all over the world inspecting the work of teachers in rock schools, I still felt I was in an alien space because I associate playing the guitar with being relaxed and at leisure, and usually having an audience and a couple of drinks. I hadn't brought any. First mistake. There's a complex relationship between alcohol and adrenalin. Flashback to a lunchtime gig at The Railway during The Nantwich Jazz and Blues Festival: all the guitarists in the area were in the pub. My hands just wouldn't work; the more I concerned myself with this the worse I got.

Someone sent me a double Jack Daniels. I was OK.

The same thing happened at The Hand and Trumpet but I had a hangover. So alcohol can inhibit me from allowing the flow in two ways: not enough or too much! Yet I recorded *4 Hours in Georgia* after a heavy night and very little sleep but other factors overrode this. I did have a couple of drinks and they said I was on a roll. Everything was new and exhilarating and I was able to utilize the adrenalin of curiosity and excitement and survival.

On the other hand, adrenalin arising from failure and tension is inhibiting. I didn't do the basic preparation at Jason's so I was physically uncomfortable: on a low chair with the guitar digging into my chest, my little finger on my right hand uncomfortable on the finger plate, causing my hand to be more unstable. The state I was in because my hands wouldn't work caused me to concentrate too hard on technique. Nothing flowed.

To be fair to myself, though, I was recovering from my second hand operation and my hands were painful, and tired very quickly partly because of that. I had underestimated the effect of the second operation and I wasn't match fit. The last time I had played a full song was ten months previously; I thought my daily strumming was enough but it wasn't.

Another reason my performance had no edge was because there was no element of urgency. I wasn't paying for the studio time and I could redo it if I wanted. Complacency is the enemy of spontanaiety.

Also, because I don't like digital recording – you don't get the interaction of voice and guitar – and studios are places where they fabricate things, I can't get rid of the thought that this isn't right: music should be a live experience – authentic and honest. Perhaps I should do one of these perfected recordings but I don't like the concept. I think all recordings should be live – the nearest thing to the experience of being there.

I'd broken my own rules.

But the day wasn't wasted. To calm myself down I played "Reckless Disposition" at a ridiculously high volume. Jason thought it was terrific. You do need adrenalin – you shouldn't perform if you don't feel nervous but this time the adrenalin was a nuisance. I just couldn't settle down. I was much better after lunch and a couple of bottles of beer. But I wasn't happy with the CD and did it again a few months later.

I just don't like recording.

Musical opportunities often come out of the blue – or should I say blues? In 1998 I had the opportunity to fulfil a wish. I went to the homeland of Blind Willie McTell, Tampa Red, Kokomo Arnold and Curley Weaver.

I went to Georgia to sing the blues.

Notes: Section Three

(1) Leadbelly: "I'm Sorry Mama".

(2) Nina Simone's 1960s live performance of "Mississippi Goddam".

(3) Fred McDowell: from an undated recording made in the late 1960s in Jackson, Mississippi, and released on Capitol Records SM-409 some time in the 1970s.

(4) Quoted from Hand Me My Travelin' Shoes by Michael Gray, published by Bloomsbury.

(5) Big Band Life and Segregation in the 1940s: hubpages.com.

(6) New York Times, Friday 2nd December 1988.

(7) www.earlyblues.com/chronology

(8) Library of Congress Recordings.

(9) Bo Carter: "Banana In Your Fruit Basket".

(10) Carl Rafferty: "Dressed With The Drawers".

(11) www.Zirconbleu.com

(12) Leadbelly: "Gwine Dig A Hole".

(13) Blind Blake: "Notoriety Woman Blues".

(14) Leadbelly: "Whiff on Me".

(15) Blind Blake: "Rope Stretchin' Blues Part II".

(16) Leola B. Wilson: "Black Biting Bee Blues".

(17) "Sweet Home Chicago": done by several performers, notably Robert Johnson.

(18) John Henry Barbee.

(19) Michael Gray: Hand Me My Travelin' Shoes, Bloomsbury Publishing.

(20) Mississippi Fred McDowell – taken from a transcript of an undated recording made in the late 1960s in Jackson, Mississippi, and released on Capitol Records SM-409 some time in the 1970s.

(21) Georges Adins, who went to meet John Estes in 1962, wrote about him in Jazz Journal August 1963.

(22) Part of the Alan Lomax Collection.

(23) For more detail see Michael Gray's Hand Me My Travelin' Shoes, Bloomsbury Publishing.

(24) Prestige records USA, Transatlantic Records Limited.

(25) Living Blues Jan/Feb 1998.

(26) Santa Cruz Sentinel quoted at www.arhoolie.com

(27) Bob Groom, Blues World Magazine 1967.

(28) www.oafb.net

(29) The All Music Guide.

(30) Quoted from the sleeve notes of Blind Blake's Blues in Chicago in the Classic Jazz Masters series.

(31) Recording engineer: Can you do a dozen in an hour?

Blind Blake: I can do as many as you want, boss!

I've read this somewhere but I don't remember where and if it isn't true I still believe it.

(32) Jas Obrecht: Talking Country Blues with Ry Cooder, in Guitar Player July 1990.

(33) Hand Me My Travelin' Shoes: Michael Gray. Bloomsbury Publishing.

(34) MTV: Unplugged 1993.

(35) Quoted by his daughter Cora Mae Bryant in Living Blues Jan/Feb 1998.

(36) Bob Groom, Blues World Magazine, 1967.

(37) From an undated recording made in the late 1960s in Jackson, Mississippi, and released on Capitol Records SM-409 sometime in the 1970s. The question marks denote a high-rising inflection.

(38) Jas Obrecht: Talking Country Blues with Ry Cooder, in Guitar Player July 1990.

(39) Andy Smith from a conversation at Custom Amplification, 2006.

(40) Jas Obrecht: Talking Country Blues with Ry Cooder, in Guitar Player July 1990.

(41) Jason Woolley is a guitarist and bassist who has performed nationally and internationally. He is the Principal Consultant for the Rock School 2006-2012 Guitar Bass and Drum syllabus and a freelance composer, producer and sound designer.

SECTION FOUR

Georgia On My Mind: Dream Fulfilled; Illusion Lost

I went to Georgia on the strength of a brief encounter! It was a risk to take a plane into the unknown but I had always dreamed of visiting this place so prominent in blues history, and when the chance rock'n'roll circumstance arose, I was ready for it.

I wasn't ready for what it did to me.

That Old Sweet Song

One afternoon in 1997 a fleshy bloke with a goatee and a Southern drawl came in. He spotted my twelve string Dobro and his eyes gleamed. Love at first sight. This was Tom Hubbard: blues musician, from Georgia, USA. He was in the UK for an interview and like many far-flung musicians had found his way to my shop.

If Dobros were cars they'd flash their headlights at oncoming Dobros. I've had the twelve string Hendrix Dobro since 1976. They are usually made from mahogany or plain maple. The Dobro Roy Rogers has is ordinary maple; Tom had a mahogany one. My instrument is extraordinary because twelve string Dobros are rare anyway but this is made of special book matched flame maple – tiger striped – and would have cost the buyer a serious amount of extra money. It might have been made as a presentation instrument, like the one Dixie came across which was made of bamboo and had something like "Emmy-Lou '82" instead of a Dobro serial number. A supplier of laminated bamboo for kitchens supplied this material to Dobro – plywood giving the correct amount of density and rigidity for the resonator function. Des has that guitar which was made for the supplier's daughter. But I digress.

Tom Hubbard from Georgia offered to buy my twelve string Dobro for £3,000. I refused the offer. He offered £2,000 plus a vintage National. I refused; he was confused! "This man has as many guitars he *doesn't* sell as he *does*!" The Dobro was not for sale because I played it and when I did play it Tom was astounded: "Man, that's awesome!" He took a tape of my songs and when he contacted me from the States, he said he hadn't stopped playing it and that he would organize some gigs for me. This was a yearned-for opportunity to play the blues in some of the places of their origins.

In a Radio Stoke interview (January 1998) I spoke about my excitement and apprehension at playing the blues in America. Although many people had said that mine was the most authentic-sounding blues performed by a non-American and I knew that I had done the groundwork properly over the years, I still felt humbled. Nevertheless, in March 1998, full of hope, I went to Georgia. The Georgia visits – four altogether – are chronicled in a daily journal, which in parts, echoes the themes and rhythms of the music I respect.

Uncle Tom's Cabin

My time with Tom Hubbard and his wife Kathy, at Newnan, forty miles outside Atlanta, in a typical single-storey wooden house I regarded affectionately as Uncle Tom's Cabin, was a direct exposure to some of the Southern themes which had dominated my musical studies. Nothing prepared me for the huge scale: the epic weather systems; the stark, rugged landscape not softened by the springtime blooming you get in England in March; the vast stretch of suburbs where you'll find no pedestrian; the varied and often deadly wildlife. Nothing prepared me for the large contrasts: lavish and formal Southern hospitality co-existing with some narrow and forthright racial views; the KKK still having some left-over rights and everyone going to church. In Georgia there are people holding placards saying "any job for a roof" and lines of shacks – think of the worst pigeon loft – mixed in with huge, ostentatious mansions such as that owned by Evander Holyfield. Nothing prepared me for the ubiquitous gun culture: everyone owns one and they'll shoot you for being in the wrong place or doing something on the wrong day. There are no gardens to soften the boundary between home and wilderness either and in spite of swings on verandahs, there is a Spartan element to the way of life that isn't to do with wealth or lack of it. It's in the culture: summed up by the austere lounge in Hoyt Hubbard's brick-built house whose upright chairs symbolised a Victorian sense of rectitude. No lounging in the lounge!

Snakes In Tyres
"I done give them snakes hell!" – Hoyt Hubbard

I appreciated the country pursuits, the wildlife and the farm tours with Tom's father, Hoyt. Originally used for cotton, Hoyt's 260 acres is now dedicated to leisure activities like shooting and fishing from the large artificial lake. Within the rural scenery there were abandoned cars and trucks almost assimilated into the undergrowth, as if a fairground had dropped some of its paraphernalia.

There are dangers too: although I walked every inch of Hoyt's land, I was extremely wary of snakes, not being used to them. Water Moccasins are two to three feet long and as fat as your wrist. Deadly poisonous, they live near water and they give chase! Being handy with the broom, Hoyt's wife Peggy had killed one that came in the house. King Black snakes lurk in barns and there are some highly coloured numbers that just fall out of trees. Highland Moccasins live on slightly higher ground and are equally poisonous. The locals know which places to avoid but I was nervous, even though I was given a gun with snake shot in it and as soon as the temperature rose, I became housebound – a bit embarrassing if your blues name is Snakey Jake!

Hoyt had been furious about a black farmer who had allowed tyres to accumulate on his property, because this is where these snakes take cover. There are other dangers: the swampland on Hoyt's land had swallowed a whole tractor and various cattle but my Enduro riding made me more capable of facing this challenge. Good job too!

Mississippi Burning

Just as snakes permeate this landscape – perhaps more luridly in my imagination than in reality – another sense of unease is apparent across these former cotton fields. My video footage takes in a rough blue cross marking the grave of Old Blue Eyes, Hoyt's dog, and a startlingly white water tower with a black lettering: COWETA COUNTY (1) which dominates the skyline. My camera eye returns to the tower time and time again; I was mesmerised by its incongruity in this pastoral landscape. It is this iconic presence that allegedly appears in the film *Mississippi Burning* (1988) based on the murders of three civil rights workers in 1964 and the power of the Ku Klux Klan. Hoyt received a fee from the film company.

There is also footage of an old building: a one-storey brick-built cottage almost throttled by climbers whose branches have yet to show their spring growth. I was offered this shack that once housed a black family, plus half an acre on Hoyt's land in exchange for my Dobro – the one that his son Tom coveted so much. What a strange idea to own so cheaply the sort of place many of my musical gurus had lived in.

The water tower dominates the sky like an alien craft.

I had some very revealing conversations with Hoyt about the white Georgian attitude to African Americans, whom he still calls "niggers". He recalled how, as an enlightened and astute farmer he would make sure his black hired hands had a rail so that they didn't fall off the truck transporting them to the fields! Other farmers were less mindful and could end up with two or three of their cotton pickers having fallen off. The feeling was not one of concern for their safety but of the inconvenience caused to the farmer when he was short-handed. Hoyt also described black people being shackled by the sheriff for real or trumped-up crimes and the locals being allowed to thrash them with thongs: thongs which had silver dollars threaded through them as if to emphasise the economic hierarchy. It's easy to see how lynching could occur. I wondered naively how such a callous attitude could persist post-Civil Rights. Hoyt was a decent enough man.

I decided it must be to do with the way the white supremacist categorises people. With surprising neutrality, Hoyt regards black people as he does his stock – and with less human feeling than he has for Old Blue Eyes. Control and a certain amount of self-interested care and paternalism are necessary to get a good return on your business. That's all. He believes that all black people are lazy and inferior. He doesn't hate them but his world view is absolutely secure and that is that.

Hoyt's son Tom said, "I'd like to piss on Martin Luther King's flame." There is an eternal commemorative flame to the great Civil Rights leader in Atlanta and this is how Tom gave vent to his hatred. He has a far more emotional attitude to black people than Hoyt, hating without knowing any. When Tom visited my shop, he came back from the local supermarket absolutely fuming: "Them niggers wouldn't get off the sidewalk!" he raged. It's discouraging to feel that nothing has budged in the hearts and minds of people like Tom. At least Hoyt doesn't compound his racism with hate.

Fortunately I did meet some people with liberal views during my stay in Georgia and I was able to take refuge with them when the white tower seemed unconquerable.

It's easy to judge someone like Hoyt Hubbard but I liked him. He has the views of a conservative farmer, belonging to a time when racist attitudes were the acceptable norm. The British have nothing to be proud of. They treated their workers equally badly; they supported slavery until it became an economic no-no; they behaved unspeakably in the colonies. What I did take issue with was Tom's racism; he was born into a different era and his racism is an anachronism based on hatred. Tom is a bully and like all bullies a coward. "He's a prize steer with no horns," Hoyt said of him.

Tom would have led the lynch mob.

The shadow of the Ku Klux Klan still passes over the State: every year they hold a televised meeting on top of Stone Mountain – the site of the reincarnation of the Klan in 1915 – courtesy of an unrepealed law giving them the right to hold celebrations there. More depressing: it's attended by thousands of people harbouring unrepealed prejudice.

Gun Law

I never did get used to there being a loaded handgun on the breakfast table next to the coffee pot. Like the snakes and the lingering sense of oppression, guns are endemic in this part of the South. I am familiar with the gun as a sporting accessory and I enjoyed the lessons I received from the "Georgia boys", but knowing something is not the same as experiencing the peculiar position gun owning holds in the US. I was completely taken by surprise when someone shot at me for drinking on Sunday! It didn't make me feel any better when it was explained to me that this was just a warning shot – Georgia boys never miss. I soon noticed that Tom always took his gun when he answered the door and that all the road signs off the main highways were full of gunshot.

There was also a very awkward situation with a sheriff. I took the car 400 yards to run the battery up then across the fields to have a walk, during which I collected a couple of fir cones. On the return journey I was pulled up by the sheriff: "STAY IN THE CAR!" He gave me the third degree about trespass and demanded to know what I was doing. I showed him my passport and said I was collecting a couple of fir cones for my girlfriend in England. That must have sounded pathetic and I must have looked frightened of his gun, handcuffs and truncheon because he let me go. "I didn't want to shoot you," he said.

For trespass?!

Gospel, Atlanta Braves And Silver Dollars

Yet, as a contrast to this territorial aggression, I experienced hospitality which was as wholehearted as it was formal. When Hoyt said grace he included good wishes for me, before a good meal of fried okra, purple-eyed peas, cornbread, biscuits, pan-fried flavoured chicken and lemon meringue pie – all home-made. A nice woman gave me an Atlanta Braves baseball hat when I visited her house. This was not a trivial gift; it would be treasured by anyone owning it. Hoyt gave me a silver dollar which happened to be from the same year I opened my shop; he regretted he could not give me a 1949 silver dollar – the year of my birth.

For all its pleasantness and upholding of family values, it seemed to me that with this hospitable culture comes an insularity, a lack of vision and a narrowing of possibilities. Apart from visiting one another's houses, the only other social activity is church-going, dressed to the hilt. Yes it is true that people eat out a great deal; restaurant prices are very cheap. But these weren't social occasions: things were much more basic, more single-minded than that. This was about eating. There are few bars and social drinking is frowned upon and relegated to ne'er-do-wells.

But going to church is big amongst the majority of Southerners, black and white. The churches appeared to be segregated. Martin Luther King said that the most segregated hour of Christian America was eleven o'clock on Sunday morning. I didn't attend a church service and this has surprised some people, since the blues are linked to gospel music but I had a good reason for my fastidiousness: as a non-believer I felt I had to avoid voyeurism. But I could hear the gospel music; it was fantastic, with fabulous harmonies and the experience reminded me of the old tin church in Stewart Street, Crewe where you could feel the walls bulging with sound during services.

You Can't Buy A Pitcher On Your Own

Hospitality notwithstanding, I found the dearth of alcohol perplexing for a Brit used to a pub on every corner and one in between. I was surprised how small a part alcohol plays in the day-to-day lives of people. As a committed drinker I felt it needed recording: "Hardly any bars but a church on every corner!" Another journal entry makes reference to surreptitious drinking: "TJ invited me round the back, gave me a polystyrene beaker and a jug in a blue shroud – Crown Royal Whisky". And how joyless it was! The echoes of Prohibition and bootlegging are still around. This feeling is supported by the draconian drink laws in this part of the US: Sundays are dry and if you have an open liquor container in the car, even if empty from a previous day, it's a serious jail offence. For a man who has punctuated a good part of his life with alcohol, I became just a bit pre-occupied with my supplies!

As well as the strict laws on alcohol there are other examples of Puritanism still rife in the Bible Belt. Perhaps the law against sodomy is fairly understandable in such a God-fearing society but oral sex is still forbidden for married couples and *dancing* is still illegal in Newnan!

Continuing this theme: alcohol rationing exists at a place called the Yacht Club. You are not allowed to buy a pitcher of beer on your own. The idea that you might consume four whole pints of beer is not acceptable even in such a bohemian environment.

My Old Friend The Woodpecker In The Walnut Tree

I did enjoy my first visit to Georgia in spite of the alcoholic anxiety and I wrote a piece of music: "Magnolia and Honeysuckle" in honour of this garden state. What Newnan lacks in wild life, it makes up for in its wildlife: buzzards by the dozen, heron, grebe, red cardinals, birds with blue tail feathers bright in the sun, male and female woodpeckers, wasps that could eat you, butterflies as big as sparrows, beaver and glimpses of deer disappearing into the trees in the flash of a white tail. I enjoyed sitting on the swing verandah seat listening to birdsong and the sound of insects' wings in the Georgia sunset – a trickle of orange and gold light gradually diminishing, the trees darkly silhouetted against the evening sky.

And I thought about Burl Ives.

I'm Goin' To New Orleans

One of the highlights of my first visit to Georgia – "off in brilliant sunshine: tight jeans and a big belt" – is the trip to New Orleans. The journal entries record my eager response to this road movie with its fast-moving scenery:

Flattening out – pines replaced by deciduous just coming into spring bud – temperature climbing – light intensifying – field full of donkeys followed by field full of llamas! Trees wear grey beards here – possums instead of hedgehogs dead – soil is getting sandier – dead armadillo on shoulder. Three Rivers Bridge 3 miles approximately – right Mississippi, left Florida…temperature rising.

And so was the emotional temperature rising. Tom and I stopped overnight at Gulfport where the rich brown colour of the Mississippi mud in the Gulf of Mexico reminded me of the Shroppie Union, and we found the bizarrely named and never to be forgotten Seafood and Shoe Repair Shop, and dozens of twenty-four hour pawn shops ominously close to the casinos.

In New Orleans I was soon walking through the French Quarter and the energy of the walking is captured in my words: "Had first crawfish with margarita, walked around, bought voodoo dolls, Cajun spices, T shirt, post cards, couple of beers".

But perhaps all pilgrimages are marred by the anticlimax of arriving. I was struck by the absence of music on this short trip. At one point Tom and I visited a blues bar offering: "5 nights Karaoke, 1 night house Rock 'n' Roll band, 1 night Ladies Night, 1 night once a month for out of town Blues band". Perhaps we were just unlucky and short of time but once a month blues in a *blues* bar?

I've spoken to other musicians about this musical paucity and they agree. Des read an article written by BB King which substantiates the view that you'd be lucky to find the music Bourbon Street and Beale Street are famous for.

I collected my Mississippi dirt and I recorded the sun: a ball of fire dropping over my left shoulder as we left this legendary place, "till next time!"

A commitment I meant at that moment.

The British Blues Invasion

Musically speaking, the high points of my trips to America were the interviews at WRFG ("Radio Free Georgia"), the recordings at Whippoorwill Studios, the gig at Fat Matt's and the Labor Day Blues Festival.

Tom, a locally known musician and recording artist, had told the radio station about me and that's how we came to be on our way to the studio, listening to the programme *Good Morning Blues* advertising us several times as "The British Blues Invasion – Shaky(!) Jake with Tom Hubbard and live playing". Well – I *was* used to people getting my name wrong: I've been referred to as "this brilliant blues player called Smoky Jake Johnson from Crewe" before now. (2)

My first interview at WRFG was with the Blues Professor. He was a good DJ though not such a good communicator and I was a bit nervous. I was able to advertise my gigs and recording and mentioned a deal I had with Pyramid Records to distribute my CD in the US and in Manchester UK. I answered the usual questions about my musical background, stressing that I hadn't wanted to just come to Georgia as a tourist, that the country blues was my "main thing" and that I had met Son House, whose "Death Letter" was to be my first live number on the show. I followed this with another dramatic song: Woody Guthrie's "Vigilante Man". The interviewer remarked, "When you sing, you definitely don't sound so English," – praise indeed.

We agreed it was ironic that I had been able to meet great American musicians in the Sixties as the result of their own countrymen not giving them the musical, let alone political and social status they deserved.

Tom and I did a duet of Bobby Bland's "Today I Started Loving You Again" giving this soul number a country edge, followed by a recorded version of "Dust My Broom" by Snakey Jakes' Dead Skunk Band. The session ended with a rendition of Mississippi John Hurt's "I'm Satisfied" and a recording of John Hurt at the Newport Festival which I thought was a nice link with the past.

Done And Dusted

In retrospect this first interview with WRFG was less satisfying than the later ones partly because the content was less extensive and because the interviewer seemed less enthusiastic about the music than the other interviewers. Perhaps I was more relaxed the second time and I could also talk about the newly recorded CD: *4 HOURS IN GEORGIA*. The title refers to the location and the amount of time it took to record at Whippoorwill Studios, Smyrna, Georgia. My journal entry for Thursday, 12th March 1998 is surprisingly brief about it:

Off to Whippoorwill – arrived 10.50 and started sound checks. 11.15 – first half done and dusted before lunch using my 12 string and Will's Maple Guild 6… lunch at The Old Hickory House – main course brilliant – pork and barbecue sauce on garlic bread with fries and salad $4.95 and Brunswick Stew – not so good – $2.25. Back to finish last 4 and master. Finished by 4 with 6 Honey Browns.

But I do have a reputation for just getting things done. It looks as if I was more interested in the food and drink than the recording studio but on the next page of the journal it is obvious what an emotional impact the recording had had on me: "I realised it was the anniversary of Mum's birthday – coincidence or what? Well I made it. BLUES IN GEORGIA; a mountain climbed…JUST STEEL & WOOD".

There must be a song in that last line.

"It's Always Better Live."

The interviewer for my second appearance on WRFG was Black Jack, a civilized and gracious conversationalist. He was enthusiastic about the music and there was a good sense of informal communicative equality in our dialogue, with him contributing some of his own musical anecdotes and passions but always with deference to the professional musicians. He remembered sitting around in a place called Mandy's Carwash listening to Junior Wells and seeing Muddy Waters in Chicago in the Sixties. He regarded Muddy Waters's *Folk Singer* album with some awe.

I was at the end of my second visit to Georgia and was in the WRFG studio to talk about the CD I cut during my first visit. The interviewer was agreeably surprised that the cover showed me standing in front of the windows of the WRGF Studios, immediately after my first interview there. It was by now a legend that I took four hours to record the album, with one-take tracks, "as it happened" including lunch. Black Jack played contrasting tracks: the drama of "Black Ace" and the intimacy of "I'm Satisfied"; the exciting vocals and heavy slide of "Death Letter" and "Friend of the Devil" sung in an understated, folkie way.

The interviewer responded positively, especially to the slide guitar work and invited me to do a live number, on slide. "Dust My Broom" was the choice. "It's always better live," was the verdict so I followed this with "Pay Day" and received applause, especially from AJ, the interviewer's wife. More was to come. I gave the jazz classic, "Stormy Weather" a plaintive country edge using slide. This prompted a celebrity response. Curley Weaver's daughter, Cora Mae Bryant had been singing along to this and called the radio station to say it was "the best goddamn blues" she had heard.

Curley Weaver, Blind Willie McTell, George Carter, Tampa Red and Kokomo Arnold are all representatives of the early slide tradition in Georgia. Weaver and McTell were musical partners and friends: busking in Nashville and recording in New York (1933). Curley and Cora Mae's mother lived with McTell and his wife. I felt a connection, through Cora Mae, with these great musicians. A blues festival in honour of Blind Willie McTell is held every year in his birth place, Thomson, Georgia.

Cora Mae has had her own musical career, playing at one time with Tommy McClennan. From the early days The Skunk Band admired McClennan's version of "Bottle Up and Go": it's a good vehicle for his characteristic growly voice. We did a rock version. As a soloist I also had a refined version with finger picking. Considering what Cora Mae said about white men and the blues:

white boys now, they don't hardly make no blues. Mostly they copy after us. I don't know of any blues they made. They just can't do it. They can play it pretty good, but they can't sing it at all. They just ain't got the voice for that (3)

she paid me a huge compliment. I realised how great a compliment when I read about Michael Gray's encounter with her. (4) He describes how she expressed "disbelief and contemptuous unimpressedness" when he tried to interview her about her father's life with Blind Willie McTell.

Cora Mae Bryant died in 2008.

Two more live songs: Sleepy John Estes's "I'd Been Well Warned" and "Vigilante Man" followed, and the interview ended with very sincere wishes for a welcome return. Very sincere. It was good to have such an appreciative interviewer as well as an accolade from a celebrated blues woman.

The commercial break included an advertisement for an anti-KKK rally.

Fat Matt's, Blind Willie's And The Voodoo Rooms

Playing the blues in Atlanta gave me a sense of musical context. It's not possible to say any one place was the home of the blues but being a large conurbation, Atlanta was a focus for blues musicians – somewhere to play to the biggest audience.

Fat Matt's is one of those places I dreamt of playing. It's long-established and reputedly the haunt of Blind Willie McTell, who played there and at other places in the area such as the corner of Peach Tree and Vine, further on. Tom's video shows it buoyant and increasingly busy, the clients concerned with the serious business of eating but there is an appreciative response, especially to the slide numbers. As I record in the journal: "An old couple really enjoyed themselves, complimenting me several times. Sat right at the front – 2 feet from my feet – direct in the line of fire".

An easy hospitable venue with free beer for the entertainer – the waitress bringing me good quality traditional Southern food on the strength of my English accent – in retrospect this was the only venue on my Georgia circuit with any atmosphere. The *clientele* were from all walks of life and there were blacks as well as whites. The black people at all the other venues were serving.

The gig at The Voodoo Rooms was less well attended and less lively but in spite of the small audience I received good hospitality: free beer, refried beans, sour cream, black olives and tortillas, and people were genuinely interested in me.

My visit to Blind Willie's: the 1997 winner of the WC Handy Award: "Blues Club of the Year" was not as a performer but to see John Mooney (Bluesiana), considered one of the top two bluesmen in the State. A Son House disciple. My reaction was mixed:

good tight drummer – double bass – he played a lot like Son House but lacked a little firmness, using a thumb pick and heavy rhythms and relying on the old foot, his vocals not being anything like his recordings.

Marietta Crystals, Java Blues, J.Paul's, Roosters, Harry's

During my second visit to Georgia, in October 1998, I did several gigs and experienced many contrasts. The first one took place at Marietta Crystals, roughly a hundred miles from Newnan: local by American standards! It was an upmarket venue and I received $85, $45 in tips, free drinks and sold five CDs at $12 each. It was hard work – they expected three hours from me. After the Gig from Heaven came the Gig from Desolation Row at Java Blues, a club on the edge of extinction in the same square as Marietta Crystals. The manager was pissed; the assistant manager a space casualty from the Sixties and a man-eating blonde offered to let us take her every which way but loose. It was a veritable zoo and a close escape.

In spite of the flamboyant publicity, the gig a few days later at J.Pauls was not a very nourishing experience either, although the money was better than at Java Blues:

Well big neon sign: International English Recording Star but no punters except a few rednecks listening to country. I had requests hollered from Lynyrd Skynyrd to James Taylor.

Fortunately, things were better at Roosters in Douglasville the next night:

...a really nice blues bar with food and drink which Jerry the owner said was all on the house and the barman Chris made sure of it. Great first set – Jerry asked me for a CD for his jukebox. I cheekily swapped it for a $15 Roosters T-shirt.

Things were less good at Harry's a couple of nights later, where there were eight customers and Tom had to hassle for his money that was then thrown across the bar. I had received some praise from one of the other musicians: "That's smokin' Pete," he said as he shook my hand but I was appalled at Tom's treatment – docked $25 for not playing until 1.30 in an empty club. Familiar territory.

It got worse. The next gig at Rupert's was cancelled, the management being the same as the doomed Java Blues. This was the second club I had seen off and at this point I began to feel frustrated and disappointed. Although there were positive experiences, the second visit was characterised by a sense of diminishment: gigs cancelled; interviews postponed; uncertainty about payment; places closed down; money becoming scarce as the sun's heat dwindled. My welcome had worn thin. When I was preparing to leave there was tense cleaning taking place around me: "Oh my bed's gone and the washer is on cleaning my sheets 'fore they're cold".

Another song lyric?

Performing in unfamiliar places, the welcome and the hospitality become very important – it's how you judge whether an experience, is good or not. I've often spoken about the loneliness of solo playing: how insecure everything is and how exhausting it is to play unsupported. You are dependent on the kindness of strangers and if it happens it is as significant as the fee. I suppose this echoes how it must have been for those early blues players, busking for bread, more or less. How difficult it must have been for them to experience the lack of respect they encountered. It seems to me that people performing on this particular circuit of venues still have low status, no matter what their musical ability is and managers are reluctant to pay them if the audience has been thin. Yet there was good feedback: Tom's drummer said, "Who's this Snakey Jake character they keep talking about on the radio?" Another friend of Tom's – Glyn – rang and said, "Snakey Jake was the talk of the blues programme this morning," and this lifted my spirits.

The anomaly was that my talent and status were appreciated but not at the bleak edge of management where an empty venue was the issue. At best, things were all a bit cheerfully amateurish; I had over-estimated Tom's influence and this began to depress me.

Labor Day Blues And The Golden Ghetto

I returned to America in late summer 2000 for the Labor Day Blues Festival in Georgia: a high spot in my career. I was jubilant about recording *4 Hours in Georgia* as a dream realised and I'm proud of it because I sang the songs as the old guys did – it's honest and the same recorded as live – but a CD is something you do for others; the live performance was more real and the experience of the festival hasn't faded. I was performing with my best mate and we were well placed on the bill. I still have the T-shirt with the list of performers: bizarrely the top of the bill is actually at the bottom of the list, like a countdown. We had an appreciative audience and we even found a bar we both liked!

During this third trip to Georgia with Des as my companion, some of the contrasts and anomalies I had already experienced came into heightened relief and our time was characterised by ideological conflict and boredom, as well as some exciting encounters with musicians and intellectuals. Although I hoped to make some money performing because each time I leave my business I lose money, the previous two visits had not reassured me. But this trip I had the good fortune to be sponsored on both sides of the Atlantic.

Keith Bellamy – Bert Bellamy's middle son – likes the music his father liked and comes to see me perform. Perhaps on the strength of this, Keith sponsored my third flight to Georgia. A generous impulse: "Don't get one of those flights where you have to change at Newark – get one that goes straight through," he said as he gave me his credit card details. He also arranged for me to use the Crown, Nantwich, as a free venue for a gig that earned £500 to help with my American expenses.

Unlike the previous times I was not dependent on Tom Hubbard for hospitality. I had been invited by Black Jack – who did the second interview at WRFG – to play at the Blues Festival: an event organized by WRFG. The deal was that I could bring Des and we would receive free accommodation. I had made an independent link as a result of the interview and the fact that *4 Hours in Georgia* had reached number one in the blues chart. My circle of contacts in Georgia had widened.

For the first few days we stayed at Heartfield Manor, Inman Park: a mansion referred to as the "B&B" in my journal and owned by our hosts Harlan and Sandra. Harlan, a left-wing intellectual who has co-written a book about local history (5) had set up WRFG, "a peoples' radio station", had run it, and was still associated with it. His home was a beautiful building with balconies, wooden floors, good quality traditional furniture, a stunning staircase, books, paintings, displays of archaeological artefacts and comfortable sitting areas. Des and I had five-star adjoining rooms and a shared balcony complete with praying mantis. Heartfield Manor was a cultured environment, with an atmosphere of calm spaciousness where creative people were welcome and where the conversation would cover many topics: literary, social, economic, political, artistic, musical… Des and I enjoyed the communal intellectual stimulation of the night-long discussions and we found their liberalism refreshing. We were also intrigued by the proximity of musicians such as Pete Seeger and parties that carried on until breakfast, unattended by us as yet. Des and I were conserving our energy for the next day: Festival Day.

After breakfast we walked a mile with our instruments to the festival site. The Labor Day Blues Festival was held in a very large walled complex: an old factory, partly dismantled with the roof and windows gone so that it most resembled a walled garden. I recorded the intensely humid weather, "hotter than Africa" and how grateful we were for the hospitality suite with its cool water, beer and food – all free. Then the inevitable waiting. I stayed on water till two o'clock then had three beers; Des stayed with water.

There were a hundred performers all with their own agendas and it was difficult actually getting on the stage. Because of the egocentric behaviour of one of the bands half way down the list, whose long-winded attention to their own equipment threw out the timings, we were squeezed into a half hour slot. We felt that this band had been disrespectful and annoying. Fortunately the audience was attentive and relaxed – a family audience. The event was well attended and festive yet there was a sense of intimacy and close contact between audience and performer.

Francine Reed was headlining; Beverly "Guitar" Watkins was the penultimate act with Des and I before that. The Producers played Eric and Blind Blake well if a little contrived. We had to cross "Down 'n' Out Blues" off our set list. These things happen. Ours was a difficult set with pints of sweat and fried feet! Not only that: our first two numbers were played without either of us being able to hear ourselves, although all came right for our rendition of "Shine" with kazoo solo courtesy of Des and black guys shouting "Shine!" and laughing every time the word came up. Then the twelve string did its usual job.

Musicians are used to things going wrong but I have no tolerance for heat. Des had a more equable approach, pointing out that the musicians from the bands were mutually supportive and kind to one another. Anyway the hospitality was stunning and we relaxed into it to watch

Francine Reed moving and singing effortlessly, at one with her music. I was impressed by the sound balance: you could hear all the instruments and, importantly, the singer's voice with its story. There was clarity and a space for each instrument; a laid-back sense of musical professionalism. The other musicians stood back and let her do what she's good at. American twelve bar blues is so much less frantic and busy than the UK version. There is an ebb and flow in the music. Hear that piano; hear those vocals; there is none of that loudness that prevents the audience communicating, either. In the UK you would have a *melée* of sound and then vocals on top of that.

Francine Reed received her well-deserved award for lifelong blues activity and sang like a goddess.

Things were hectic. The day after the Festival Des and I were interviewed at WRFG at 7.30 in the morning. We hadn't made it to bed until about 4.30 after a night of talking on the porch. It was a very shaky start but the interview was good. I performed "Louis Collins" first then stitched Des up to sing a song. He wasn't going to sing originally but I put him on the spot by announcing over the air that he would be. So he retaliated by singing at a pitch that would make it hard for me. He sang low and I sang from my boots! I finished with a thrashed "Groundhog" then there was another call from Cora Mae saying how good she thought we were. Quite a long conversation and what a compliment.

Because Harlan and Sandra were expecting other guests, Des and I were moved to Dunwoody, a gated condominium with a gymnasium and apartments forming a quadrangle built round a large swimming pool. It was one of many: a vast development of hundreds of apartments as far as the eye could see, aimed at Atlanta executives, or people on short-term contracts or people waiting to purchase. It had a shifting impermanence, like a hotel, which it resembled, and steel security gates for which you needed a pass card and number.

Our apartment was modern, luxurious and spacious. We were asked to keep this exclusive stockbroker arrangement to ourselves because none of the other musicians were receiving anything. Rhonda, the complex manager and our host was connected to the radio station so that's why we were there: another five-star plus experience all on the strength of my musical efforts.

We named our gated accommodation the "Golden Ghetto". It was a sterile environment with no sense of community – not even in the pool. We played some music to stay sane and counteract the flatness; my journal entries for this time express a heavy sense of waiting around, of too much TV and beer, of expeditionary quests to find food and drink that suited our pocket. Why do people pay so much to live in an open prison? It was comfortable enough but there was a lack of stimulation and in spite of the luxurious trappings, we were short of cash and we missed the sense of community we experienced with Sandra and Harlan. Their mansion had a different kind of exclusivity: it was a cultural *salon* whose doors were open to musicians and writers but where mere money wouldn't gain you access. It was intellectual dynamite and reassured me that not all Americans are bigots and racists.

We were invited by Rhonda to a "blues fest" but we declined because we were hard-up; we were waiting for a phone call from Tom Hubbard to make arrangements to go on to his place and I wasn't that keen on the sort of music offered. She was offended but the Tom Hubbard connection was important: I wanted Des to see the aspects of the South I had experienced in Newnan and also felt it was disrespectful not to visit him since we were in Georgia.

Finally, we left Dunwoody and started a long hot journey, our discomfort emphasised by Des' bag splitting open and our lack of a vehicle in a country dominated by freeways. If you arrive somewhere without a car you may as well be carrying a loaded gun – people are that suspicious of you. We arrived at Little Five Points: a haven for me throughout my times in America. Phew! The Pabst was sweet – three pitchers before Tom arrived to collect us.

So, we found ourselves with Tom and Kathy in Newnan. Events were not auspicious: travelling a hundred miles to play to a nearly empty room followed by our "usual sponsored beefburger" sums it up. The journal pages are labelled: "Day 12, Day 13, Day 14" but nothing is written there. Was I too busy? No. The pages are empty because there was nothing to write. Perhaps this sounds a bit pathetic and perhaps if I'd had a manager in Georgia things would have gone better. I've always managed myself and never knew how to ask someone else to do it. After the amount of publicity I received with my CD I was presuming someone would contact me with some gigs. In retrospect they were no doubt presuming I'd been signed up at my age!

On the fifteenth day we persuaded Tom to drive the 400 miles to Nashville via Chattanooga. As with New Orleans my expectations surpassed what was possible. Considering Nashville's musical significance and its importance in the Civil Rights Movement, it was a bland experience characterised by urban and rural sprawl spanning several counties. Then my journal records Day 16: "back to Newnan and the wrath of Kathy".

There was a nasty incident. A black family's car had broken down and to Tom's annoyance Kathy went out to them with the phone. "I'll go get my Glock." Tom loaded and primed his gun and placed it on his knee. "You can't trust this black shit." When the black woman and her ten-year-old son came into the house to use the toilet, Tom's like John Wayne playing with the gun. A ludicrous but menacing display and I felt devastated. Des felt worse. These people presented no threat; Tom just wanted to humiliate them. It was the culmination of lots of small incidents that had Des and me ringing Sandra to ask for asylum then fleeing as political and emotional refugees to the freedom of Harlan and Sandra's home. She sounded so sweet and kind – I was crying with relief. "The same two rooms are ready and waiting for you," she said.

This bust-up had been brewing for some time. Although I was grateful to Tom and very fond of Hoyt, I felt more and more stifled by the cultural barrenness at Newnan and couldn't identify with their values. If you're just visiting a place you're better off living by their rules and although there were some difficult moments in America, I was able to shut out my feelings and get on with things in the interests of my music. But only up to a point and that point had been reached: my nerve went at the moment Tom's racism threatened a woman and child in his own house – the very antithesis of hospitality.

The intensity of my relief testified to how troubled I was about the clash of values.

Interestingly, Des and I realised that our experiences at Newnan and at the Golden Ghetto were aspects of the same thing: both equally narrow and fruitless. The short, expansive stay at Heartfield was the best of all the Georgian times in terms of human values. But wherever we stayed, the squalid shacks of the poor were always visible. How can a *verandah* be squalid? These were and I felt intrusive when I photographed them.

Fourth Time Lucky?

You'd think I wouldn't want to go back to Georgia. But I did go: on the strength of musical promises I went once again for my music. One of the gigs was at Blind Willie's in Atlanta; the ideal twelve string guitar for this came my way and I learned Blind Willie McTell's "Reckless Disposition" to honour the occasion. Yet in spite of my musical high hopes my fourth visit to Georgia in April 2003 was characterised by loneliness and dwindling resources. I was genuinely poor, increasingly unable to earn any money and trapped for three weeks.

This was much worse than Leeds!

Bad Moon On The Rise

The omens were not auspicious: I arrived with a gastric bug courtesy of the airline and Tom was late to collect me. I was unimpressed by Jim the new lodger and found I had been relegated to the couch. "Virtually next to the road…I feel like an outlaw" I wrote in my journal. Back home, my dog Dobro had been bitten and now, coincidentally with my (unusual) chronic headache, the worst type of weather was hitting the state: "turn to news program – worst storm and possible tornado to hit Atlanta ever. Golf ball then baseball hail. Freeway blocked. Windshields smashed in cars". References to home as "Blighty" are quite frequent in this final section of my journal and express an "up against it" siege mentality as my sense of isolation and danger increased.

My anxiety about those at home manifested in troubling dreams and a blister on my ring finger. I was clearly not where I wanted to be and then I was hit by another kind of bombshell: a big festival was attracting every big name in the music industry so my gig at Blind Willie's was postponed. Expecting to earn six hundred dollars in three weeks I was now upstaged and down to forty dollars. Desperate to get an early flight home but prevented by the rules and the cost of an alternative ticket, I was sentenced to a further twelve days in worsening weather:

Evening – WW III broke out – never known anything like it – lightning and thunder, torrential rain – power's off – beer's warm. Everything including the new 'Woodstock' will be an absolute washout. Writing by candlelight.

Warm beer! Could things possibly get worse? The weather deteriorated:

More tornado warnings – house shaking like bomb attacks. Tornado is now heading for Newnan – 10 minutes – headache is back…the foundations of the house are shaking again and a waterfall is pouring from the sky. Oh!!! For England.

Good grief man! Get a grip! I got an itch. When the storms abated there was a stifling and uncomfortable heat, accompanied by insect bites that inhibited the normal functions of living, let alone creative effort – speaking of which, by the fourth visit six of the original clubs available for gigs no longer existed. There was an abysmal jam session with an out-of-tune bass, poor keyboards and a shit drummer which even the Mexican lunch didn't compensate for. Could things get any worse? Well, yes. My credit card was rejected during the last alcohol run, leaving me broke in more ways than one with two more nights to go. It was my darkest hour.

The power was off again.

My actual poverty reflected the poverty of musical experience that had shattered my American dream and the violence of the weather punctuated the gun-riddled racism I had lived amongst. There were two main reasons for the musical desert: many once-available venues had been shut down and we had no control over the economic forces in action there. In spite of the promises Tom had not been pro-active where he did have some control. He hadn't done any organising; he had not checked dates; he wasn't on the case. He hadn't seen the implications of the biggest music festival since Woodstock with regard to my Blind Willie gig. Tom Hubbard's musical career had imploded and he was certainly not nurturing mine. Probably too depressed.

But I can't *blame* anyone because my illusions were crushed. I had created them by having large expectations of people and places – expectations for which I had no real basis. Knowing what I know, why did I expect audiences to appreciate the country blues? I had anticipated something far more vibrant and inspiring but the US had no more musical pizzazz than the UK at that time. Where were the blues? It appears that I had taken them home to Georgia but the welcome had only been partial.

It had been my dream to play the blues in Georgia, to touch the places touched by my musical heroes and I had achieved this and celebrated it as "a mountain climbed". The only way after this was down and sure enough despite a few musical high spots, the impetus ran out and the fourth visit yielded nothing but a sense of hollowness. Not only this but the things I had read about racism had been enacted for me as part of the Georgian way of life I experienced at Newnan. Although a non-believer in the conventional sense, nevertheless I have a well-defined set of values. My music is the nearest thing to a spiritual dimension in my life and my hatred of the bully is part of my humanistic ideology. The music I love and have championed over the years defines the experiences of an oppressed people; despised, hated even, by people such as Tom, whose sense of white supremacy is absolute. I was never going to be able to reconcile my stand against bullying in all its forms with Tom's perpetration of it.

The conflict between Tom and I was not really personal. Tom looked after me during each of my visits and was kind enough to compensate for the lack of gigs by recording some of my songs. I'm grateful for this. The conflict was between two sets of irreconcilable ideas. The last visit to Georgia completed my rejection of Southern values in particular but also American values in general. I couldn't forgive Georgia its lack of respect for musicians, its racism, its crass materialism – on our way to New Orleans I saw a double-stretch black Cadillac limo with jacuzzis in the back – and its violence. It does seem a strange country where people believe they're free but where there is so much violent threat: a procession of police vehicles and aerial reconnaissance seems to be the accepted norm.

It is no coincidence that I felt nauseous the minute I arrived and throughout the final visit; nor that the heavens were torn apart by tempest and my musical Odyssey had been reduced to trips with Tom to inspect meat! The gods were angry. During my first trip, coffins in Albany were floating out of graves because of flood waters and Tom Hubbard joked about the old bluesmen coming up to meet me. Perhaps the statement was far more apposite than either of us knew.

The hurricane put a stop to the second 'Woodstock' and Tom Hubbard's house and barn have since been destroyed by hurricanes; the connection is severed.

Maybe.

I returned from Georgia exhausted, broke and disillusioned. And now my other hand was going.

Notes: Section Four

A lot of the quoted material for this section comes from my Georgia Journal.

(1) Coweta County, of which Newnan is the county seat, was ceded by the Creek people in 1825. The Koweta Indians were a sub-group of the Creeks. It is one of the few Georgia counties to have an African American museum.

(2) Thea Gilmore interview: Total Guitar August 1999, Issue 59. I forgive her – it's a good name!

(3) Living Blues magazine, Jan/Feb. 1998.

(4) Michael Gray: Hand Me My Travelin' Shoes, published by Bloomsbury Press.

(5) Living Atlanta: An Oral History Of The City 1914 -1948 by Cliff M. Kuhn, Harlan E. Joye and E. Bernard West, forward by Michael Lomax, University of Georgia Press.

SECTION FIVE

A View From The Edge

I've lived my life balanced on the edge. Out of my depth, out of my mind, in love, in danger, or about to die, there have been times when the rush of adrenalin has given me such exhilaration that jumping out of aeroplanes seemed completely rational. A sheriff threatened to shoot me but not for riding my horse to work – different movie! Flooding potholes, flamboyant women and exploding petrol tanks have all challenged me. I've saved lives, been threatened with knives and I've ground a man's head in the gravel.

But the danger of losing the use of my hands was the worst.

Hand Over Fist

Facing Incapacity

I arrived back from Georgia to confront worse things than my disillusionment and economic penury. I faced a second hand operation with no guarantee that it would be a success. The idea that I wouldn't be able to play music was excruciating. If I couldn't play my guitars I knew that depression would make me indifferent about living on. Not a suicidal impulse: just a slow, sad decline. This was a starkly passive idea for someone so used to active risk-taking.

Lethal Weapons

This sounds bizarre: my hands were registered with the police as lethal weapons. My disembodied hands! This is how it happened. My father and I saw six youths kicking hell out of a lad; my father told them to stop; one of them went for him. It ended with three of the thugs hospitalized and me arrested. I had used skills and knowledge learnt from training with the famous heavyweight wrestler Count Bartelli to protect my father and also the set-upon youth. I had not broken the code of honour stipulating the protection of others and self-defence as the only circumstances for such action. When all was explained the charges were dropped but the police re-designated my hands as lethal weapons.

The Wrong Arm Of The Law

There came a time when I had to resist using my martial art skills even though I needed to defend myself. It was 1978 and Penny and I and our son had been to the Crown at Audlem to fix the sound system and collect some money. It wasn't very late – about 9.30 – and when we got back to Crewe I parked in Catherine Street to get some fish and chips for us. Very domestic and ordinary. I was following the hot vinegary smell to the chip shop when a police car drove up and stopped. A constable approached: "I believe you've been drinking. Blow into this bag." I was amazed. "Come off it," I said, "I've only just got my licence back and I haven't had a drink." No reply. Then: "You're under arrest!" At that I was forcibly shoved into the police car. "There's a baby and a thousand quid in my briefcase in the car," I said. "She can look after that," he said. But Penny was frightened and couldn't drive.

As we got towards the door of the police station the PC twisted my arm up my back. "If I was going to escape I'd have done it by now," I said. With that I was frogmarched into a side room and the PC started to beat me up. Severely. I'm not just talking about a couple of punches: it was elbows, feet, fists – the lot.

After a few minutes the Duty Sergeant entered; he didn't join in but I was on the point of retaliation and I knew the consequences of that, not just for this thug but also for myself. He would have been in hospital and I would have been in trouble. "Get rid of this madman," I said. My assailant left the room and the Duty Sergeant politely asked me to go to another side room for a breathalyzer test. "Certainly." It was negative, of course. "What's all the trouble, then?" he asked me. I explained my side of the story and he seemed satisfied.

By this time Penny and Nathan had been dropped off at her father's house and my car had been brought to the station. The Duty Sergeant called for someone to escort me out – the same one who'd beaten me up. "I'm not going down those stairs with him because one of us will end up down the bottom of them. Whichever one – I'm the loser." So he called an extra escort. At the bottom of the stairs the PC who had beaten me said, "Your number plate's dirty." I replied, "Get on your fucking knees and lick it, you cunt."

I was so badly hurt Penny's father insisted on taking me to Leighton Hospital and my injuries were photographed at the instigation of the medics. My letter to the Chief Constable included them with the solicitor's letter outlining what had happened to me in which, among other things, attention was drawn to my training with Count Bartelli and the restraint I had shown.

The reply was an unveiled threat and in no way addressed my complaints: "as the owner of a shotgun certificate you will be aware that this can be revoked at any time". My solicitor suggested I let the matter drop and predicted a sideways move for my attacker: a bully since school days.

It's as if I sing the song of that savagery and it happens to me again and again. But something worse than a physical beating had harmed me. My naïve belief in democracy and justice and the police being there to protect these was also knocked out of me. I'm slightly angry with myself for not continuing with my complaint about police brutality: not in South Africa; not in the Southern states of America but right here in my own hometown. But I had my reasons. I had insider information that the police had a thick file on me, even in those early days. I think they suspected I was a gangster using my business as a front for drug-dealing! I was making a lot of money: every lad wanted to be in a loud band and the market in vintage instruments was doing well. All my assets were legitimate but the police were on my case and that's why I didn't pursue the brutality issue.

PC Thug was transferred.

Any Substance In It?

Mushrooms In A Pencil Case

To redress the balance, I have another story in which the police were courteous, good-humoured and tolerant. My girlfriend and I were decorating so everything had been moved upstairs, including me. There I was with a glass of malt whisky, Radio Four, a Wilbur Smith book and a big spliff. My contentment was shaken by a horrendous bang like a cannon followed by a galloping noise coming up the stairs. Eight police officers – two of them women – spilled in like the Keystone Cops and consumed all the space. A drugs bust. But in spite of the numbers – or perhaps because of them – the whole thing bordered on the hilarious. Did I know what I was smoking? Well, yes. They found some dried mushrooms in a pencil case in my girlfriend's drawer. Asked if I knew what these were, I took the rap. Magic mushrooms are actually more illegal than cannabis. I was interviewed in a good-humoured and non-threatening way, even though the police made it clear that I would be going down to the station to be charged. But the really gratifying thing was that they allowed me to smoke my spliff and drink my drink all the time I was being busted.

This time nothing bad happened to me at the police station and I was even released in time for last orders at the Leisure Club. Eventually I was fined £100 for the resin and £100 for the mushrooms.

The good humour continued. I remember what my barrister said in my defence and that makes me laugh too: "Mr. Johnson is a well-respected business man of the area, brought up in academic circles. What could be more natural than to smoke a spliff – or cannabis cigarette? It's just like having a G & T."

Dead Giveaway

People make roaches for spliffs by tearing bits off business cards (for example) so the presence of cards with corners torn off was a dead giveaway in drugs searches. Incidentally – no-one tore my cards up because it was too difficult and because they had nice photos of nudes and guitars on them!

Fudging The Issue

Alcohol has been my main stimulant and some would say I was an alcoholic. I refute this but then I would, wouldn't I? My best friend died young partly as a result of alcoholism and the effects of abuse are irrefutable. Apart from the physical toll alcohol has a devastating effect on judgment. A musician I knew had been in the shop having a drink with me. Quite a drink. He stumbled off, only to return later. Finding the shop closed he had tried – using that strange logic drunks have – to get in by scaling the back fence. He fell, of course, crushing two vertebrae. Somehow, he made his way back to the shop front, where I saw him: ashen-faced and clutching the security bars on the shop window.

This had all the hallmarks of farce but I immediately saw the danger of his condition. I had to get him to hospital. My dilemma was that I was over the limit for driving but there was no time to sort anything else out: this was an emergency. So I drove him to Leighton Hospital, by which time he was in a very bad way. Fortunately I was able to deposit him with two ambulance men and drive off. Very quickly.

It's quite possible that my intervention saved his life. His crazy drunkenness led to a stupid decision: in a sober moment he would have got over the wall by standing on the handy dustbin!

Or he could have knocked on the front door.

I was more likely to get high on fast cars and music when I was young and I didn't take drugs till I was thirty, although they were readily available. In some dubious venues I'd even been paid in pills! The first time I took drugs was after a partner and I split up. Whitty offered me a joint and I spent the next two hours unable to move but aware and laughing. Then it became more a part of my life though I've given up on it recently: the quality's not there and the more you use, the more you need. Unlike cannabis, cocaine is good for concentration and also helps you imagine and play things a little more adventurously. That's why the jazz musicians use it. I've had no personal experience of using heroin; it wasn't around much in my youth. By the time it was there I'd already seen the cases. Fastidiousness also plays its part. I wouldn't want to vomit horribly and as for injecting myself…

During our irresponsible bachelor period Dave Evans and I dabbled in almost every illicit drug. One night, pissed and stoned, we were dipping joints into the residue of amyl nitrite. What I forgot was the bit about letting it dry off. There was a sudden sheet of flame a foot long on my spliff. "Dave – put it out!" He did – once he'd stopped laughing. I used to go to business meetings in respectable places, dressed smart. I smoked Consulates which I'd bored out with a guitar string and refilled with weed.

Amyl nitrite comes in a bottle like smelling salts. They sell it at sex shops and it's known as "poppers". It's supposed to be an aphrodisiac if you take a big sniff of it. It's like glue sniffing – it gives you a short high – a quick whack.

Wayne Davies (Slim). (1)

My drug experiences have been fun mostly but I have seen at first hand the scourge of heroin addiction. Addicts need a minimum amount of the drug to maintain a crude stability: a vantage point from which they can vaguely cope with day to day living and in addition some means of getting the sought-for "high". That's why a heroin addict will also smoke crack and the alcoholic will drink large quantities of spirits against a background of beer or wine. I've seen the sheer drudgery of being an addict: the daily grafting – the everyday tyranny of having to get the money to get the drug. By whatever means. I've also seen at close proximity the high financial cost of addiction: people losing their cars, businesses, properties, in order to finance their habit. Their chaotic and obsessive lifestyle cancels out holding down a job of any kind. Similarly, coming off a drug whilst associating with people still using is virtually impossible.

Whatever problems led them to take heroin none can be greater than the huge problem of being an addict.

Yet not everyone had a bad drugs story to tell. A friend's mother came on a bus from Bridgemere with a cannabis plant under her arm for me. "In my country they grew this between potato plants to keep pests away," she told me. "The men came home smoking pipes very happy!" Mike Slaughter ("That's laughter with an *S*," he used to say) would make fudge containing all sorts of substances. He'd offer it round in the pub. You'd refuse because fudge and beer don't mix. But then he'd say, "No – have some *fudge!*" so of course we all did.

Extreme Sports

Whupping The Toffs

Coming from a background where people were sick: my mother an invalid, my brother having TB gland and people dying young, I enjoyed having a fit body and I precociously went in for the extreme end of the sporting spectrum. I've done athletics, cycling, potholing, wrestling, canoeing, swimming, Enduro-riding, skiing, climbing, flying, yachting and parachuting, and enjoyed the opportunity to be determined and resourceful, to balance the danger against the thrill. To survive.

I have two medals dated 1962: one for cross-country, the other for athletics, awarded by Nantwich and Acton Grammar School. I broke all records. This was the only time both medals had been awarded to the same person on the same occasion. There was a magic event when Nantwich and Acton Grammar School was competing against a posh Chester school attended by the Headmaster's son, who was also competing. The entire senior cross-country team (including my brother Roger) from Nantwich overtook the posh team (including the Head's son). Not only that: competing in the junior cross-country team, I overtook them as well. It was a sweet moment.

I'm interested in excellence and that's why I admire the Olympic ideal, though not the reality. Yet I haven't single-mindedly pursued expert status in any sport. If you have some aptitude I believe that it's relatively easy to become good at a sport but to become *expert* takes a massive amount of time, commitment and endurance. That part of me has gone into music.

In A Hole

I remember a very dangerous situation. Aged 18, I was out with my brother and about ten others, potholing in Lancashire. There had been two entrances to a particular set of caves; my brother and I had taken the riskier route and there was a problem with fast-flowing water. At one point Ralph was swept off his feet trying to cross the water. He went like a cork and I had to act fast. It was a weight thing: I was able to put my feet on the bottom and grab Ralph who was much, much lighter. But there was more drama to come. When the two groups were united, the leader mistook the way in deteriorating conditions: water was rising in the tunnel and we had to climb through a waterfall. The leader lost it: "Run for your lives!" he shouted. He couldn't swim! We had to make our way to a large cavern to wait for rescue.

There we waited and waited in near-total darkness, conserving our carborundum lamps. I remember the differing levels of morale. Some were silent; some were cheerful; some were very panicky: men were breaking down in tears. Their panic flared and subsided, flared and subsided – the worst case was an ambulance man. I suppose he knew all about the fragility of life or perhaps off-duty he had relaxed his guard and therefore lost control. I was surprised: a bit of water round the ankles and they thought they would drown. But we were in a cavern the size of St Paul's Cathedral! It was a nightmarish idea that it would gradually fill up with water but not a reality. I didn't lose heart; I was convinced that I would be OK. I was with my big brother – the best caver in the country – who had informed the rescue team of our intentions beforehand and I had confidence in my own abilities. In tricky situations I can maintain my composure and respect the expertise of those who know more than I do. My brother and I made chocolate drinks by melting chocolate in a tobacco tin over a candle in order to cheer people up and I led the singing. Like rugby players, potholers have a repertoire of bawdy songs with phrases such as "winky-wanky bird". It's surprising what you remember.

We were there for well over a day until the rescuers found us. When I eventually emerged from the cave, a familiar face greeted me: a girl from college. Fortunately there's always a good-looking girl to cheer you up.

A Weighty Matter

On another watery occasion I was not with a group: I was Scuba diving off Anglesey. I'd read the manual but I lacked experience. Over the side I went, down into the sea, down and down until I reached the bottom. But why couldn't I move? I realized I had too many weights. I could have panicked at this point but I remained rational. Should I fling off some of the equipment I'd invested so much money in? If I jettisoned the weights would I be able to retrieve them later? Why was I even allowing this consideration to jeopardize my safety? There I was, on the bed of the ocean, unable to move, having this debate with myself.

Meanwhile the situation was resolving itself: after a while I realized I was becoming more buoyant; my feet weren't so heavily on the floor. I soon sussed out that although compressed air must weigh a lot, things would get lighter as time went on: all I had to do was consume it. I didn't need to chuck off the weights and I would be more careful with them in future. This tricky situation was the consequence of my extreme reluctance to join clubs but fortunately I dealt with it.

Carpe Diem

Pete didn't just take musical risks. We were staying in a cottage near Porth Beach. He knew not to swim near the river but he went snorkelling on his own. When I went to call him for our meal I found him gasping and spluttering. He had swum into a plastic bag and put himself into danger. But this carpe diem *attitude permeated his life. If the water looked inviting he would jump in, fully clothed if necessary.*

Linda Johnson. (2)

Fire And Water

I once nearly perished by fire – twice by water. I had taken the lead during an Enduro race and was first to refuel. Satisfaction turned to horror as I realized that the over-zealous man in charge of the fuel in the transit van had started to fill my tank up whilst the bike engine was still going. Not only that – he was allowing it to overflow! That alone was enough to set things alight, even if the engine had been off – which it wasn't. I was shouting, "No! NO!"

Eighty gallons of fuel exploded – blowing me off my bike. I got the full brunt of it because I was the first to refuel – none had been used yet. I was on fire; my bike was on fire; the transit van went six foot in the air; three other vehicles besides were on fire. I managed to drag my bike and myself into a nearby trout stream. Amazingly no-one was hurt. But this is why I hate relying on others: they can make stupid, dangerous mistakes. "I might have known it would be you," was all Brammer could say.

Once at Criccieth I was surfing in a fibreglass canoe when some idiots in a big old-fashioned heavy double wood and canvas canoe lumbered up over the top of me. I was unable to shift it and thought I'd bought it. The big canoe was the right way up; I was upside down and pinned on the bottom. But fortunately my brother Roger came running towards the boat, kicking it off and other people joined in the rescue.

Another time on the River Dane with Ralph and a group of kids, I went over to rescue one of them who had capsized his canoe. Unfortunately all his mates were trying to do the same. There was no way through this logjam of rescuers so I resolved the dangerous situation by swimming with him under his canoe.

On the first occasion the help was constructive; on the second it was obstructive but this is what you deal with if you take risks.

Taking Risks

In doing dangerous sports and in dealing with threatening situations I have always known I was risking death. To me death hasn't been the issue. I've minimized the odds by calculating risk; I've taken the risk if the payback was worth it. It's a delicate balance. But the scenario has never included the idea of serious, life-changing injury. If I'd thought there was a real possibility of being an amputee in a wheelchair, it would have stopped me doing it. So why could I contemplate death but not injury? What was the psychology? I suppose your survival confidence persuades you that you will escape both injury and death. Experience, physical fitness and training in a variety of techniques can convince you that bad things won't happen, especially if you add good luck and good judgment into the equation. Other factors involved in survival are your state of mind, your cardiovascular system and the size of your lungs. And the fight or flight hormone adrenalin. So in entering the arena of extreme situations you create an invincible mindset and this might be foolhardy and delusional but paradoxically, it also helps you survive.

Just Walking The Dog

Hooded Menace

These dangerous or edgy challenges were all chosen and to a certain degree controlled by me but some situations are unpredictable, irrational and shocking. You don't expect to be in danger whilst walking your dog. One evening I took Dobro out to a business park just off a very busy road. There are woodland areas and open spaces for people to enjoy and it's well used by dog owners. We're all on nodding terms. I was in a bad mood because I'd just had a row with Zoe. She never walked the dog – originally bought for her – it was always down to me. I noticed a hoodie riding about on a bike very slowly. He passed me so many times that I felt compelled to acknowledge him. The youth averted his face. There was a woman walking her dog I recognized from previous occasions.

The next day, I had stopped at some traffic lights. Someone from a car behind got out and gestured to me to pull into the area by the post office. There was a second woman in the car she was driving: the woman I had seen walking her dog. She was in a condition of trauma judging by her general demeanour. Then I noticed she was black and blue and her hair was matted with blood.

Her daughter explained that her mother had been attacked at the business park the previous evening. She had seen me and recognized my very distinctive green and white camper van. Had I seen anything? A man had dragged her mother into the bushes and rained blows on her head with a rock. Her dog – off its lead – had returned and sat on her to protect her. The man ran off.

The poor woman eventually made it back to her car and drove it with the horn permanently on, such was her distress. Site security phoned the police who were now looking for witnesses. After my conversation with the victim's daughter, I contacted the police to offer my information about the youth behaving suspiciously and was shocked that they were not in any hurry to speak to me. But something else shocked me more: the realization that if things had been different that evening, it would have been Zoe walking our dog. She could easily have been the victim. I felt very emotional about this and about the woman and about her dog protecting her, and it occurred to me that Dobro would have torn him limb from limb if he had attacked Zoe.

The police arrested the youth and he was sent down. I have no doubts about what I would have done to the bastard.

Grey Power

As I've got older and greyer people have underestimated my strength. I was jostled at a bar by a paratrooper. There were several of them and their arrogant, elitist attitude annoyed me. "Firstly, you don't know how hard I am," I said, "secondly, I'll just be a little old man in court." I don't know if he got the subtlety of my threat but his mate said it was well put.

I was walking the dog along the Nantwich canal; it was Bank Holiday Sunday in the daytime. Four youths wearing hoodies were spread out along the towpath fishing – one of them sitting on a camp bed. They had two pit bull crosses harnessed but not on a lead. I had Dobro on a lead and I was anxious about how he would react when the dogs approached us, which they did. I've seen Dobro hurl a boxer in the air like a toy so I asked the lads to control their dogs. They poured abuse over me. "Fuck off you fucking cunt you old bastard. Dye your hair you dirty old fucker." The one on the camp bed said he'd got a knife and he'd stab me. I lost my temper and threatened their tackle – fishing tackle that is. The first thing to hand was a rod rest which I pulled round the youth's neck. He went very white. "Where's your knife now?" I shouted, furious. "Where's his knife?" I asked the rest of them. It was a rhetorical question. He got paler. I cooled down. "Make sure your knife's closer next time and watch who you threaten." Something had annoyed me about his ill-prepared and foolhardy threat. I let him go and I realised that throughout this I still had Dobro on the lead.

Good job for them and their dogs.

But as I walked away they still did the name calling. I've thought a lot about this nasty incident and come to the conclusion that I don't blame them. I don't blame this generation for wanting to knife or gun down the generation of people who have, or have had, what they don't have. It's war; they've got nothing and no prospects and no power. You've got a nice house – let's trash it. You've got a nice car – let's trash it. You want us to behave in a certain way that you think is right for you – fuck off! I'll stick a knife into you. And they would. They would risk being incarcerated to do it. This senseless, almost random violence, triggered by the tiniest amount of resistance to their behaviour is in the media all the time.

The paradox is, these kids with impoverished outlooks live in a society of excess; even the poorest people never go hungry. My camper-van was splattered with eggs the other day. Kids had obviously stolen eggs from Sainsbury's and then they did this mindless thing. They live in a society in which eggs aren't food because they never experience hunger. This is one of the reasons Zoe likes to go to Tanzania; she feels the values are more real and more sane and to an extent I agree with her. It's terrible to come across these young people who have no values. The revolution in the Sixties tore everything down and didn't replace it with anything.

But I wasn't being stupid in tackling the towpath kids although I was outnumbered. They were spaced out along the canal bank. I knew that if things got any uglier I could take one at a time and I might not have needed to set more than two waterborne examples. Dobro would have joined in if I had been in any danger. I only spoke to them because I was genuinely concerned about the welfare of their dogs. Dobro is a massive dog and there is some Rotweiler in him. He has claws that come right out like a cat. But they were too busy reacting violently to realize this, or to know that although I am older now I can still handle myself the way I was trained to do. The skill is still there; the instinct is still there; the adrenalin does the rest.

This isn't the only time I've been threatened with a knife. Within the past three years someone came into the shop and threatened me. Fred was here to witness it. The bloke in question had phoned me about selling me an amp and I had agreed, though no arrangements were made. Then one day he just appeared out of the blue with the amp and expected me to pay him. There were two problems: I don't have a lot of cash lying around so I need advance warning. The other thing was that he didn't bring the flight case for the amp. This was important; it was a beautifully made mahogany cabinet, purpose-built by a master carpenter and worth £200. So: no deal. The bloke was furious and that was when he threatened me with a knife. I phoned the police at this point and he went. This would be at eleven in the morning.

A bit later I had a phone call: "I believe I'm lucky to be alive?" It was my apologetic assailant. He'd been talking to John Darlington.

A police constable arrived at five. Too late mate.

The Hands Dealt By Fate

There's one thing over which I am powerless. The situation wasn't caused by a big bad policeman or over-indulgence or risk-taking or the foolishness of others or neglect or accident. I have a problem with my hands – a genetic legacy over which I have no control – which recently became a crisis because of complications. All the survival skills I had developed, all the lucky breaks I might have, all the cursing in the world could not help me in this particular instance. All I could hope for was that fate would decree a skilled surgeon who could do as good a job on my right hand as had been done on my left hand in 2000.

Losing the use of the hands is something to be feared by anyone but for a guitarist it has an added misery. Do you know the origin of the word "basket case"? It referred to the men with terrible injuries who were carried limbless, in baskets, from the battlefield in World War I. It was easier and safer to remove a whole limb than to try to keep a wound clean. It's amazing what human beings do to overcome disability, though. I remember Harry, a war veteran who had lost the ends of all his fingers to frostbite. He survived Paschendaele and the Somme and when he returned, his mind was affected by shell shock and he was deaf.

Childlike and gentle and large, with huge ears, Harry was looked after by a couple who had lost their son in the war. He played the piano with his enormous hands – hands like Fats Waller – but because of his shortened fingers only used the black notes. In spite of being deaf and disabled he could play anything at all, including all the hymns at the Salvation Army Citadel.

I found myself thinking about Harry when my first hand – my left hand – was becoming disabled. It's an amazing thought that you can find yourself experiencing events whose causes go back centuries. Dupuytren's Contractures: a condition inherited from the Vikings, causes the tendons in the hand to contract, owing to the presence of scar tissue. Hard pads of flesh develop and pain arises in the elbow. Like Harry, I gradually adapted my playing, instinctively changing the position of my fingers to get the notes. Imagine the frustration of a thousand trivial acts such as the permanent cupping of the palm, making it impossible to rub shampoo into my hair without it all spilling. Untreated, the condition can only get progressively worse, not only preventing you doing ordinary things but also inhibiting and preventing a skilled musician performing the one thing he needs and loves to do. It is ironic that artists, musicians and athletes often lose the faculty essential to their art. Beethoven became deaf, for example, and Monet had problems with his eyesight.

My left hand had suffered contractures in each digit, creating a claw-like condition. I had customised slides made in order to accommodate my bent little finger and managed to play guitar for years with this increasingly difficult complaint, before seeking medical help. But things reached crisis point. I felt dreadful about the prospect of being unable to play any more and went through a period of pining, when I lost weight and became very depressed. I was even able to contemplate the loss of some fingers so long as I could carry on with my music. Des insisted I did something. So I saw a consultant who greeted me as, "Mr Johnson, the world-famous guitarist". The first operation, which took place between my third and fourth visit to Georgia, involved the stripping of the tendons of the scar tissue. It was a success and determination to play replaced the need for physiotherapy. I initially used a glass as a slide. My spirits rose enough to eliminate the anti-depressants although I knew that the condition wasn't cured and could recur.

I took comfort from examples of musicians who play in spite of handicaps. In 1928 Django Reinhardt's left hand and right side were badly burned in an accident. He created a new fingering system around the two fingers on his left hand that had full mobility. (3) Tony Iommi of Black Sabbath had an accident at the sheet metal factory where he worked, which left him without the tips of two of his fingers. (4) Jerry Garcia had a hand accident aged four when two thirds of his right middle finger was accidentally amputated by his brother splitting kindling. (5) My namesake, Pete Johnson was an excellent boogie-woogie pianist who lost part of his finger changing a car tyre. (6) Some musicians

I know have had serious hand operations and they're back out there, myself included. I heard this amazing story on the radio about a German aristocrat who was a classical concert pianist who had lost an arm in the First World War. He practised playing one-handed for about eight years and symphonies were written specially for him. Listening to these, you can't tell that he has only one arm. I admired this dedication.

Although these were good role models I couldn't help feeling flat and apprehensive when my second hand became bad. The condition manifested differently in the right hand which was afflicted mainly in the little finger: the contracture had not gone to the second joint but I was worried. I had no way of knowing if things had gone too far. Would my second hand heal as quickly as the first? The operation was scheduled for twelve noon on 7th June 2008 and I had a gig on 8th July. Things were tight.

Unlike the first operation I was left in a lot of pain; it felt as if the middle part of my hand had been gouged out. But every cloud has a silver lining: whatever drugs they administered gave me a night-long hard-on. I met all my previous partners in a long libidinous dream. More please! I was soon back in the shop – I needed to do things. What I did manage to do was set fire to my bandage trying to light a cigarette! But there was a feeling that an obstacle had been removed; the sense of waiting had gone.

After two weeks my hand was still very painful – the removal of the stitches had been agonizing. I had an infection and an inadequate dressing; the consultant I saw last time hadn't seen me, and the surgeon was dismissive and uncommunicative. This was a serious situation for a musician. The slow recovery, the poor and often contradictory aftercare, the realization that this was a botched job made me angry and frustrated. On top of that, Zoe was putting pressure on me to socialize!

I did play guitar but it was intensely painful and the scar rose after half an hour of playing. The flesh on the palm of my right hand looked grey and dead. It took ages to improve and it never did to the extent of my first hand. My debilitation as a musician had repercussions when I did some recording and it left me bored and depressed and restless and powerless and ashamed. I was on the mend but this wasn't enough. I was desperate for change and gripped by loneliness – a combination of grief for the past days of activity and the acknowledgement of an incurable condition: old age and death. I remembered the party pace of life but heard only its ghostly echoes. Everything was off-key and all my misery was focused on my hands.

By August 2008 my hand was breaking out in blisters at the slightest activity. I presumed it was associated with the operation but on visiting the doctor I found this was coincidental. I had a rare condition called Porphyria – something mad King George suffered from, though mine is not the same strain. There are various contraindications: alcohol, cigarettes, sunlight, herbal remedies, stress, trauma – all these can affect the condition. No-one seemed to know much about it but my own gut feeling was that it did have something to do with the trauma of the operation on my right hand, which triggered the genetic predisposition. I didn't think there was much to be done. Whilst waiting to hear about the biopsy I lay off the drink a bit and that made me short-tempered, especially when people came up with their own diagnosis and prescriptions. At the end of the day I couldn't really see myself giving up drinking. As part of the fabric of my life – part of the ambience of my musical performances – giving it up would need a radical change in lifestyle. It was all very depressing

In the end, the feared liver damage was not there. So I went to the pub.

In the past I had always used my willpower to survive difficult physical situations and avoided hospitals at all costs. It's related to the visits to see my sick mother when I was very young.

I once fell downstairs having got up early one morning for a pee. I went cartwheeling down and felt every step – slicing my arm open on a nail in the wall and breaking five ribs. I wasn't even drunk. There was blood everywhere and I knew it was serious. Dobro was just whimpering by me and Zoe had to lock him away because he would have been distressed by the sight of me on a stretcher.

After five days I got up to go to the toilet. I was still in agony, my underpants were stuck to me with dried blood and I hadn't had a crap the whole time. There was a hole in my back – room for a tennis ball – where my ribs were stoved in. The doctor told me that I would always have that. I discharged myself as soon as I could hold a pen, then I went up to Peckforton and subjected myself to a trial of endurance: I did some vigorous climbing. I knew if I expanded my rib cage to the maximum something had to give. It gave. It was excruciating. Then I went back to work.

The medics were amazed that the hole had disappeared.

Now I had *two* weird chronic conditions and medical science had no cures for either of them. But there was to be no radical self-help, no Peckforton moment for my hands: only the anticipation of further operations and less music and also dealing with a crazy condition no-one knew anything about.

Less music. Was I finally going to lose my balance? And what would become of my 'girls'?

My Girls

Decisions

My incapacity together with the contraction in business and musical opportunities, forced some decision-making on me.

Loving the freedom of living close to the skies and the seasons, I seriously thought about selling up and making a living giving music workshops and doing gigs whilst travelling about on my boat, as Eugene did. I used to give music seminars in colleges and community centres and I've also taught people how to play and – more importantly – how to perform. As an interpreter and arranger of music my reputation also stands up so there is no question about my qualifications. But there are contraindications: I wouldn't be interested in teaching anything other than the country blues. Also, I know every pub, every venue in the locale and most would be unsuitable in one way or another. Where are the people who would be interested in this minority music and who would be prepared to pay in the current climate?

But the economics was less important than an emotional involvement I couldn't relinquish. Suppose I sold my shop and made a living as an itinerant musician: what would become of my precious guitars – each vibrating with memories stretching back beyond my birth? Leaving space and security to one side, the extremes of temperature and humidity on a boat would damage them and I couldn't bear that. This had nothing to do with their considerable market value – I just wouldn't want these lovely instruments to deteriorate. So they'd have to be sold. Then the only guitar suitable for a canal boat would be one made of plywood or a National and this would confine my choice, preventing me from suiting guitar to mood.

Losing my 'girls' was too big a loss to contemplate.

So I compromised by selling the upstairs flat just at the optimum moment, keeping the downstairs shop and the business – at least it's ticking over. This accommodated my guitars and released enough capital to buy a new, larger boat and pay a few bills. My solution reflected a workable compromise brought about by a combination of love and economic hard-headedness. This is how I've lived my life.

I am an acknowledged expert when it comes to sourcing information about musical instruments and musical equipment; my information is good because it comes from the heart, not the catalogue. During the thirty-six years I have owned this business I have come across many interesting instruments some of which I own. Any decisions about lifestyle changes had to consider the fate of my collection and my emotional attitude to it.

The composition of my personal collection has changed periodically because I don't hang on to things for the sake of it and recently the problems with my hands had raised another issue. If a guitar isn't being played I sell it. Every one of the guitars in my collection has its own beauty, its own character and its own story. They have often been photographed and I have a guitar for every conceivable occasion.

I would like to introduce them whilst they're still around.

Elvis And The Gibson Blues King

Each guitar speaks differently and if I had to choose only one it would be this guitar. My 1936 Gibson Blues King 169 is unassuming, nicely proportioned and shows a bit of wear. It's a perfect blues guitar and can do nothing wrong as far as I'm concerned.

I paid £180 – the going rate – to a bloke from Caernarvon who brought in a load of unusual stuff. This is the guitar I've had for the longest time: thirty-five years is far longer than most marriages and I know it intimately. For it to sound its best I have to play it for a couple of hours. Foreplay. I've thought about the physics of this and come to the conclusion that it's something to do with the molecules of the vibrating surface.

I'm so attached to this guitar that I've even worried about it wearing out. I worried to the extent of trading in a £600 Orange Marshall for another, more recent Gibson Blues King. But this 174 wasn't as good as the 169 so I got rid of it to Pete Hughes for £1,500 when I realised the 169 would outlast me!

I have a photograph showing two Blues Kings: the 169 one I still own and the Century of Progress guitar which was actually made to commemorate a trade fair in Chicago in 1936. The latter was purchased by Elvis Costello via a shop in London called Andy's which used to sell guitars on commission.

1923 Martin 0018: Best For Ragtime

I've had the 1923 Martin for twenty years. Like the Gibson it's nicely proportioned but blonde, not brunette. Early Martins don't have a name on the headstock; both name and serial number are inside. This guitar came from Andy's, in Denmark Street London: one of the biggest vintage guitar dealers of the time, which, as we speak, is being sold because all the buying and selling which was its stock-in-trade has moved to eBay. Someone from Andy's had a Gibson Les Paul of mine worth £600 for which he wanted to give me a 1923 Martin 0018. I awaited the package.

When it arrived at the shop I just left it there. On the floor. An acquaintance in the shop wanted to open it. I prevented this. I drank tea for an hour, contemplating it. I opened the packaging to reveal the cased instrument. The annoying acquaintance again tried to interfere. He wanted to take the guitar out. I vehemently prevented him. Drank more tea and did some more contemplating: looking at it from various angles lying in the case. Finally – and by now the insensitive gooseberry had gone – I took the instrument up. (I nearly said I took it into my arms!)

Andy had said the guitar had a mahogany body – incidentally some more modern Martins are made out of mahogany – but it hadn't, even though it was a 0018. It wasn't featureless like mahogany. This was koa: a hardwood from Hawaii used for making ukuleles. This 0018 Martin was doubly unusual: it was made of koa, not mahogany but it was wood-slashed koa, not quarter-sawn koa used for the Martin 0028 models which were more ornate, the wood having been cut in cross section and having herringbone trimming.

What was the explanation? I believe that a piece of koa deemed to be too big for use on a ukulele was used to make this Martin 0018 unique. There's another way in which it's unique: models made of koa have K as part of the serial number. This one doesn't. It's a one-off.

Koa is a precious wood from Hawaii and its use was banned in the Twenties because it was becoming scarce. You had to put your name on a tree and hope it would fall down if you wanted an instrument made of koa.

I like the way that everything in the Martin is understated. The fingerboard is ebony but they've not over-embellished it. Other sizes have more ornamentation but this is modest. It's also very light – like a violin – and has ivory tuning pegs nicely yellowed and mellowed, the brass machine heads handmade. Everything about this guitar is lovely in what I can only describe as a modestly *right* way. I love and respect this guitar. It's more limited than the Gibson but it's still a fabulous instrument and a great guitar for ragtime: very precise like a piano, very crisp, unlike the Gibson which has a drawl, a slur, making it suited to the blues. The little Gibson swears, if you like. The Martin has a warm resonant depth. Between the Gibson and the Martin I've got everything I need.

People ask if the Martin is my favourite. I don't have a favourite instrument; which instrument I play depends on my mood and what I am trying to do. Certainly some things sound better on the Martin but the Gibson is versatile enough to play anything. I hope I never have to choose.

Unfortunately neither the Gibson nor the Martin is much used these days because there is no longer an audience for them. But I love them and I use them.

1932 National Style O Resonator Guitar

Whole books have been written about the resonator guitar: it had its own art deco style that placed it between the two World Wars and made a short, glamorous impact before the electric guitar strutted onto the stage, flinging out redundancy notices.

The era of the Big Band created a demand for more volume in a guitar so that it could be heard in larger venues. Banjo players could play and be heard in a jazz or dance band context but guitarists couldn't – hence the creation of an instrument with greater resonation in performance and recording. Resonator guitars are made mostly of metal and have an aluminium dish that resonates and acts as a loudspeaker. Various methods were used: the Weissenborn is a Hawaiian guitar whose body goes right up the neck, giving bigger volume for resonance. Nationals used the same idea, increasing the resonating surface. Django's guitar had an inner table to increase the volume and resonance. It's such a Heath Robinson thing it's untrue! A French guy's quirky design idea. He went on to develop plastic guitars in the Fifties. They weren't bad – nice plastic.

The first resonator guitar was developed by the Dopyera brothers, using plywood made out of hardwoods but later they diversified into other materials. The National guitar, invented by the Dopyeras, and produced in Los Angeles between 1926 and 1939, was the bridge from acoustic to electric instruments. The brothers fell out over the Tricone – one of the most expensive guitars ever made. Nationals were about $62 new; the Tricone would retail at two to three times that price. There was a split and that's where Dobros entered the scene. The Dobro was cheaper.

Resonators were doomed to a short life for two reasons. Parallel to their development, pioneering work was taking place in the Thirties on the electric guitar, which would put an end to all amplification worries.

Rickenbacker, then part of the National team, was making electric lap steel guitars at this time and Gretsch, also part of the National team, was developing electric guitars. Fender, the other contender, was a radio repairman who produced an electric guitar in a modern design that was easy to manufacture. The first electric guitar was produced by Gibson as early as 1936 and as soon as Charlie Christian started playing electric guitar, the sky was the limit.

The second reason was that the development and production of both types of instrument was discontinued because of the war effort. Resonators didn't survive the War; electric guitars did.

My 1932 National Style O resonator is the loudest guitar I've ever played. It's the resonator equivalent of the little Gibson – it slurs and swears in the same way. Vast and resonant, rich and blue: it's a blues guitar with a wonderful tone.

The body is German silver – not plated but silver all through. Later, as the world political situation worsened, leading up to the Second World War, steel and brass were used instead of silver. That's how I can date it at 1932.

Complete with serial number, this guitar has the appearance of being well used. There are two pale brown patches on the front where you can see the different coloured metal underneath. There would be steel then copper then nickel over the body. The surface plating has worn and the typical engraved patterning of Hawaiian trees on the back is now very faint. It doesn't tarnish. The resonator is made out of spun aluminium and costs £50 to replace. They probably use pressed aluminium today.

It's metallic and machine-like and perforated and decorative. The reflecting metal takes some getting used to after the traditional wood, though it retains the traditional curved 'female' shape. It is also strange side-by-side with the more angular, dynamic shape (often with phallic protuberances) and bright shiny colours of the electric guitar. But I like to imagine it owned by somebody rejoicing in its modernity and reflecting the foxtrotting couples who were soon to be parted by war.

These vintage instruments are imbued with history. Although aimed at white dance bands and Hawaiian musicians, the resonator was used by blues artists and white hillbilly performers. The blues sounded good on this instrument which adds depth and drama to a performance. Also, being a combination of art and technology, Nationals and Dobros looked very contemporary and desirable, like some cars do.

Until 2006 I owned three Nationals, collectively worth about ten grand. Such instruments are special and precious but not only in terms of wealth. Once, when I was broke, I advertised a National for sale at £800. Someone said he'd buy it off me. "Just a minute – don't you want to play it first?" "Oh – I can't play!" "You can't have it then." So I ended up selling it to someone for £600. But he could play it as well as I could so I was happy to let him have it.

1936 National Tricone: Came Out The Back Door

Whereas the 1932 National took me into the realms of the imagination, my 1936 National Tricone took me into the library of research. This is another one-off instrument I own, though its story is contentious. In 2002 I made some enquiries about its provenance and value, and had a very helpful letter back from National. (7) They say the guitar is definitely a unique piece though I don't agree with their conclusions.

This guitar appears to be an early 1930's National Tricone, Style 2/Wild Rose pattern with a Spanish neck. At some point in time a craftsman has lovingly modified the original engraving pattern and supplanted it with one of his or her own liking. This is most unusual. I would say it was probably done sometime in the 1960's as the musician is playing an Appalachian dulcimer which had gained popularity during that time. The headstock and fretboard have non-original inlays and outlays that were probably done during the same period. This guitar, in original condition, would sell here in the States [depending on condition] between $4000 and $6000 US Dollars. However, being modified, it is hard for me to say if that price would increase or decrease. It is my opinion that collectors and/or vintage dealers would tend to decrease because the original ? of the instrument has been modified.

The serial numbers of these instruments were stamped into the body below the tail piece/strap button in the late 20's and early 30's. Later, the serial number was stamped into the headstock. Double check those areas. The number would help in dating the original guitar.

Regards, Donald L. Young, Vice President.

There are a number of things I can say in refutation of this letter.

I don't agree with what they say about the Wild Rose style – it's quite crudely done and not up to the standard National achieves. It seems unfinished and amateurish to me and it doesn't have the same consistency of engraving standard, being quite shallow. I think it might have been done by an apprentice as a practice piece and then scrapped. Then I think one of the workers had the reject body.

This point is borne out by the fact that there is no serial number stamped into the metal below the tail piece or on the headstock.

When I got this guitar there was no pillar inside it. A guitar has to have this or it will collapse, so I think it was made as an ornament and not as an instrument. I had the pillar put in because I wanted it as an instrument.

It has been alleged that the engraving on the back of the guitar was done in the Sixties. They say the man looks like Elvis. In those boots?! They also point to the Appalachian dulcimer in it as being a Sixties thing, yet the Appalachian dulcimer has always been popular for certain types of music. The folk boom of the Sixties popularized it but it was around before then.

Another reason I don't think the engraving on the back was done in the Sixties is that in order to do this, the owner would have to take off the nickel, do the engraving and then re-nickel it. Now I think my guitar has the original nickel. It looks like 1930s nickel. So the engraving would have to be done at that time, before the plating went on, not stripped off in the Sixties, engraved then re-plated.

So, I think National are wrong in their conclusions.

This guitar is a one-off – a bastardisation of the style 97: the rarest one. The neck is a standard National with inlay work in mother-of-pearl and abalone. The body is brass nickel-plated. German silver ran out because of rearmament in the Thirties and that's how I can place it at 1936. There are fairly conventional designs on the front but the back is a complete surprise. There's about eight hundred hours of work in the design on the back, which I think comes up to the National standard even though the person who sold it to me said, "Someone's drawn on the back of it with a screwdriver" – a travesty of the truth!

I gave £2,000 for it. The cheapest plain Tricone I've seen was $6,000. The amount of decoration on these instruments varies. Style One would be plain, Style Two would have a bit of decoration, Style Three would have a lot of decoration and Style Four would be extravagant – covered in bloody chrysanthemums! But mine has a whole picture.

So this guitar is an amalgamation. It is typically National but there are a couple of things that are atypical and a unique back. I think someone has taken it home and worked on it, assembled it and had it plated at the factory. It has a badge: a deep red shield with "trade National mark" written on it. National badges were manufactured like a stick of rock then sliced. This badge isn't verifiable although I have found similar badges. The fact that it has no serial number also indicates that it was put together outside the factory.

Oh – and the sound? It has a wonderful tone: soft and mellow. Three cones and a brass body give a more subtle tone altogether than the style O or other Tricones made from harder materials. The 1936 National would suit jazz musicians or Hawaiian music but with this guitar my imagination wanders – and wonders – more in the direction of the mystery engraver.

1934 National: Amazing Grace

I had a third National in the collection until 2006. It was a 1934 model of manufactured plywood and although this instrument was less glamorous than the other two, I was surprised by its volume and depth of resonance. It had a more 'ancient' sound than the others and I think the wooden ones sound a bit better than the metal ones. It seemed appropriate to play "Amazing Grace" on it. I sold it in 2006 for £1,000. It went to a good home in Liverpool.

Electric Dobro Made By Mosrite Under Licence

I've had an electric Dobro made by Mosrite under licence for about fifteen years. It's made of decent quality mahogany, though not the best.

Tom Hubbard had the twelve string version of this. It's extremely rare and works acoustically too, though it does sound better as an electric guitar. The only modification is the fact that there is no cover over the bridge. The best reason for this that I can think of is that it was made for country players – they place the palm on the bridge to get a different sound. Zero fret is another Mosrite feature. It's a great idea for setting the action because it doesn't rely on a nut being cut so precisely. The neck is very much like an electric guitar and too thin for me. I like a chunky neck.

I like the sound. It has dignity: there's a remote, old-fashioned sound to it.

My Mosrite Dobro has been greatly admired. Interviewers have asked me about it and people have wanted to own it. About four hundred of this particular type were made under licence in the Sixties by Semie Moseley.

Twelve String Dobro: Good In Any Language

This particular twelve string Dobro was made in 1966. I bought the guitar and the case for £120. I have subsequently been offered three grand and it's probably worth more.

There's a photograph of Roy Rogers playing a twelve string standard maple Dobro and it's a beautiful instrument. My twelve string Dobro is made of flame maple with tiger-striped sides. To have this type of maple would cost £700 extra. I bought it in 1976 from an American guy who was going back to the States and who didn't want the bother of it.

If the provenance of this guitar as the one owned by Hendrix could be proved, it would be worth £200,000.

I have the same interest and pride in guitars as is often shown by the owners of vintage cars and pedigree animals, so I have personal knowledge of the whereabouts of four of them: my own, the one owned by my Georgian connection, Tom Hubbard, the one owned by famous American slide guitarist Roy Rogers, and the one I saw advertised on the internet described as a "Jimi Hendrix type" but having no provenance. I have a photograph of this so-called Jimi Hendrix 12 String Electric Dobro (estimated value £4,000 to £6,000) which was auctioned at Bonhams for £7,000 on 18th August 1994. I feel dubious about it: the serial number is not available and the year of manufacture is alleged to be the late Sixties, when this is actually from the mid Sixties. No authentification is provided. Moreover, although I have seen Hendrix play such a guitar, it was a blond one, like mine, not mahogany like the one in the photograph. Bonhams should put me on the payroll!

When I was staying in Georgia with Tom Hubbard I did enjoy the rarity of having two twelve string Dobros around. An entry from my Georgia journal testifies to this:

Spent 1-2 hours rebuilding Tom's 12 string mahogany Dobro…played 2-3 hours with Tom – 2x12=24 …lowered the action on Tom's 12 string courtesy of Hoyt's farm workshop…the only brace of 12 string Dobros together. Will photo them later and probably record them.

Banjo In A Gun Case: The Bombay Connection

There are a couple of instruments that are not guitars but which I like to have around for a variety of reasons. I have a pewter banjo with a lovely sheen, made in Birmingham in the 1920s by Riley-Baker, an arms manufacturer, then exported to Bombay and retailed by F. Rose and Co. This piece took the eye for more than one reason. Its metallic nature is reminiscent of a machine component: there is something cog-like about it. The back of the banjo is like a National, with engraved designs. The screws are gun screws, and the headstock is ornate and shaped like the headstocks of Indian instruments. It's a curious amalgamation of Western manufacturing and Eastern ornamentation, understandable only when you know it was destined for the Indian market. There's another surprise: its red satin-lined leather case is a gun case. I have a leather case I used for my own gun and the type of case used for transporting a gun is very similar to this banjo case. I love the way all these old cases have individual clasp designs. There are also cartridge spaces inside the banjo case and that clinches it for me. I'm fascinated by the similarity and it is curious that the banjo and its case, linked as it is with an arms manufacturer, somehow links together two of my own passions. I came by this extraordinary instrument when someone brought in a family heirloom for refurbishment. After refurbishment they decided to sell the instrument to me. It always attracts a lot of interest.

It's currently worth £750.

Defeated The Experts

My one-stringed violin looks more like an invention than a musical instrument. It doesn't know if it's in the string section or the brass section! I bought it from the antique shop next door to the Nantwich Road shop – the same place I bought my gramophone. This curiosity dates from the turn of the century and is called a Home Model Stroviol. There used to be orchestras of these strange-looking instruments. The studio model has a more ornate curly brass horn – rather like the early gramophone. My version is an economy version with a tin horn yet it has an exquisitely carved ivory nut. These nuts would have been mass-produced from off-cuts in the days before ivory hunting was illegal. It's impossible to put a price on such a curiosity. Even *The Antiques Roadshow* couldn't explain what one of these was.

We used to put our stash of drugs in the tin horn.

All my dealings with guitars and other musical equipment, all the introductions to new instruments and blue instruments and instruments falling apart or needing admiration or a new owner, all transactions involving money, bartering, pain, love, loss or cunning – all this took place in my shop which was more than a shop, and that's where we're going next.

Notes: Section Five

(1) Wayne Davies (Slim) interviewed by Sandra Gibson 30th January 2007.

(2) Linda Johnson, interviewed by Sandra Gibson. 4th November 2008.

(3) Guitar Gods: ed. Rusty Cutchin, Flame Tree Publishing 2009.

(4) Ibid.

(5) Wikipedia.

(6) Ibid.

(7) Letter from NATIONAL Reso-Phonic Guitars Inc. postmarked Santa Barbara.

SECTION SIX

Custom Amplification:

More Than A Business

"No-one knows more about guitars than Pete; he could go on Mastermind."

Zoe Johnson.

"This shop is unique because of the man. A traditional music shop always has to have something else going on, such as repairs, collectibles, tuition. But the shop always revolves round the owner. Usually modest people. Nice people, on the whole."

David Rushton. Inter Music.

"It's just the only music shop as far as I'm concerned. The others aren't musician's shops – this is the only one that deals in pro. equipment. Everyone else deals in commercial crap."

Wayne Davies (Slim).

"When I was 14 Pete gave me a guitar and amp. He said I could just take them away! So I took them away before I could even play and he let me pay every week. 'How much can you afford?' he asked me. So I paid £4 a week out of my dinner money. He's a bloody beautiful bloke. I love Pete. But for him I wouldn't have played. My band Chapel of Rest toured Europe. He's a bloody beautiful bloke."

Ian Moore.

"My son's at university. I've got some stuff to sell."
"What kind of stuff?"
"Stuff in the hall."
"What kind of stuff?"
"I want to get rid of it."
"What kind of stuff?"
"It's big and it's orange."
"What do you mean – it's big and it's orange?"
"It's a big orange box with another box on it."
"Without seeing it I would say it's worth £200."
"That'll do. Can I bring it now?"

Conversation with man on phone.

"When we were about sixteen and hiring amps we'd phone Pete's shop and he'd say, 'Oh, I'll just hand you over to our hire department,' and the voice that said 'Hire department' was still his voice! A good sense of humour."

Ade White.

Shop Stories

Focal Point

My business has mirrored the economic climate and cultural preferences over the years and at one point it nearly went under. But after nearly forty years I'm still here and if you look around you can read the history of my musical career, my business and current lifestyle. I've often made jokes about its location in a sex 'n' drugs 'n' rock 'n' roll triangle at the top end of Edleston Road, Crewe, which included a methadone centre (now relocated) a 'private' shop (newly painted) and my music shop: Custom Amplification.

Custom Amplification is more than the neutral name conveys. It has been the centre of a network of musical talent, the focus for lads in pursuit of that ever-elusive perfect amp, the home of instruments beautiful, trashed, eccentric, abandoned, expensive and vintage. It's been a social space – more than that: it's an extension of my living space – on occasions it *has* been my living space. It shares my idiosyncrasies. People have described it as "Aladdin's Cave", "a bit of a dump", "the start of an adventure", "Motorhead's dressing room", "The Old Curiosity Shop", "the only music shop there is". Disparate things are stored haphazardly but I know exactly where everything is and everything has its own importance.

When I first started going into the Nantwich Road shop I didn't belong to a band. That didn't last long – the grapevine worked efficiently. Dave Evans, a keyboard player, walked in and said to me, "I believe you want to play in a band." It was like a speakeasy – talking about gigs – and that's how bands got together. "We're short of a bass player…has anybody got…do you know anybody with..."and that was it – sorted. And Pete gave generous support of one kind or another. Being a musician it didn't matter if you were rich or poor – if you needed an amplifier, Pete would say, "Take that one; we'll square up later." We were never short of equipment and Pete never charged a thing. He's a great bloke – I must admit it whilst he's out of the room.

Wayne Davies (Slim) (1)

When I had the Squier I took it to Custom Amplification. I'd seen it from the bus. Loads of people knew about it. I knew it was owned by a personality. He did the job; he fixed my guitar. It's a weird shop. It doesn't look much at first but when you go in it's got a lot of very nice guitars. Old guitars but they're all quality guitars.

Dec Higgins (2)

Move Over Dali

Amongst the conventional things for sale there are unusual items of furniture: a juke box disguised as a cupboard with leaded glass windows, an old wooden gramophone side by side with enormous dense black speakers and amplifiers: monuments to past and future sound extravaganzas. There's an accordion with salmon pink decoration, an ancient and abandoned wind instrument leaning against the wall, faded advertisements for gigs, current requests for drummers, a chunky wooden box, a gourd-like, face-down mandolin and a guitar strap for every taste: powerful black or multi-coloured or smiley-faced or intensely pink. A Sixties Futurama Duosonic guitar with "Bender Jobbycaster" printed on it is the lone survivor of a rogues' gallery of naff instruments. And in the window there's a clarinet: pale brass in black fur, its cleaning cloth pristine white.

At the back of the shop guitar cases lean together, wearing polythene covers to resist a storm and a group of guitars on stands gathers near the piano like a barber's shop quartet. There's a large inflated replica of a Guinness on an amp next to a huge metallic wedding cake of drums and a Gallotone guitar, its name faded by time. On the counter is a spectrum of plastic plectrums in every conceivable colour. Like penny chews.

Some days the shop is fuller than usual. Occasionally there is a flight case in the repair queue: an industrial amp rack on robust castors, edged with aluminium, designed to house several amps for a PA system – reminding you of the sheer scale of amplified music. Scratched and dull and scuffed, amps and speakers always bear the scars of their life in transit. Many will soon be redundant; the trend is towards smaller equipment.

Music shops are full of chance meetings between unrelated objects, or items altered in some unnerving way that changes their appearance, or objects so obscure that only the fanatic or the antique dealer or the historian can guess their identity. When an electric guitar is reduced to its carcass of moulded plastic, it looks as if it's made of old fashioned washing soap. How naked a guitar looks without its strings! What about this ceramic model of our mascot skunk next to a cool brass canal boat and this tiny tin of cider with the encouragement to "pull ring in case of emergency"? High on a shelf is an ancient washboard, a couple of claxons and some tubular brass, with some incongruously small American flags and a product for cleaning steel and bronze strings called "The Swipe".

Spirits

Sometimes, when the shop is closed and silent, its walls lined with curved shapes, the eye is drawn to the back walls where the atmosphere changes and where I've placed portraits of blues gurus: Arthur "Big Boy"Crudup, Blind Lemon Jefferson, Blind Boy Fuller, Sonny Terry, WC Handy, Robert Johnson, Blind Willie McTell, Bessie Smith. Guardian spirits. A little apart from these photographs is a pencil drawing of me. If this was a film it would be in sepia tones at such a moment. Then the camera would focus on the montage of more recent coloured photographs, each with its own rock 'n' roll story.

Comings And Goings

You can't separate the shop and the stock from the people who come to the shop, and you can't presume that they have come merely to buy something. For some it is entirely transactional of course but there are many other reasons. A jovial Liverpudlian brightens a wintry day just to remake contact: "I still talk about you, Snakey Jake!" He used to bring in amps for mending when he was on the road many years ago and now he speaks about someone in Tasmania who still asks about me! *Tasmania?*

There's a wild boy at the door one day when I'm closed going, "Oh fuck! Oh fuck!" and I open the door expecting some hassle and he says, in an Eton accent, "Terribly sorry to bother you but do you have a high 'E' guitar string?" Well of course I do.

Various fierce bikers come to talk about bikes and guns and guitars: they're interchangeable. The man from next door visits once a fortnight to return the tenner I lend him once a fortnight; a man with a boxer's face is terribly disappointed that I don't sell leather cloth; a small square man with a hearty complexion staggers in with a huge square speaker and speaks fast about a blown horn as if he's in a perpetual hurry but he's just out of breath; white vans drive up, disgorge their contents and drive off; a well-dressed woman with an air of academic inquisitiveness looks in at the window; Joey Shields is looking at everything with the enthusiasm of a child, wanting me to get him a hundred quid home recording studio; a mother is buying her son's first guitar, "I'm going to regret this – he can't even play!" One busy morning it's students looking for percussion instruments – such as primary school children use – for a photo shoot.

Sometimes my customers bring with them a whiff of fame...or notoriety. There's a gentlemen's outfitter who comes in to buy banjo tuners who went to Lonnie Donegan's last birthday party. A bloke with a long pigtail and a beard brings tales of piracy in the backwaters of Cheshire and boats so old they have moss growing on the interior and the music scene in Crewe now that The M Club is on the ascendancy and will this be bad news for The Limelight? There's gossip of someone with at least forty-seven collectible guitars and an E-type in a hermetically sealed bubble plus a TVR and foreign thieves at large.

You'll find all sorts of people wanting to touch, buy, sell or swap all sorts of instruments, amps and speakers. People dither at the door and go away again; people bang on the door when I'm closed; fail to turn up for an appointment when I'm open; breeze in when they're cheerfully out of jail; slope in when they're depressed. A policeman is enthusiastic about a musical project for local kids; periodic reps. bring music shop gossip.

People haul in stuff from car boot sales, from the attic, from the tip, stuff "as seen on eBay", stuff left to them by relatives, stuff stolen, borrowed, or abandoned, stuff they're weary of collecting or stuff they love but have to sell because they're broke, need drugs money or are living in a small space. Millionaires are just as likely to come through the door as someone wearing all his clothes at once with a dog on a string. Come in on some days and I'm teaching a couple of fishermen to play guitar – great manual dexterity from all those years of tackling up! One day it's my drummer Melvyn bringing me laminated recipes and photographs of a Scottish-themed wedding, shaking his head over the Glaswegian tendency to deep-fry pizzas. Sometimes there are famous visitors from the past, like the Incredible String Band.

For some reason the shop attracts a lot of blokes called Lee. There's one: tall and lean and restless who's got quite a rock 'n' roll past. He'll never run to fat – his mind's as mobile as his body but always on the subject of music. He was keen to find a Telecaster and admired one I had in for £350: "I've been looking for a good Tele for ages you know. It's not heavy either, is it? I'll come back and play when I've got a bit more time. That's lovely, that is. A good Waylon Jennings…I've got this Gretsch – I don't know what I think of it really. It looks good and if you play rock 'n' roll you need to look the part. It's just got to feel right…Andy Boote… breathtaking…is he still well into that?"

I think the leap here comes from the fact that Andy also plays a Gretsch and he wants to know if he's still Vavooming. But it's hard to keep up with him. Lee's stylistically good across the board and has been with a Hendrix-style band – not just doing covers but writing stuff in the style as well – that very nearly made it but for a horrendous event. One of the musicians got MS and murdered his mother – just walked barefoot to the police station and handed himself in.

Safe Bed

Some people are not only concerned – or not concerned at all – with the things I sell. It's a sociable space and we drink tea and put the world right, and in recent years I've had my baby granddaughter with me on Mondays. Some will be in to discuss jobs I want them to do, or jobs they have done: mending and refurbishing musical equipment or my camper-van.

My son Jordan did his Work Experience at Pete's shop. He never shuts up about it. He says it's the only shop he's been in where you have a siesta time: just sit back and chill. He remembers Pete cutting through someone's incessant babbling by playing slide guitar. He looked sideways at Jordan. It was one of those moments.

Wayne Davies (Slim). (3)

Over the years I've given people a temporary roof. One of the most recent was a singer-songwriter friend who had fallen out with his sister. I stored his few possessions – a medium-sized black bag and a nice brown leather jacket – and gave him a bed whilst he found somewhere else to live. Part of the problem between brother and sister was that she was rationing his beer; the other problem was that her TV was tuned to the God channel at all times.

I was quite glad when he left though – he had buckled the electric fire and de-potted Zoe's plant in no time.

When my son needed a refuge for himself and his two young daughters, and there was no other way I could find to keep them safe, I took what I felt to be a big risk to our relationship. I asked Pete if I could move the family into our one-bedroomed flat whilst things got sorted out. It was a matter of several months and it was not easy, as can be imagined. But Pete was absolutely marvellous and I don't know what I would have done without his support.

Zoe Johnson. (4)

I've never had a problem sharing my space. Whether people are mad, stinking, egotistical, passing through, depressed, impoverished or getting divorced, as long as they respect the house rules – trust is one of them, so no locked interior doors – I'm very tolerant. The shop is an extension of my living space: it's where I do business, socialise and play music. It's been the scene of practical jokes, wardrobe malfunctions, spectacular drunkenness, good news drifting through the letter box, police raids, bad news over the telephone, knife threats, parties…and people are welcome to share it with me. Most folks know instinctively how to behave but if anyone starts dictating or influencing the atmosphere, putting other people off or making it seem like *their* front room, then I don't like it. Narrow-mindedness and hypocrisy are out. Why do people who drink alcohol feel able to criticise drug users?

Tea And Sympathy

Not everyone needs a roof; sometimes they just need a listening ear or a sympathetic space or a good turn. You have to be astute and diplomatic and compassionate because people bring in more than just their musical buying and selling needs. So many stories walk in through the door: from the hilarious to the tragic.

Pawn Shop Blues

A musician friend and customer took the heroin trail and pawned his electric guitar and amp. He probably got £100 or less for them and needed £130 to retrieve them. The pawn shop makes a weekly charge as well as giving you far less than the items are worth. Anyway, he was almost in tears when he came in because he didn't have the money to get them back. I wrote him a cheque and told him to bring the stuff to my shop where there wouldn't be a weekly charge.

However, the pawn shop wouldn't accept a cheque because – unbelievably in these times – they were on the verge of closing. It was strictly cash. Pawn shops can be as inefficient as any other business, I suppose. Unless people know the value of stuff they don't ask the right prices: they overprice and underprice and it doesn't always balance out.

My bank agreed to pay some cash over to my customer as long as I sent a covering letter. So the customer's daughter took him to collect the money and then the equipment, which I now hold for him. I trusted him; I've done it before for him but there's a safeguard anyway. If he doesn't pay me I have equipment worth far more than £130 – the Fender amp is worth £250 in itself. I'm compassionate but I'm not daft and unlike the pawn shop I do know the value of things.

One Of My Business Cards

A guy had phoned earlier in the day to warn me that he would be bringing in some speakers and an amp he wanted me to sell. He arrived and I helped him with a huge Trace Eliot speaker. Then a woman brought in a 240 watt Ampeg. Next I helped the guy to haul in another enormous red-carpeted brass-tacked speaker with a slack front.

But this was serious bass equipment in more ways than one. The couple had brought in more than musical equipment: they had brought the heaviness of their grief.

The woman's son had been diagnosed with cancer and died seven weeks later. At forty-one. He was a customer – his parents had found one of my business cards among his papers – described as slim with a blond pony tail. I couldn't place him because this description is an archetypal one when it comes to bass players. Their distress was palpable and there was nothing I could say or do other than the practicalities of selling their son's equipment: "Can you leave it till Thursday? I'll have a look at it and give you a price." "It was all working."

Unlike the poor guy.

The mother wiped tears from her eyes and they both went off to their empty car which waited across the road. The poignancy of the situation had everyone in tears. I can listen but how do you help people who have lost someone? I usually say that crying helps.

Six String Banjo

Not every encounter is emotionally demanding. Performers come into the shop with travelling tales and we swap musical anecdotes and sometimes compliments. A type of transaction I really enjoy is when I can use my musical knowledge to solve problems. A lady wanted to buy a banjo for her son. Hers was a musical family: she played guitar and sang gospel but she was a bit anxious about being able to help him with a banjo and this was what he wanted. I showed her a six string banjo: a surprisingly large and round object, two-tiered and with a chalky skin. It was a Remo Weather King Banjo head made only in the USA. I thought this would be the compromise between a guitar and the conventional banjo. The son could then go either way: to the guitar or the five string banjo. I reassured the lady that she would be able to help him, since it was open tuned and she could play guitar. She left a deposit, told me she was delighted to have met me and promised to be back. A mutually positive experience.

Off-Centre: Fairy Dust, Coffins And A Speaker

I've noticed that things can be a bit bizarre at times: nothing to do with madness or alcohol or musical high spirits. There's a different kind of surreal strangeness I can't explain. Fairies with pink organza wings at the window the same moment a bus with "SNAKES ON A PLANE" on it sailed past, for example.

One August day, Bob "The Builder" brought in some partially renovated guitars for me to complete or re-contract but that is not the most interesting thing. He had also brought a selection of fossils for me to show to my father-in-law. Each item in the collection was individually wrapped and labelled and incongruously stuffed inside a briefcase complete with combination lock. A briefcase full of stardust.

The same summer – picture the scene: the shop is dominated by a guitar case containing a new-looking bass guitar, open on the floor, like a coffin. Myself and several lads are standing round it, like mourners. Apparently the pick-up has fallen out. There's a gig tomorrow and the earliest I can give it any attention is Thursday. They ask if I can hire out a bass guitar. No I can't. Do I know of anyone that can? No I don't. The sick bass guitar: a reissue of a 1950s Fender Precision – £500 new – is beyond immediate help. There's a defeated, hopeless atmosphere about the place and particularly around the defunct guitar. The chief mourners: The Designs, from Winsford, slowly close the case, pick it up and file out in silence.

A couple of minutes later there's a cheery face at the door and a man of medium build in a black suit and black tie enters soundlessly. He has what can only be described as a habitual smile. He is softly spoken with a Welsh accent and it turns out he needs a Mini Studio to put his guitar through. I'm always happy to serve this regular customer – it pays to keep in with the local undertaker!

I had a battered speaker that had seen a lot of mayhem. It had the dust of a thousand gigs on it and was more grey than black, scrawped down the sides and where the wood showed through you could see that good quality plywood had been used. At this point in my observations Jo Elensky came in: a man with a clipped, brisk, manner and an active mind; on the move all the time and nobody's fool.

"Need a bass guitar, Pete – cheap – for a beginner. No – he might need something a bit more styley. I know this is the current vogue. I think he wants something a bit more rock – he's a beginner. Got anything else coming in?"

"You want something about a hundred quid?" I made a phone call while Joe paced about restlessly.

"You got any rocky looking basses about £140? I'll pop up later or tomorrow for it."

Jo had decided to return on Friday. Meanwhile he was regretting something he didn't buy years ago! It was always hard to follow what he was saying because his thought processes are faster than he can express them. He's always moving on, mentally and physically.

"Is this a genuine – ?"

"No it's Chinese. Actually, they're not that bad, you know."

"The problem is they went for cheap."

"Plastic bits fall off; I asked if they could make them stronger. They said yes. Why haven't you then? No-one asked us."

"Crewe's not big enough to support three shops, is it?" The conversation had taken a sudden swerve.

"No."

"I could do with a decent drum kit. If someone comes in – silly money – something modern and tasty. I've set up a stage at the factory." Another swerve.

"I actually turn quite a bit of stuff down; quite honestly there are not that many people playing. I'll have to pop up and see the new set-up." (I rarely stock drums – they take up space and I don't know enough about them.)

"I'm not tempted to play again myself, though. Still doing vintage guitars?" He was on the move again.

"Not so much vintage: just older. Everyone knows what they're worth. There are inflated prices for certain things."

Jo Elensky – the man in a hurry – left in a hurry. He had been here less than five minutes but speaking in the short hand of two men involved in the music business, we had covered a great deal of ground. I met Jo many years ago at Wasp Music in Manchester. He set up a business at the same time as me, making speaker cabinets originally in Salford. He decided to go for the top end of the market, split off from Salford and bought a state of the art computerised factory in Knutsford. This became Ohm Industries and he was into big money. Jo's latest venture is the Vienna Opera House where he has fitted a sound system.

The rebated speaker cabinet I was contemplating when Jo Elensky zoomed in is one of Jo's…

Buying And Selling

I make most of my money from expensive items. In the old days sales were staggering, never mind the profits. Things like leads and strings and straps I considered more of a service rather than for profit. My prices for strings, for example, haven't changed for twenty-five years. But times have changed: the Chinese Industrial Miracle is upon us; there's no longer any money in being a recording star; people don't pay for CDs and live music has degenerated into tribute bands. Yet some things stay the same: finding bargains, making something from very little, close encounters with musical instruments and their owners are still a pleasure.

Bartering And Haggling

In this business it isn't all about cash or plastic. If I know and trust somebody I will be patient about payment. I suppose it's more about knowing the value of things than about insisting on cash. People can pay for goods by exchanging or part-exchanging instruments. I've been doing this for a long time and I can very quickly assess a business situation. I won't be messed about and I don't like people underestimating me. If a deal isn't completed and then someone wants to re-open it, I'm likely to change the starting point. If someone won't give me a fair price I'll wait for someone else who will. I don't get tense and I don't pressurise anyone. I try to think what's best for the customer and I will order stuff or send them to another shop. If people come on my day off I'm not afraid to send them away until I am officially open. At one time I allowed people to hassle me for things after closing time but it got ridiculous and now I'm more protective of my time. If people are interested they will come back. Anyone phoning out of hours will hear the snooty phone lady saying, "Your message will not be recorded."

I also know that once people go out of the shop they might not be back, whatever their present intention. But it's on my terms. It's my territory. That's why I could never do a car boot sale of my goods. I have too much self-respect; I wouldn't be on my own territory and it would be bad publicity.

I've spent my life bartering – it doesn't matter what it is. *Sea Feather* was exchanged for a Trimin and a Ford V8 Coupe: a two-seater with a dicky-seat in the boot. I swapped a V12 Jag for a Les Paul and some other odds and ends because I had a company car and wanted to sell the Jag after six months. An appreciation of one good machine or vehicle can easily be transmuted into an appreciation of another type. Bartering is not just about money – you have to add in the pleasure you have had from temporary ownership.

I know Reg Banks well because he used to run the Hanley shop: Custom of Crewe. I remember having nearly eighty classic guitars in stock in the Seventies – we often discuss the system of bartering that took place then. Motorbikes, bikes and even a crossbow were traded in for instruments and equipment. I took the crossbow to show Jo Olenski at his factory in Salford. There were photographs on a wall and Jo indicated one: "I hate that bloke!" he said so I aimed at the image and shot the bolt. Unfortunately, I had overestimated the sturdiness of the partition wall and it went right through into the electronics factory next door, scattering the startled employees!

A View From The Skip

My personal sound systems came as the result of a combination of bartering and scavenging. I need a system for my modern equipment: radio, CD player and DVD player; I need a different system for my record player.

Some people make a good living from the throwaway society; they have a licence to salvage from skips at the tip. It's amazing what people dump and some of it ends up in my shop. I know a couple of "scrappies" and one of them who has a contract and a container at the posh peoples' tip at Brereton brought me a modern amp – worth £300 new – for which I paid a tenner. I use this with my modern equipment.

All Change At Crewe

My 1960 amp has old-fashioned valves like turned pepper pots and industrial sized knob controls. Its origins are noteworthy. It came in for repair and Barry repaired it. Impressed by this example of old British engineering, I asked the owner what he would be using it for. He wanted to use it for his modern recordings. I offered him a modern transistorised amp to try. The customer was impressed by the improvement on the valve amp when it came to playing recordings made by modern technology and we did a swap. I was pleased to be able to use the old technology for my vinyl records and the customer likewise had the appropriate means.

The valve amp is more suitable for vinyl, for which it was designed, along with the vintage Sixties speakers I have. If I want it to sound like music, if I want atmosphere, it's a record I listen to. If I want to analyse it, I use a CD. It's clean; it's clinical; it's not music – just a computer simulation of it. A lot of musicians are coming round to favouring vinyl. CDs are not, as was thought, indestructible; vinyl has longevity if you take care of it.

Time, Patience And A Drawer Full Of Odds And Ends

I've collected stuff for thirty years. I have stuff only guitar dealers would have anyway but nowadays you wouldn't find most of it even there. It's obsolete. It's really satisfying to root through it and find a replacement slot head screw for an old guitar.

Most modern screws used on guitars have the Phillips heads: the cross head.

A Guitar Fit For A Quarryman

Having the correct replacement parts is important and makes you feel satisfied with the completed job. I had a vacant-looking guitar: worn and without strings in the shop for twelve months. It was a Gallotone Champion – the same guitar used by Quarryman John Lennon – that had seen better days. This guitar belonged to someone I've known since he was a teenager – the Gallotone being his first guitar. He asked me to do it up and I found the right replacement machine heads for it. I was pleased because I believe that replacements for old instruments should be in keeping with the character and original structure of the instrument. You have to be aware of idiosyncratic features like the variations in distance between the holes in a headstock or the headstocks being three to a plate rather than separate. The distance between pegs and the holes on the actual spindle of a machine head both matter. It's important that the spacing on a machine head is the same as on the actual guitar. It's also important where the hole is on the actual peg to ensure it will clear the headstock and allow the string to go through the said hole.

Some machine heads, such as Gallotones, have the hole at the centre of the peg and some have the hole close to the end of the peg. It's important that this hole clears the headstock to allow the string to pass through it. Barry renovated the plate for the Gallotone and fitted it on. It looked good.

Classical guitars also have three on a plate, like the Gallotone but modern electric guitars have separate machine heads. The position of the holes is critical because it needs to clear the wood. With more modern guitars the hole is in the centre and modern machine heads are more difficult to repair because they are made of diamond chrome, which is almost impossible to drill. They are also a specific tapered shape. All idiosyncrasies in design create difficulties if repairs or modifications are attempted and that's why I always try to renovate instruments with original and authentic parts if possible.

Speaking of Gallotones: one of mine was purchased for £10 at a car boot sale and brought into the shop where it malingered in a corner for two years. One day Keith asked me if he could turn it into money and then we would share the proceeds. It fetched £400 and was shipped to Canada.

Two From Very Little

My requirements for a Skunk Band situation are specific. None of the guitars in the shop would suit my purpose unless I re-stringed them with thicker string for finger picking. I managed to get two suitable guitars for next to nothing – from scrap. Objectively speaking they're worth £100 but not really for sale.

This is the story. Lee wanted a Telecaster I had. He gave me £100 and an old Squier which had Seymour Duncan pick-ups worth £200.Yet the guitar itself wasn't worth that – the body had been rubbed down and it sounded all right till you started going up the neck. Anyway, Slim sorted that and now the Squier is rehabilitated and of course it has these posh pick-ups. Guitar number one.

Enter Lee number two. Lee had a Fender Strat and wanted me to take off the pick-ups and pick guard and fit a different setup altogether. I asked him what he wanted to do with the originals and he wasn't sure. So I offered him £75 and we did the deal. I had a Fender body I'd paid £25 for years ago and a neck which I had by me as a weapon against potential robbers, and Slim grafted them together. Then the electrics were done with the Fender pickups and wiring harness, and a white scratch plate with US on it. The 'weapon' neck completed by Slim looks well against the deep green he has used. He would accept nothing for the job and the guitar was now ready for my appearance at the Whitmore Barbecue. Guitar number two. Both guitars had components worth more than the saleable value of the instruments.

Everyone Wants Valve Amps

I have a Simms-Watts hand-built British amplifier I exchanged for a drum – equivalent value of £60. Someone had left it at the tip. I put one new valve in and cleaned it up internally. It will go on the internet for about a grand but there's no way of calculating the value of the intuitive knowledge that led to the transaction and the subsequent refurbishment of the amp. Everyone these days wants valve amps since they were resurrected by The White Stripes. Musicians also want point to point wiring – wiring done by hand – rather than circuit boards, which are machine made.

A lot of car boot items find their way to my shop, especially banjos and guitars. I have a Grampian PA set in a box which dates from the late Forties and which cost £20 from a car boot sale. It is worth £250 to £300 on the open market. I tend to accumulate items and then focus on photographing and selling them on the internet. Well – my son Matthew does.

To eBay Or Not To eBay

My son buys and sells on eBay. Everyone buys and sells on eBay. I know I should be more interested in eBay but I can't be bothered with it. Buying and selling is complex enough without bubble wrap and queuing at the post office. Reg told me he sold a 1958 Vox AC 15 amp – broken – for £2,000 on eBay. The guy wanted it for the case. Slim buys new Chinese guitars because it's the cheapest way to get the parts for the guitars he makes. But I really can't be bothered with it – it's part of the madness of commercialisation.

I use eBay to shift stuff from the shop that might otherwise take some time to move in a business this size and in this town. The internet gives scope to find that specific customer for that particular piece of equipment.

Matthew Johnson. (5)

Sixties Guitar Collection

A pair of ornaments or a full set of dining chairs always has greater value than the single divorced item. It's similar with guitars. Historical significance and being in a collection adds interest and value. I had a collection of electric guitars representative of the type of thing young aspiring musicians of the Sixties would have coveted. Originally, they were not worth very much but sold as a historical collection to a London shop in the early Nineties, they went for £600: a considerable amount for what I regarded as a heap of junk not worth the effort of selling individually.

The Black Pig

You can take renovation too far.

Henry Marsh, also an accordionist, played keyboard with a group called Sailor. Some time in the Eighties, when I was playing at the Oakley Centre, Henry Marsh, disguised as Darth Vader, came as a guest with Paul Elson who was playing drums. Although he usually played keyboard, Henry played guitar for me. We managed a five minute rehearsal before the gig. Anyway, to cut to the chase: I got him a state of the art keyboard (worth £1,200 to £1,500) for about £800 plus expenses incurred by my journey to London to purchase it. When he collected it from my shop he gave me a 1957 Les Paul – the one he had played at my gig – for which he had been offered £250 (a stupidly low offer) in

London. This was for the great favour he felt I had done and out of respect for my musicianship: "You've got more charisma on stage than anyone I've ever played with," he said. He has kept in touch over the years and has often phoned for personal advice.

I loved that electric guitar. It had P90 pick-ups that someone who had released records in the Sixties had owned. It was made before the company designated their products into Les Paul Standard and so forth. It was scruffy: I remember that part of the purfling on the underside (as you play) had been lost but it had been played such a lot that the wood was smooth, not rough where the purfling had been. I used it when I played with the Skunk Band and all the younger musicians fought over it on jam nights.

After a few years someone bought it off me for £1,500 – well, £750 plus two guitars. Henry Marsh maintained that it had always been black, certainly from when he had it in the late Sixties. The new owner had it restored – scraped back – to reveal a Les Paul Gold Top. Perfect. With the finish still intact. The restoration cost him £800. He sold it for £3,000 – possibly more.

It had been a good, useable stage guitar and although it was beautiful restored, it didn't feel like the Black Pig. It was less comfortable. Something more than paint had been taken away.

Georgian Treasures

Regardless of anything that was happening during my four trips to Georgia: heat, tornadoes, hailstones, snakes, being ripped off, getting drunk, being feted as a Blues Legend, eating lavishly, driving a tractor, being disappointed, getting arrested, trying to cross roads, having headaches, talking to Cora Mae, escaping persecution, watching crap TV, wearing mirror shades, being broke, getting shot at – regardless of anything and everything my interest in musical instruments never failed. Every such encounter is recorded in my mind and in my journal. My interests and my good business brain always work in harmony no matter what the circumstances.

Visited some vintage guitar shops and clocked different prices of English amps and cheap American products in the UK. Bought a 1928 Tricone, mint for year: $5,000. Just have to find the money now…called at pawn shop. Interesting Stella 12 string – 1940s: $90.00 but how do I bring it back?...On the way back called to see a couple of interesting instruments: 1947 Gibson 8 string pedal steel $500,00 and 1928 National Tricone, beautiful but $5,000 and not that impressive on tone but requires a good clean and set up. Got my picture taken with it though…arrived first music shop, sold 2 pedals Fuzz Face: $150. MXR Phase 90 (orange): $75 and good contact: Marty's Music…phone or fax: vintage instruments, pedals, Hiwatts etc. 2nd shop sold my National… (6)

Even during the fourth rather unsuccessful visit to Georgia, beset by ill health, awful weather and loneliness I noted the following:

meat run via music shops in Atlanta. Some nice guitars: '46 Martin 0021 – $4,500. Great. National Triolion: $1,500 sensible and some cheap disc mics… stopped at Dirt Cheap Music bought '58 ES 125 mint – $550 and a Guild D40 $450 ideal for here plus Shure condenser $80. Great. On to posh Atlanta shop and bought MX 802A in sale – $70. I'm smiling now. Some posh condensers: $599 down to $99 mmm!...to music store bought 6 mics – $500 and MX802A – $60. (7)

I think I always manage to combine my enthusiasm for the beauty of the instruments with some down-to-earth valuations and an eye for a bargain, but I'm always fair or try to be. I bought the stuff on my card and that's how I ended up with no beer money!

Reason To Go Acoustic

If you look – sometimes if you don't look – there's a story behind every transaction. January 2007: I watched a young man painstakingly unwrapping a guitar from two black bin liners. Then a tiny amp emerged: a hundred quid's worth altogether. He wanted an acoustic guitar so I tuned it for him. I hoped for some sort of exchange. The quiet young man sat down to play the new acoustic guitar – £99 on the price tag – he took no time at all to decide. "Yes, I'll have that. I used to have a band but I got electrocuted and nearly died. My dad says hiya – Mike Harradine."

The decisive young man of few words was only 24 years old. His was a very good reason for changing to acoustic.

I had also been decisive: thirty seconds to decide the deal. Sometimes it takes considerably less. Slowed down, this is the process: the guitar he was trading was a popular instrument: a Vintage SG Electric. I hadn't got one in the shop and I knew it would sell. I had two more of the acoustic guitars he bought so I could let that one go without a thought. The amp and the electric guitar balanced exactly the value of the acoustic guitar. It was a fair deal. He had a compelling reason to sell; I had a sound reason to buy.

"Say hi to your dad," I said as he left the shop. I've known Mike Harradine as a customer for a while.

Guitars On The Move

A man (mid thirties) came to the shop with five guitars: all in very good condition. He had wanted £600 but ended up taking a black Les Paul Studio (worth £595). I told him that if he wanted the *copper* Les Paul it would cost him another £200. So in he came on the following Monday, bringing in *another* guitar plus a big pedal multi-effects and returning the black Les Paul. He gave all these to me in exchange for the esteemed copper Les Paul. No money had exchanged hands.

One of the six guitars – a BC Rich – had a snake design on it and I didn't think it would shift. It was the last guitar I'd have bought in but this was part of a deal. It was the first to go.

Guitars were on the move. A young man came in on the same Monday as the great Les Paul exchange and bought it – the black one – along with a Marshall Half Stack. This time money exchanged hands: £550.

Parallel to this, another instrument – a nice twelve string Crafter Acoustic – had a deposit the equivalent of a hundred quid on it, part of which was a guitar and another one was out on approval, on trust, to a man I've known for thirty years. Some transactions take longer to go through than others and it's a process you shouldn't rush.

In April 2007 Reg brought in three guitars. One was a cutaway resonator. Another was a tenor guitar: it's got the same chords as a banjo though you can tune it to play like the top four strings in a guitar. I thought Des might be interested in that. The other was a Dobro Lap Steel.

There we are – surveying the wares like punters at an antiques fair; for a while there is an air of unresolved deeds. Eventually, and without anything perceptible happening, the deal is agreed: I give Reg two lap steels and Reg gives me two guitars and £250.

There's not much call for tenor guitars or lap steel guitars: they're just the quirky type of thing that turns up and you never know who will want them.

A Beautiful Gypsy

Some guitars are inherently special, or special because of their connection with a person. Or for both reasons. Near Christmas 2006 a Tacoma came into my life. I bought it for £325. I liked it. I liked the fact that there were no markers on the fret board – why spoil a nice piece of ebony by cutting it and inserting pretend abalone or pretend mother-of-pearl? I liked the fact that the ebony was wider, more like a vintage guitar. It fitted my hands better. Size matters. There's a Taylor Dreadnought in the shop; it's worth £1,000. It looks impressively large but it is normal for that type, though too big for me. It's all about the waist. I fit better with a slimmer waist – that's what the Tacoma has in its favour – the ones with a thinner waist fit on the leg better.

The rosette reminded me of a Spanish guitar and it also had a see-through pick guard like on a flamenco guitar. Many – probably the majority of electro-acoustic guitars – have an equalizer that compresses sounds, evening out the highs and lows. I don't like that. The electrical feature of this one didn't do that and I was thinking of keeping it for that reason, and also in order to protect my vintage guitars from over-use and wear and tear in pubs.

I think talent should be respected; a musician should have an instrument worthy of their talent. A beautiful young girl with auburn gypsy hair and classical good looks came to the shop with her father. A talented guitar player, she was looking for an instrument and I suggested this recent American acquisition: the Tacoma. She played it and her face lit up – a good sound. I told them that even if they didn't buy it from me, they should think about getting a guitar that matched her talent. They said they'd think about it.

They didn't come back. So I've been playing that guitar as if I've been playing it all my life. It has a lovely mellow sound and it makes me happy and I lose myself in the music for a while. It was love at first sight and also linked in my mind with the beautiful guitarist.

Post Script

The girl's father did get in touch again about the guitar. I told him he was too late: I had withdrawn it from sale. It's the only electro-acoustic guitar I have and I like it. I think they're worth in excess of £1,500 new.

Falling At The Last Hurdle

You can never tell whether a person will buy or not. They can be on the point of buying then for some reason they don't. If they don't do it there and then the chances are they won't. A musical instrument is an important and intimate purchase so this doesn't surprise me. One day in May a tall black girl in a striking white jacket came in to look at a flute nested in a dusty black box with a torn label. She was about to start flute lessons. She was interested in how it fitted together and I was able to reassure her that I had such instruments checked out by someone with more knowledge than myself. She was completely absorbed and anyone present would have been convinced she intended to have it. When we got round to the payment she couldn't remember her PIN. I sensed the girl's disappointment when she couldn't take the flute with her. She promised to return.

But she didn't.

In my business you get used to the psychology of buying and selling; you have to assimilate the indecisiveness of people. One moment they're being ruled by their head, the next by their heart. Sometimes they just want to look and have no intention of buying, even if they behave as if they do. Some are genuinely indecisive – vague about what they want or afraid of making a mistake. In this case it might have been embarrassment that kept the flautist away or perhaps forgetting her PIN was her subconscious mind saying no.

That's Why I've Got No Tattoos!

Speaking of indecisiveness: a man with an uncertain air about him brought in a Marshall amp and speaker. He asked what the cash deal would be.

"£400. The deal would be worth more if you took a guitar." There was much silent pondering and things were being weighed up. It wasn't clear what the man wanted though he hadn't said no to the guitar offer.

"Acoustic or electric?"

"Electric."

"Anything in particular?"

"I've already got a Fender and a Strat." He didn't seem to be drawn to anything in particular and the uneasy silence continued. Then he indicated one.

"What about that one? How much is that?" This was a black Les Paul Studio.

"I could do you that one for £400. You see them from £395 to £495."

"What's it sound like?" I couldn't get to it without climbing on the amps. And while I weighed it up the man switched his attention to another one: a Gibson Sonex. So I climbed on the amp to get that one down and the man plugged it into his own amp and tuned it. It sounded mellow. He turned it over and over, looking the length of it. Then he asked to look at the previous one: the black Les Paul Studio. So I got that down.

"There's some weight in this one!" He crouched down to tune it, play it. He looked at the head. There was a deep sigh. I switched an extra light on.

"It's had a bit of use, this."

"It's twenty-five years old, innit?" The man with the shaved head and the earring looked along the body to the head as he did with the previous one.

"Any case for it?" I brought a case and the man put the guitar into it.

"Give us a swap for that." He had made a decision. I took the hanger off it, closed the box and snapped the catches.

"That can only go up," I assured him.

The man lingered to buy plectrums and strings and then showed interest in another guitar: a white guitar with a satin finish. This was a Washburn that was made in the US. I got that down for him and he was very drawn to it and I knew this; I understood this air of uncertainty I've witnessed so many times.

"I'm shut till Thursday. See how you get on with that Les Paul for a couple of days then you can swap it if you want."

"Might see you on Thursday. Might do." But he still didn't go. Something in the window caught his eye: an Effect Processor.

"It does everything but make tea," I told him. "If you don't know anything about pedals, this is what you have until you do."

"I need a really good all-round amp for the guitars I've got. It's the sound I'm after – like AC/DC."

"Well – start by sussing out what sounds you actually use then you can get pedals that do that. Buy it, take it home, try it, swap it or have your money back if it won't do."

"I'll see how I get on with this."

And off he went, the man whose heart responded to a guitar he didn't take with him but who might be back. He had actually taken the guitar he first asked about: the black Les Paul Studio but his heart went out to the third one: the Washburn. He could have had that plus a hundred quid in exchange for the amp and speaker. I was pleased with the Marshall amp. It was light enough to go on an aeroplane; you could probably take the speaker as well. And it was equipment from the late Sixties which is like hens' teeth to get hold of.

The indecisive man came back several times to change his guitar. "That's why I've got no tattoos – I can't decide!" He ended up with a copper top Les Paul Studio. I think he should forget about tattoos. It's a slippery slope!

My hero is Ritchie Blackmore of Deep Purple. I named one of my sons after him and had his name tattooed on my arm. If you look closely there is only a black area where the name should be. I had to have the name blacked out because the tattooist had spelt it, "Blackmoor".

Wayne Davies (Slim). **(8)**

Presumably the same level of scholarship that produced "Hendricks" on another unfortunate arm.

Sometimes you just don't know what the agenda is because it looks as if no-one is sticking to one – they're all over the place. You don't know if people intend to buy anything or just want a browse; you don't know if they want to buy what they say they want to buy. You don't know which transactions are about necessity and which are about love. There's usually a blend of reality and fantasy and prejudice when people buy musical instruments. It's like a courtship ritual: it can't be hurried; you shouldn't interfere and the choice is often incomprehensible to a third party!

To Banjo Or Not To Banjo?

One scenario involved two men in black hats, rival banjos, an elusive acoustic amp and two twelve strings – one of them derelict. The men came into the shop on a fresh spring morning in April.

"Do you have any banjos about?" asked Desperado Number One.

"Only the cheap one in the window and this one here." I showed him the pewter Bombay banjo and both men were immediately impressed by it.

"I'll tell you what I'm after; I want a decent acoustic amp." It was Desperado Number Two. I shook my head.

"Do you know any place I can get one? I've got two gigs coming up."

"It's a brilliant place, isn't it?" said the other. He was having a good look round.

"What I'd really like is an Ashdown amp."

"They're all made in China these days."

"But the Ashdown's a British amp."

"Yes but it's made in China for a British company. Peavey and Marshall ones are the best, but dear."

"I didn't get on with the Marshall but I did OK with an Ashdown. Can I just try that banjo?" The man who wanted an amp tuned and played the Bombay banjo. I showed them the case. They were both impressed by it being a gun case.

"It was worth the trip just to see that. I wish you'd got an amp though."

And this is how things meander. But it was interesting as an example of how people do know exactly what they want in spite of their butterfly minds, and in spite of my attempts to find what I think they want or what would be better for them. I thought we were talking banjos and acoustic amps and we were but only on the surface. Neither of the banjos I had in could come up to the imagined excellence of a Mastertone played in Winsford and I had, moreover, failed to have an Ashdown amp.

There was another agenda, hidden at first: a cheap guitar to renovate. The man I thought was most interested in a banjo wanted to buy the Montana twelve string acoustic – presently a heap of junk belonging to someone else and waiting to be mended – in preference to the Framus twelve string acoustic which at forty quid was a better proposition.

And we still kept coming back to the Ashdown amp I didn't have.

Curiosity Shop

Through the barter system unusual instruments find their way into my possession and I often have a cluster of a certain type accumulating in the same week.

Lap Steels

I traded a steel guitar for a hand-made lap steel currently worth about £500. I think its owner probably didn't like it; there's something cold about it but people do find lap steels bizarre in the way the body, though curved, is small and it also has to be played horizontally. The strings are high above the fretless finger board and you press hard down with a metal bar and there it is: the unmistakeable Hawaiian sound.

I had another one up my sleeve: a 1937 Gibson lap steel. It's a nicer looking instrument made from a solid piece of mahogany and sounds altogether sweeter than the 1947 instrument. Again, there are no frets because you don't press as far down as the finger board but the finger board is marked so the musician knows where to put the slide. This one is worth about £600. People are surprised that such old instruments are not worth more but few people want them.

What Does A Dobro Hound Dog Have In Common With A Single-String Violin And A Wind-Up Gramophone?

In early spring 2007 I acquired, by a circuitous route, a1972 Dobro Hound Dog which will retail at £800. In some circumstances it could fetch £1,200 and to the right person it's worth the money. Dixie had phoned to tell me about it being in Route 66, Hanley. I turned it down. Then Reg from R&B on Nantwich Road phoned me saying he had it and was I interested? Like Dixie, Reg knew my tastes and this time I succumbed and did a deal. He relied on me to know the going price for the instrument. I gave him a little Washburn plus £200. This gives an insight into the inner workings of the trade: people having knowledge of other people's specialist interests, the existence of some trust in fair price-setting and a system of bartering.

The Dobro Hound Dog is a lap guitar with a square neck and very high action. Everything about this instrument is associated with dogs – the bar I use is called a "Lap Dawg" and you've just gotta play country, not blues on it. I decided to treat it as a toy for a while – all I had to do was develop a liking for bluegrass!

Lap Dobros were developed as long ago as the 1920s for the Hawaiian music *aficionado.* It's easy to produce the echoing Hawaiian refrain: melodious and resonant and warm, through complicated picking and key changing. The sweet tones and volume levels were just right for this music, which is produced using a bar to alter the pitch of the notes by applying pressure on the strings. The strings do not touch the frets and the 'wobble' or tremolo effect is only achieved by pressurising the strings with the bar. It is possible to get a similar effect using a slide but it's never the same.

The Dobro Hound Dog resembles the ordinary Dobro in having the trademark resonator which meant it would easily stand up to other instruments on single notes. Before the resonator it was impossible for single lap guitar notes to be heard above the sound of the other instruments, hence its popularity until the advent of electrical amplification.

The steel resonator has fan shapes and openings for the sound. The curvilinear shape of the wooden body is a little flattened across the top and there are two holes with steel mesh for sound to come through. It works on the same principle as a wind-up gramophone. With the Hound Dog the bridge acts the same as the stylus and the web takes the weight of the strings, transferring the energy from the strings to the resonator whilst at the same time supporting the strings. The sound comes out of the body of the guitar, which acts as a 'horn'. Some have more holes, thus greater volume and tone than others.

The Hawaiian equivalent of the Dobro lap guitar does not use the same principle to produce volume. For example, the Weissenborn Style has a hollow neck, tapered to the top to maximise sound. There are some examples in *Acoustic Guitars* by George Gruhn and Walter Carter. The photographs show beautifully made guitars: decorated and carved, not by computer but by hand: an art form in their own right.

I have an extraordinary piece of equipment: a single string violin. The bridge acts as a stylus and the string sound, played by a bow, is amplified by the metal horn which has a small resonator or diaphragm where it is joined to the rest of the instrument. With a wind-up gramophone, vibrations are picked up from the needle onto a diaphragm and into the horn, which amplifies it. Then, in the cupboard there's an extension of this horn effect whose volume is controlled by the opening and closing of the cupboard doors.

My innovations in sound amplification in the Seventies were based on the same principle.

Brown Is The New Black

Sometimes the form an instrument takes is to do with technical innovation; sometimes it's about image – there are fashions in musical equipment as in anything else. For speakers and amplifiers the conventional colour is black – the colour most associated with power – so amps that are not this colour stand out. When I serviced Des' two Sherwood acoustic amps and a Laney acoustic amp, people noticed them. Apparently, brown amps are produced for the acoustic market; wooden ones are currently in vogue as it looks a bit more folkie.

I also have a Marshall amp, unusual in that it is covered in blue – French navy – to be exact. Every now and again Marshall produces limited edition coloured amps. This one is four years old and worth about £295.

One Of Those Orange Things

Orange amps originally built by Matt Matthias are worth a lot of money now and are still being made. Orange was actually a shop in Denmark Street, London and it was painted orange, hence the amps were called Orange Matt amps and the orange was the company logo perhaps to parody Apple.

Me and Dunc were looking in the window – we'd be thirteen/fourteen – and saw a great big orange thing, a great big bright orange thing with a white front. It was called "Orange" and there was no writing: just symbols. Size of a microwave: tall and fat – not like Marshalls which are long. We honestly didn't know what to make of it because it was so strange and we didn't like to go in and ask because the place was always steeped in mystery – like one of those shops that kids pass and it's full of cobwebs and the beginning of some adventure and we didn't like to ask as well because Pete would say, sternly or grumpily, "It's an Orange..." whatever and we'd have to cover our ignorance and slink out saying, "Yeah, we thought so..."

Jim Farmer. (9)

There isn't very much you can do about speakers: they're just big black boxes but the manufacturers do try to make them distinctive. In a corner near the back of the shop stands a tall tower of a speaker, rather *art deco* in design. This is a WEM as used by Pink Floyd: and can be seen on the *Ummagumma* album cover.

The shop is frequently dominated by monolithic bass bins and horns. Each set would have cost £800 plus new but will fetch only £100 a set these days because everything is being scaled down in size.

Zob Stick

The Zob stick I have is a piece of rough-hewn wood, four feet long with piles of bottle tops attached by nails and a biker's boot at the end. The top of this rhythm stick is carved as a phallus – originally embellished with a pair of red PVC balls which fell off at an exuberant moment. The Skunk Band made good use of it: it's an effective percussion instrument and makes people laugh.

Displaced Tuba

Another thing that can't help being humorous – preposterous – is the tuba. I swapped a sousaphone for mine. It's been painted maroon, navy blue and bottle green with jaunty pale blue highlights on the pipework and primary red and yellow on the valves. It looks festive in a faded kind of way and has obviously seen some action. I think it has probably appeared in a pantomime.

Toys

In some respects music shops are like toy shops: full of shiny objects laden with the latest gadgetry and as much to do with fantasy as with reality. You only have to look at some of the expensively produced brochures supplied to the trade – they don't bother with information – it's all image! I would expect this if it was aimed at the customer but they must think that the retailer is equally susceptible to impulse buying. As a retailer I require hard facts.

Desirable Object

Speaking of which there's a Paul Gilbert white horned guitar with F holes painted on. The volume knob looks awful; there's a switch in the middle you can't see and with three pick-ups there's nowhere to play it! Normally there's space for your fingers between pick-ups but no matter where I put my hand I've got £50 worth of pick-ups interfering! It has upside down machine heads and I think it's naff but there are people who would like it and put up with the annoyance for the novelty.

But the persuasive power of the world of the guitar as desirable object is all there in the catalogues' words and images. The instruments have virile action movie names: Revolver, Shredder, Fastback, Liberator, Apocalypse Special Bass, Paul Stanley Dark Star; or names that proclaim supreme expertise: Sovereign Special, Sovereign Pro, Blues King, Session Master Special and so on. There's a style to suit every performer: Traditional Double Cutaway, Aggressive Double Cutaway, Aggressive Carved Body are all on offer and necks can be Bound Set, Sculpted Bolt-on, or have a Select Spruce Top. Then, if this advertising copy doesn't get you, you might be tempted by an endorsement from a rock god such as Paul Stanley of Kiss. Or surely the sight of a black shiny guitar outlined in white, decorated with mother-of-pearl, sporting aristocratic Seymour-Duncan pick-ups, lying in the black velvet bed of a pristine guitar case, *actually within reach in the shop* will do the trick?

As favoured by Motorhead and all yours for £600.

The Economy

If I Were A Rich Man

For me wealth creation started as soon as I could ride my bike. Aged six I'd collect some jars, cycle down Weston Road to the marl pits and catch minnows, red doctors, frogs and newts, to sell to my mates for pennies – a penny ha'penny for a red doctor. Later I'd do paper rounds to fund my growing interest in music. I didn't hoard my money – I put it to good use: musical equipment, racing bike, nice guitar, scooter, big motorbike, sports car. All through spotting the bargain, doing things up, wheeling and dealing: the pattern of my working life.

When I started Custom Amplification all the right conditions came together: my business acumen and innovative skills, the explosion in pop music, a young generation with money and the desire to play loud music, the growing interest in vintage instruments.

So why am I relatively poor? Leaving aside the vagaries of the economy, the simple answer is I'm not a millionaire because I've spent my money!

A friend of mine treated himself to a red Porsche for his sixtieth birthday. Why wait so long? This should happen when you're young enough to enjoy what money buys – then you won't have any regrets in old age.

And that's what I've done. I've invested my money in hedonistic experiences. I always had enough money for the guitars I wanted, the sporting equipment I needed and the vehicles: terrestrial, marine and aerial I drove, and through this I met all sorts of people. These opportunities sustained me far more than the security of a large bank balance and because I experienced things when I wanted to, I have no regrets that I am now poor.

Of course, there were other contributory factors. The good luck in my life has been offset to a certain extent by those occasions when the timing has been out, when someone has let me down, when bureaucracy trampled over me or when a tiny detail had the power to dominate everything. Perhaps I was never single-minded or ruthless enough to be a millionaire because I split my focus: losing time in an abortive career as a white-collar worker, and then when I did get my own business I divided my time between that and playing music. Music – not money – was at the core of things and I chose the type of music that was never going to be commercially successful. In this I knowingly followed my heart and not my head – with no regrets.

I also have ethical reservations about wealth creation and the way commercialism pervades everything. I have respect for wealth that has been earned through hard work over a period of time but not for celebrity wealth that comes easily, overnight and for slender talent. There's something wrong when a footballer says he can't manage on forty-seven thousand a week. There's something wrong when the florist's bill exceeds what a hard-working ordinary man can earn in a year. There's something wrong when naturally talented people can't afford the instruments their skill deserves because vintage guitars, like vehicles, have become investment items, divorced from their purpose and kept in bank vaults to accrue unearned wealth.

I have lost money by refusing to sell vintage guitars to people who were not musicians.

My life has been punctuated with the deaths of people I have known, worked with and loved. Seen through the filter of grief, some of life's problems have seemed petty, including making money.

I'm a survivor because my lifestyle has always been underpinned by hard work and a stable business. I've taken some risks but all my decisions have had a basis of calculated wisdom. I've accumulated some assets because I've always needed and had a safety net. This has moderated my hedonism – if that's not a contradiction in terms – and that's why, in spite of her scorn for my conservatism, I fight Zoe's desire for me to sell up.

Bricks And Mortar

Having a business means you need suitable premises: space and security for the stock, a working area, room for development and The Nantwich Road shop had all this as well as being in a prime commercial position. Business went very well in the Seventies – so well that I opened another shop in Hanley in 1973. But times became very edgy when the economic climate in Britain took a downturn in 1976 and from banking three to four thousand pounds a week, I was only taking a few hundred pounds. The Hanley shop was the casualty – that went in 1976. Within three months of me deciding to sell Hanley and consolidate Crewe, I had notice to quit Nantwich Road: there was to be a road widening scheme. Thus began a period of unrest which took me to the edge of bankruptcy until I had established the Edleston Road shop as a going concern.

No matter how good at business you are, you have little power over the big boys whose plans ride roughshod over individual hopes. My shop on Nantwich Road was compulsorily purchased: my end of the block was to be demolished for the wider road into Mill Street. Preston's the chemist and post office (number 41) was on the corner of Mill Street and Nantwich Road: that was going. Gasket Breakers and a couple of other shops were the premises in Mill Street that were going. Next to Preston's was Stancie Cutler's antique shop, (number 43) then Custom Amplification, (number 45) then Mr Bright's chemist shop, (number 47): all going.

When I asked for alternative premises in what has now become a chip shop on the corner of Nantwich Road and Mill Street, my request was refused. The next issue was that some of the designated places were not demolished after all and some of the businesses given notice to quit were allowed to remain. Why was my claim for part of the rebuilt block rejected whilst others were not? My success as a businessman was not in question. Years later when I was talking to the former manager of the local bank (he did some drumming and liked my music) he said, "If I'd still been there you'd have had the old bank." He had faith in me, you see; he had watched me establish my business and make good profits; I had an American Express Gold Card; I banked with him – he should know! He also knew I lived at a prestigious address with good credit rating. No: it had nothing to do with my entrepreneurial status. I feel almost certain that my lifestyle went against me. The police had their eye on me: every time I went out of the country it was logged. I suppose I shouldn't be surprised – some of the people who came to my shop had dubious reputations and criminal records, and when searched my business cards would be found on them. I have committed minor drink and drugs offences myself. But I've never deserved to be treated like an outlaw.

I had a proper tenancy agreement with the council so I received just under four thousand as compensation for the broken agreement. But for me the loss of the Nantwich Road shop represented an economic downturn and I wanted to remain on this main road where there were so many good memories. The premises to which I moved in Edleston Road were in a less dynamic position and reflected the setback in my fortunes. What I got in compensation couldn't compensate me.

I gradually built up the Edleston Road business and reached a point in 1990 when I could stop renting and purchase the premises. I raised the mortgage and then met the sort of unfair circumstances I loathed: the price was increased by ten grand and I was told that if I was unwilling to pay that price, the shop would close for six months for refurbishment. In other words I was stuffed. Anyway, I raised the extra money but felt an enduring bitterness for the perpetrator of this exploitative opportunist act. It was legal but unethical.

Business has deteriorated since the glory days of the Seventies, not just because of national economic fluctuations but because fewer people are hiring these days. People used to be too poor to buy outright so they had to hire equipment or make an arrangement to pay gradually. Musicians now have more money and – until the Crunch – better access to credit so most established bands own their equipment. With the influx of Chinese goods it's cheaper too. Because clubs and pubs are closing there are fewer venues and therefore fewer people playing music. Business has seasonal fluctuations as well. The worst months for selling have always been those without an 'r'! Most people don't choose to spend summer studying the guitar.

I went to Pete's shop as a boy customer 35 years ago and Pete allowed me to have a drum kit and pay for it weekly. I couldn't have had it but for his support. It was £350 – a lot of money in those days. A lot of young musicians would have gone by the wayside but for Pete Johnson.

Phil Doody. (10)

The spasmodic nature of the business was well illustrated one dismal Saturday when I'd only taken fifteen pounds by four o'clock and felt like packing up. Then I took £375 for a guitar and amp plus an order for another guitar and amp costing £250. The trend continued the following Monday when someone phoned and asked me to deliver another guitar and amp.

Vat Man And Robbing

You need fifty-seven thousand pounds turnover before you pay VAT.

There are anomalies and one of these is the discrimination made against the second-hand music business. In the world of second-hand cars and antiques VAT is paid only on the profit. In the music business it is paid on the turnover. If you sell second-hand instruments you're not getting your VAT back. If I buy new at the cost of £100 I pay seventeen and a half per cent VAT. If I sell it, it is £150 plus seventeen and a half per cent VAT.

I owe the government the difference in VAT. If I bought a second-hand instrument off someone for £100 and sold it for £150, I should have made some profit with just a little bit of VAT to pay. But if I sell it for £150 I've got to pay the government VAT on £150, in which case to make my profits the same I would have had to buy the instrument for £83.

This is what depresses the second-hand musical instrument market – and me.

There's a lot of money tied up in stock and shoplifting is endemic in our society. Some guitars are more valuable than others though any theft is regrettable. Also, value isn't only about money; sometimes it's about style or uniqueness or things having sentimental value. The top shelf guitars are higher up where the customers can't easily reach. This minimises handling. They don't have prices because I don't want to indicate worth to any potential burglar. I would hope they would go for the cheaper shiny ones. Though sometimes I don't price them out of laziness.

My own personal collection of vintage guitars means more than monetary value to me. If I really needed the money or stopped playing them I would sell them but that would be a sad day. That was why, when we had burglars during the festive season I was relieved that they only stole money and didn't touch the guitars. Several hundred pounds and a Rolex watch went from upstairs but these thieves obviously didn't want the hassle of converting goods into cash, so the shop was untouched.

Being burgled is always terrible because someone has invaded your territory as well as stealing your possessions. The circumstantial evidence pointed to one person who had insider information and the recent opportunity to size things up but there was no other permissible evidence. I'm just glad they left the guitars and that no-one was hurt.

The other day two youths came to the door. They were aggressive in their manner and I didn't let them in. I was closed but that wasn't the reason – sometimes I sell more things when I'm closed than when I'm open! The reason I wouldn't let them in was because of their manner and because they weren't speaking English. This isn't racist, although it sounds as if it is. The point is I have had experience of theft in which two people are communicating together in a language I don't know. One distracts me by asking about an instrument or piece of equipment and whilst I'm concentrating hard and trying to understand him, the other one steals something. They have a numbers advantage as well as a communication advantage over me and I don't like it and can always see it coming.

Yet language isn't always a barrier. A Polish couple came in. I think it was father and daughter. They looked keenly around and the man spoke to me in Polish. He kept repeating "Ludwig". I concentrated very intently at him, with lots of eye contact. There was no sense that they had bad motives. I understood him although he spoke no English and advised them to go to Hanley for Ludwig drums. They were speaking posh drums.

Mid-Life Riffs: Guitars As Investments

As in the art market, guitars have been divorced from their function: purchased as mere investment objects kept in vaults. Instruments which have a rarity value or whose provenance links them with musical history or the famous and notorious are much sought after. Some guitars owned by the famous dead like Lennon or Hendrix end up in Hard Rock Café and are never played again. The Japanese have bank vaults with guitars in worth as much as £150,000. There's something sad about nice guitars not being played and enjoyed.

I've noticed that a beautiful flame top, mint condition, in its case Gibson 1958 Les Paul Standard worth £245,000 is available for hire. Because of insurance considerations this instrument will only be available to film companies and rich recording artists, and at the end of the day how much better can it sound than any other comparable Les Paul? It's another example of the madness. And here's another example. Zoe and I have been sorting out our pop music. Sixties and Seventies stuff is selling, according to our research on eBay. It's surprising what you find: there's a Madonna album going for £25 but if you have the version where she's wearing sunglasses it's worth £700. They only made this cover for two months.

The way things are going all attention is on the monetary value of guitars rather than the musical value. This is throwing up some anomalies. You could buy my shop and everything in it for one Les Paul 1959. There was a mint condition 1959 Les Paul recently for sale on the internet but you had to send in a CV before you could bid for it. In order to qualify as a bidder, details of your bank account had to be produced!

It's common knowledge that there are 3,500 1959 Les Paul guitars: flame top, tobacco sunburnt, in the hands of collectors. Interestingly, Gibson only made 1,400 such guitars. Why this discrepancy? One possible explanation is that in the 1970s Russian cellos were being purchased for their backs which were put onto guitars to make them resemble Les Paul instruments.

Because most really high quality instruments are owned by companies or wealthy families that loan them out or just hide them away, those that love or need quality instruments can't have them because money, not talent, is the issue. So if you're a violinist you can't aspire to a Stradivarius.

I bought my Martin for the equivalent of £400 and it is now worth several thousand pounds. I couldn't afford to buy it now, nor pay the insurance. I paid £120 for a Dobro; another went via Christie's for £7,000 because it was similar to one played by Hendrix and Dobros are relatively rare. My Dobro doesn't owe me anything; none of my instruments do. I treat them as working tools and just take them to the pub and play them. They just bear the wear of my use.

There is another strand of collector: the middle-aged beginner. Older people are starting to invest in guitars and also in learning to play as well. I have been interviewed by Radio Stoke about this phenomenon (July 2006) and it seems that they are cashing in their ISAs and investing in vintage guitars, partly for the sheer enjoyment of having them and even playing them but also hoping that they'll prove the better investment. In my opinion playing these instruments is better than watching a bank statement but it's a pity to have left it so long. Interestingly, it appears many of these later-life collectors had serious youthful passions for motorcycles, engineering schemes and the like, which, I would maintain, predisposed them to an appreciation of quality constructed instruments.

My recommendations for good investments in affordable instruments would be a reasonably priced Gibson Les Paul, a Fender Stratocaster or a Gibson jazz guitar. The price depends on the year but the best advice is to look for something you like and then make sure it's a reasonable price by checking on the net, in magazines or with a knowledgeable and reputable dealer. Some prices are amazing: pre-CBS Fenders fetch about £5,000 minimum. These are pre-1964. But it's still possible to own a nice electric guitar plus a fairly nice acoustic guitar for £3,000. At that level you can expect some increase as it ages. A Seventies Stratocaster fetched £750 two years ago; now it's worth £1,500 so things can move fast. The age of an instrument doesn't necessarily determine its price, though. Old banjos don't fetch as much as you'd think if you're considering the age. That's because banjos are not that popular.

The Chinese Industrial Miracle: Buying A Bentley Badge And Getting A German Car

One of the most influential impacts on my business has been the Chinese industrial machine.

Then there's the China factor. Their goods are very good quality and they're flooding the market. It's a lemming-like lunacy of downward spiralling prices and lower prices don't necessarily produce extra demand. The Chinese economy is overstretching itself; they're building one new coal-fired station a week and they're having to close down factories one week in a month to save power. Then there just aren't enough ships to bring the goods out. Overproduction. The world market is not big enough.

David Rushworth. (11)

Like the Japanese and Koreans before them, the Chinese are taking centre stage as a great manufacturing nation and are making musical instruments along with everything else. These are attractive and really cheap; no-one can match them, economically speaking. These days many things we associate with UK or US manufacturing have been taken over by foreign companies. Global economics dictates place of manufacture, rather than tradition or nostalgia. Gibson has used Japanese bridges and tail pieces as long as quality could be guaranteed. For some stalwarts, this depressed the value of the instrument but I'm more pragmatic. As far as I'm concerned, we should replace Gibson hardware with German hardware, specifically Schaller, because this is superior to that used by Gibson. I would retain the original stuff for resale purposes. At one time Gibson would ship out hardware to Japan and China but these days it is actually made in these countries.

There's a new guitar: a Chinese guitar, retailing at £165. Yet you can pay £140 for a tremolo alone. It costs £25 for a set of machine heads. Just do the sums. Slim has started to make guitars and he's buying these cheap oriental guitars just for the parts. There's a new consignment of bass strings from China retailing at £9.50. They normally cost £16 to £24 a set. The cost of everything to do with music has been radically reduced, especially recording costs. You can buy a used digital recording studio for £200 – new it's only £379 – and burn your own CD for the cost of one hour's studio time.

Chinese Retro

I have a Chinese amplifier in a retro design, straw-coloured with black knobs and handle, bulls' horns as a logo and the name Shine. What distinguishes it even more is that it is the first amp to be honestly

Chinese – other Chinese amps go under well-known names. It will retail at £200. An amp like this made in the US or UK five years ago would cost £600. They were a damn sight better too but the price differential is always a factor for the customer. In order to make the same amount of money I was making five years ago I will have to sell three of these Chinese amps.

The Shining Guitar From The East

China's answer to the aristocrats of the acoustic world is a copy of a National, shiny and entirely desirable, retailing at £395 – one tenth of the going price for the real thing. Chinese resonators are done by CAD CAM (that is computer-aided design and computer-aided manufacture) whereas the real Nationals and Dobros have hand spun resonators. That is, a human being – not a computer – has sat at a lathe and spun them. Hand spun resonators are obviously more expensive; you can get the Chinese ones for peanuts.

There is no denying the superiority of tone of my National guitar when compared to the Chinese version. There are other differences. The Chinese guitar has fourteen frets to the body; my National has twelve frets to the body. That means that my guitar plays perfectly on the leg, with no stretching. The Chinese one is twice the weight and has a longer neck, making it necessary to stretch. I find this uncomfortable; I have to keep nudging it up. But I can't help but wish that these cheaper resonator guitars had been available when I was younger. They would have given the opportunity to play something like a Dobro or a National to those who couldn't afford the real thing.

The Chinese are charging half the price for solid rosewood that Gibson is charging. Youngsters don't care where their guitars come from as long as the price is OK. Both Gibson and Fender have had stuff made in the East for years. They've blown their mystique but this doesn't matter to some people; it's the economics that matters most.

It's the economics that matters when you're being ripped off, too. I have recently (2010) bought a Les Paul as a curiosity and a sign of the times. Virtually new, it has a registration number, an owner's manual and says it is made in the USA. So how do I know that it was made in China?

Seven Reasons Why This Guitar
Is the Fake Rolex Of The Guitar World

- the colour of the knobs is too dark
- the binding is too light and not wide enough.
- the frets were fitted after the binding, not before.
- all the plastic fittings are dubious – aesthetically uncomfortable.
- there is no name on the machine heads.
- the pick-up surround is too steeply angled.
- all the plastic is slightly the wrong colour.

But I knew straight away and intuitively that this guitar was a fake. I knew before my mind started the logical process of authentification. The reasons that backed up my instant knowledge came from the rational part of my brain. It is highly likely that these guitars will go on the market for the full price: £1,700. Entirely fraudulent but what can you do? Kids are being cheated because unless they have enough knowledge they can't detect fakes.

I bought mine for £200.

The Great Debates

Over the years musicians have gathered to discuss the important issues of the day such as the recent tendency for girls to wear underwear as top wear.

Differentials And Product Placement

Similar-looking guitars can have a price differential of as much as £300. The one I'm looking at now is £450 but this is because it has £200 worth of pick-ups. Price is also determined by place of manufacture; China is the cheapest, then Korea, then Japan, then Europe and finally the USA.

An instrument's popularity can be related not just to quality or place of manufacture but also skilful advertising and sponsorship. Ovation developed an acoustic guitar with a plastic back. They presented them to high profile performers who thus advertised their product so they became the most sought-after and popular instrument for a time. I'm unenthusiastic; they sounded cold to me. The idea of mixing a nice piece of wood with plastic is not appealing because the relevant movements aren't correct: plastic won't move the same as wood.

Ebony, Rosewood And Maple

Everyone has their preference when it comes to choice of materials. Most fingerboards are made of rosewood or ebony because they are hardwoods and therefore hard-wearing. Fender, however, introduced maple as a material for fingerboards. This is also a hard wood but it had the disadvantage of easy staining. The solution was to apply layers of varnish. I don't like the tactile effect of the varnish, favouring ebony every time. I prefer it aesthetically and nothing wears like it.

The Price Of Patina

As in the antique furniture trade, musicians and retailers talk about patina with regard to musical instruments, particularly those made of wood. It's inevitable that you can buy deliberately distressed instruments, known as Custom Shop Specials or Relics. Like designer-torn jeans, these items cost more than the intact ones. Just as I don't believe in complete refurbishment of old instruments because some of the character, some of the history goes, I think it's equally daft and dishonest to artificially age something. A new instrument will acquire its own patina if it's used.

John Lennon's Gallotone was sold by Sotheby's for £160,000 after refurbishment. It was de-Lennoned, and that detracts from its intrinsic value as far as I'm concerned.

Electrifying Acoustics

When someone comes into the shop to buy a guitar my first question is: acoustic or electric? You might think that an electro-acoustic guitar is a bit of a contradiction but like everything else, where there's a need it gets fulfilled. Ovation were the first to develop electro-acoustic guitars, partly in response to the need for a louder sound to combat audience noise. With the electro-acoustic guitar sound is compressed before it reaches the amp so that the equipment can cope with it. It's useful but I think the sound is dreadful. It sounds better scrubbed than finger picked but you lose something by going electric. When you play nice old instruments in finger style all nuances are possible: there's a lot of variations in light and shade, tone and volume that just wouldn't come across with electro-acoustic guitars. The acoustic guitar is more subtle, more 'human'; you can hear the human being.

It's terrible to think that the overcoming of audience noise would be an issue. The ideal, really, would be a very expensive microphone and a quiet audience. At the end of the day you wouldn't expect an actor to have electronic devices attached to his vocal chords but there's a different ethos with the theatre audience. I've played to a full house at Crewe Theatre with no amplification whatsoever; I've seen Andres Torres Segovia play to a full theatre when he was eighty plus with no amplification; I could do the Limelight with 100 watts and you'd hear every word. They've got 10,000 watts there and people in the audience have said they can't hear the vocals properly. Music has been amplified to the point where it is a noise – either that or a backdrop of musak against which everybody talks and moves.

If Health and Safety officers went into any rock venue in the country they would close them down. They're using vast wattages and there's no sign of a decibel meter. I'm shocked by the cavalier attitude towards the risk to hearing from sound equipment. At one time Health and Safety rules obliged all venues to have decibel meters: the law allowed something like 96 decibels. Above that level the electricity supply would cut out. It didn't always work: I could sing loudly without an amp and cut off the supply! People found ways to get round the tyranny of the decibel meter, such as covering the microphone, etc. I would maintain that a loud voice is probably as loud as the ears can tolerate.

Today's sound engineers don't get the sound balance right. They're using up to 80% capacity on what was once called the backing group and leaving only 20% for the vocals, which are then drowned. In the early days of the Majestic Ballroom in High Street, Crewe I could walk from one side of the stage to the other and hear each instrument in turn with vocals twice: a cabinet each side.

Acoustic Guitar vs. Electric Guitar

I've always played both electric and acoustic, intermittently. With an acoustic guitar you've got what you've got and it's self-sufficient: it sits on its own with a voice. The only other instrument that can do that is the piano. With an electric guitar you need a bass and drum and you're involved with amplification and effects. An electric guitar turns you into a party animal; it's an audacious, showy instrument played standing and strutting, and there are so many variables that can compensate for sheer lack of talent. The acoustic guitar gives a different, perhaps more serious mood, a more intimate experience. There's something about the warmth and character of an acoustic guitar. My Martin was made in the Twenties and I've had it for twenty years. It bears evidence of my playing: small marks where my little finger has nestled. Songs done on an acoustic guitar have more depth, greater resonance and every acoustic guitar you pick up sounds different – has its own character. Electric guitars can be fun and appropriate to the occasion but I just don't understand this crazy over-estimation of the electric guitar where you pay thousands for mere planks, just on a whim of fashion.

PAF (Patent Applied For) vs. Humbucking

The world of musical instruments is imbued with erudition and mystique and there are people like Rob: a self-confessed anorak when it comes to Gibson Les Pauls who can look at a pick-up – any pick-up – and say, "That screw's not right." Let me introduce you to the refinements of pick-up snobbery. I have a Gibson guitar with the residual registration which indicates that it had a PAF pick-up. The patent for this type of pick-up was applied for before 1963 and has had a certain *caché* amongst the rock star fraternity. It costs £200. A named Gibson Humbucker pick-up costs £50. It is exactly the same as the PAF but without the mystique. A PAF is a pre-1962 Humbucker but dates in this field are always a bit vague because the changeover is dubious and guitars often have the same bits on them as before the change. It is this mystique, fortified by popularity, high profile exposure and the mystery of age that gives it the added value, not necessarily as a musical aid, but as an object in itself.

The man responsible for the manufacture of the PAF pick-up did something to demystify the subject when, asked a rather breathless question said, "We had a magnet; we had copper wire and we wound it. We wound it till it was full." Of the pick-up known as the Zebra Humbucker, which is black and white plastic, the same man, who had also designed and built it said, "We ran out of black plastic."

But why trouble people with the facts?

Capo

A capo is a device for shortening the strings; it enables you to change key on a guitar without changing chord shape. They are mainly used by acoustic players. If you're playing an electric guitar you're playing barre chords. A barre is in fact a capo with the index finger free. If you put a capo on, this enables you to get the same melodies and basses but in a higher key. I feel this is cheating a bit! Most pop tunes use three or four chords and you tend to use shapes repeated up and down the neck. To change key you just move your hand with exactly the same shape. You have made your left hand into a capo. Some capos are modified to put an open tuning in.

Capos are either brass or nickel plated brass. I don't bother with brass ones: I have brass with nickel plating because brass is affected by the atmosphere. For the same money you can have a nice plating and not have to clean it. I haven't actually seen a gold capo but if gold is available it's such a thin sprayed coating that it wears off in no time. It's a gimmick.

Gibson Les Paul vs. Fender Stratocaster

I have always preferred the Gibson over the Strat. The Gibson Les Paul was designed by a guitar player; it feels like a guitar should, as far as I'm concerned. The Fender Stratocaster was a lucky accident: designed by a radio repair man. Like the Ford Model T it's good for mass production.

And the sounds are so different. The scale length is different as well. The Strat stretches your hand out. Any Gibson I play feels as if it comes from the same stable and it's much easier to play. Gibsons are more fragile than Strats; they break at the back of the neck by the headstock whereas you could kick a Strat down the road and it would be OK!

CD vs. DAT

CDs have been found to disintegrate; the Americans are having to re-record all their important information. They've gone back to tapes: Digital Audio Technology tapes which have perfect sound but not compressed sound like on a CD. The sound is stored in a tape format a lot smaller than a cassette. DAT players are used by recording studios and journalists and they are the next technology. The album I did at Whippoorwill Studios was recorded on DAT and transferred to CD.

The Music Doctor: Instrumental Transplants

If I see a guitar that needs repair then I have to do something with it.

When I was fifteen I renovated a Dobro that was in a dreadful condition. You couldn't easily get the parts then, either. I resurrected it with my own skills but also needed to call on the skills of two others, thus setting the pattern for all subsequent dealings with damaged instruments. The image of this seminal instrument appeared on my early business cards.

Quite a bit of my work has involved getting instruments repaired and restored. Sometimes, as with cars, there's just nothing that can be done except to use the spare parts. Some guitars aren't worth much, are badly made and although they could be restored, it just isn't worth the trouble. Then there are those instruments that are well made or have a certain style or are worth money and therefore merit the time and effort and money that buys renovation.

The worst cases are those where a crude job has already been attempted and botched. I have a Gibson jazz guitar L42 (circa 1940) that someone has tried to convert to electric. The butchery seems shocking and it has been given the wrong surround. I've found a DeArmond jazz pick-up more in keeping with the instrument and had a wooden cover made for it.

I have a network of skilled people to whom I sub-contract whatever I can, partly because I like to patronise such skills – many of which are dying out – and partly because I know I will get a good job. I'm essentially an ideas man, though not without my own practical skills and most things can be overcome by research and logic but Crewe has traditionally had many, many skilled people who had served seven year apprenticeships. If a cog on a machine head had gone there were guys from Rolls Royce or Crewe Works who could make you one.

In late summer, 2006 there were more needy instruments than usual. This was because one of my colleagues had returned some instruments that he hadn't been able to finish. Cockney Bob "The Builder" Snell has renovated guitars and exchanged favours with me over the years. Some of the returns were ready to be passed on to the specialists to whom I sub-contract; some I would deal with myself, and others would be used for their parts only.

To the casual observer a pile of wood standing on top of a speaker would be ideal for the barbecue but this was actually the basis for the radical repair of a Guild. There was a piece of spruce and a piece of mahogany to repair the front and the back, with elegant pencil guide lines and a piece of corrugated card labelled "rosette". Bob left these and I knew exactly what had to be done. It's wonderful that these formless bits of wood and these minimal guides can be transformed into a viable musical instrument.

There was also a lovely little Italian guitar, a hundred years old and partially restored. It was essentially feminine, with black and white contrasting purfling (a sort of decorative edge-binding, usually done in plastic or abalone on modern guitars), a decorative rosette round the sound hole and a decorative pick guard. I have a mandolin, similar in style, which indicates its Italian origin.

If you take a glimpse behind the scenes at some of the 'scaffolding' that holds a guitar's structure in place so that it can do its job, you'll see that the unseen parts of a guitar comprise strutting: the curved wood that holds back and front together and the criss-cross bracing that deals with the stresses. Without such structural elements any guitar, however pretty, high tech or baroque would just be a fragile façade.

I had a double bass in for repair, standing near the door, like a bouncer. It had been mended and was ready for collection but suffered further damage when a rep. found it impossible to resist playing it and had not replaced it properly. So its sound post had come adrift. Fiddles as well as double basses have these sound posts. They support the top. During transportation, double basses are moved without the sound post then a specialist is summoned to fit it with a coathanger-style tool. This is somehow pleasing as a piece of musical ritual.

When you first meet a double bass you're struck by the sheer presence of this man-sized instrument. The one I had was a combination of industrial utility and decorative power; especially in the head, with its wooden Viking scroll and metal keys and cogs! It was of European origin; the top was spruce and the back was sycamore or beech. If its provenance were American, the back would be maple wood. The wood was dull and there were signs of natural wear and tear where you would expect it to be: at the bottom right hand curve. But it was not this that had required attention. It was the vulnerable neck, highlighted by a strip of shiny glue at the junction between head and body that had been mended. Once the sound post had been sorted it would be ready to dance again with its player.

Sometimes an instrument has just had it. If it was a cheap instrument to start with and hasn't accrued any worth, then its not worthwhile investing time and money to mend it. If I look round my shop I see exposed guitars: neckless, stringless, lifeless, and I know there is no hope for them. I would have to spend £200 to resuscitate such an instrument and it is therefore worth more to me if I sell the parts. I write it off as a cheap knacker and salvage what I can.

A lad brought in a guitar shaped like an electrified amoeba: a nicely made piece with a mahogany back and maple top. His GCSE project. He had made the fundamental mistake of earthing it to wood rather than metal. You'd think his teacher would have spotted the mistake before he made it permanent. As it stands it'll be tricky to rectify and that's a pity – a good guitar in danger because of ignorance.

Sometimes a guitar comes from a bad home! I had a guitar in once that bore the imprint of a human foot stamping on it, splintering it in a moment of rage – a truly shocking sight. But the guitar had a greater survival chance than the warring marriage it lived with.

Dougie Wilkes

Another of the people I can rely on for renovating instruments is Dougie Wilkes. He is a guitar mender/maker who lives near Keele, Staffordshire where he has a small workshop with lovely hand-built tools from Stoke-on-Trent and all-pervading sawdust. He does a Meat Loaf tribute band at the weekends.

Dougie has learnt his woodworking skills doing car dashboards – where would you see a walnut dashboard nowadays? He's done a lot of repairs over the years; he repaired the double bass, for example and he's very good on head stock breaks, re-frets and refinishes.

But this specialist is a dying breed. It costs as much to repaint a guitar as to buy a new one, so most people would just buy new in a throwaway society. Refurbishing is bound to diminish when the valuable guitars potentially needing it are in collectors' hands and the restoration work's been done.

Barry Bray

Barry Bray is not an electrician by trade but a very gifted and enthusiastic amateur who has spent his life acquiring technical skills through helping his father make and run model railways. Sometimes he comes to collect equipment; sometimes he comes to drink tea. Sometimes both.

I sub-contract my electrical repairs to Barry, who has visited the shop since 1980. He originally worked at Smethurst and Oldham, a sewing factory in Queen Street, Crewe. This was in the Fifties. Of course, Crewe had several clothing factories at one time. He reminded me about the advertisement for Adonis Shirts painted on the factory roof that you could see from the Manchester train.

In the Sixties Barry saved up to buy a decent Jason sound system and taught himself about wiring from books. Everything he knows about repairing electrical equipment is self taught and he was soon repairing black and white televisions and other stuff for people at work.

A singer called Mark who did his own recordings and who lived down the road from Barry recommended his skills to Reg, who was complaining about the cost of sub-contracting work. So that's how the network operates.

Barry talks about how tedious it was waiting ages for parts and then how much more complicated it became when manufacturers started amalgamating parts and charging three times as much. He says that the old valve amps and the older transistorised amps were much easier to repair and still are. Recent miniaturised stuff is far more difficult to handle. I always suggest repairs for older equipment because the older it is, the more chance there is of repairing it: Barry has parts you've never heard of! Keith Marriott does the electronics on the guitars in for repair and has done since he was a kid.

Innovations
In Business

I've never become musically famous though a lot of people know me.

But I have experienced another kind of fame associated with my ability to innovate. Many of my designs were revolutionary and ahead of their time. As the name implies, my business provides the custom building of equipment. Initially I had to solve a problem with the badge that went on my cabinets: as a small firm I didn't want to commission them because the minimum number would have been too many. I resolved this by recycling the "custom" badges found on both wings of Ford transits – the accepted vehicle for bands – for which we scoured the scrap yards. An economical music-related coincidence.

The idea for the business came very early on in my career as a musician. I only had to look around at the sheer number of musicians around at that time to know there was a business supplying their needs. Parallel with the practicalities of making, hiring and selling, I was soon building up a business in vintage guitars. I'd had some business training and I was the youngest management consultant in the country at twenty-one years old. I had thirty vintage guitars by the time I opened on Nantwich Road and I started a vintage guitar boom in the North West that was written about in all the magazines. I also designed the biggest PA system of the day.

Custom Amplification
45 Nantwich Road Crewe 4779
45 Hope St. Hanley 266897
Second hand Gibsons and Fenders.
Special custom built P.A. systems and guitars etc.
Pearl and Premier Drums and Traynor and Pearl Amps.
Call Pete at Crewe for a chat. (12)

By the time I had been a Gibson dealer for eighteen months Custom Amplification appeared in the *Market Report* for Gibson. "Supplied BJ Kramer with Gibsons", it says.

Customized Slide

When Son House first showed me how to use slide he told me the slide needed to be a certain weight in order to sustain the notes. Persistent use of the slide has increased the size and strength of my slide finger. I designed my own slide because I couldn't get the right weight and size commercially. Slides are usually not heavy enough for me and usually too short. The other thing is that guitar necks have got smaller and narrower since the Sixties to facilitate pop music. As it developed, strings got lighter and action got lower so slides were designed with that in mind, whereas if you play a vintage National the neck is more like a baseball bat and it fits a man's hand. For finger picking you tend to have wider fret boards and more room on the neck, therefore you need longer slide to cover all strings. My slides were chamfered off and have a bevelled edge at the end so you can play single notes down the bottom of the guitar without infringing anything: it gives you more control over single notes.

When the problem with my hands developed I had a slide specially made: full slide on one side and with a hole in the other side for the knuckle. This accommodated what was happening to my fingers at the time. Someone from Crewe Engineering made this slide to my specifications. I get by with a much lighter slide these days; I wouldn't want to put undue stress on my fingers.

Smooth Surface

One of my early innovations in sound technology was the use of fibreglass instead of wood. Wood is excellent for housing things but is not necessarily a good deflector because of its absorption properties. The beautiful, smooth, curved shapes possible with fibreglass were ideal for sound projection. If you're trying to throw sound, the harder and smoother the surface, the better the response.

I got to know the qualities of fibreglass very well: I had made fibreglass canoes at the age of fifteen and renovated a fibreglass sports car at the age of seventeen. I also acquired further knowledge of the material whilst working at Ideal Standard and Pete Whittingham, an artist as well as a musician, who had worked in the restoration of stately homes, had also used it for fibreglass slate and woodwork to replace missing or damaged parts of buildings. So the knowledge was readily available for conversion into musical equipment.

My sound systems were acknowledged as revolutionary. Magazine articles appeared and I was commissioned to build and exhibit equipment described as "The Biggest Sound System in Europe" at the London Music Show held in the Bedford Hotel, near Russell Square. I had designed massive trapezoid cabinets – rather like truncated pyramids – to house exponential horns, vastly increasing the audible output. The intimate size of the venue showed off the exhibition to advantage.

By this time I already had a reputation for fairly revolutionary new designs. I had made Voice of the Theatre cabinets with GRP exponential horns shaped and curved all the way round like a megaphone – unlike the more basic World Leader cabinet which was straight at the top and bottom of the horn with curved sides.

During the oil shortage of the Eighties, vinyl – which is petrol-based – became scarce so I decided to make cabinets out of marine quality plywood. The trend was for equipment to get smaller anyway: speakers were high-powered and venues were getting smaller, so these well-designed and well-made pieces of furniture caught the spirit of the times. They had routed edges so they wouldn't chip and the wood was stained. I also planned luxury tour buses and cabinets that have only recently come into being.

Not all my systems were on the scale of the exhibition at the Bedford Hotel. I built up a local reputation in clubs and pubs in Cheshire and Staffordshire. The letter I sent out by way of advertisement shows how confident I was about my product:

If you would like "clarity" to come to your concert room, why not invite us along to do some demonstrations free of obligation. We can produce purpose built public address systems to suit any size building and quite a few bank balances. Our systems are already in use in the area, to the agreed advantage of the owners. If you would like to see any of these working, one of our staff can arrange a demonstration.

Crossover Or Natural Flow

If you want to separate sound, either use crossover units (very expensive and complicated) or try to use the natural flow of electrical impulse. This was an idea I had, using the fact that electricity is like water: it flows to the easiest places. Use good quality fifteen inch speakers of little resistance that will naturally take most of the power. Then, if you put a higher resistance twelve inch speaker, that will take roughly half the power the fifteen inch will take. So, I take one fifteen inch at eight ohms and one twelve inch at sixteen ohms. The horn can have a single capacitor to stop base response.

This system worked for twenty-five years and most clubs were happy with them. Some changed to more modern systems then came back and asked us to rebuild another one like the previous one – the one I innovated. We used to get orders sub-contracted from other companies that fitted machines and pool tables etc. who would provide PA systems through us.

The heyday for Custom Amplification was from about the mid Seventies to the early Eighties.

Gordon-Smith Guitars

I came across a magazine article about a guitar I designed thirty-five years ago. I felt pleased to have been acknowledged.

We knew a feller called Pete Johnson back in the early'70s who was a bit of a mover and a shaker in the rock 'n' roll retail trade. He was aware that we had ambitions to move into manufacturing, and approached us with plans for a guitar that he thought would sell. It was basically a Les Paul Jr but a bit more modern: instead of the P90 it had a tapped humbucker…Now it's one of our claims that we invented the tapped humbucker. (13)

My collaboration with Gordon-Smith started off with me taking up say, a guitar neck I'd salvaged and asking him to build a body compatible with it. After several of these prototypes we started on the actual Gordon-Smith range.

There was an article about Gordon-Smith guitars, described as "the longest continuous guitar manufacturer that England has ever produced" in the February 2006 copy of *Guitar and Bass.* The firm is distinguished in another way, too: it makes its own pick-ups. I see some parallels with my own business in terms of longevity, central control and specialization.

John Smith just picked the skills up and applied them to what was an interest and a hobby. From refurbishing instruments he gained knowledge of structure and refinements and from there he went on to manufacture his own instruments. This was the firm that I approached in the Seventies with a plan for a viable guitar: basically a Les Paul Junior but more modern. My modification would overcome the inherent weakness in the structure of this guitar which had the tendency to break at the point where the neck joins the body. I had acquired a nice neck and wanted the body custom-made with a strengthening volute. A volute is the shaping of wood on the back of the neck on a guitar. It is a strengthening piece at the vulnerable part of the instrument. Martins have a diamond shaped piece standing proud of the neck.

But there was another suggestion, too: having a tapped humbucker instead of the P90. We had a conversation about using a tapped humbucker, using two pick-ups on a guitar in the same position but I said I liked the option of giving a combination of both. His innovation cancelled the option by combining both. Whereas in the magazine article John Smith is very humble about it, I am adamant that he did invent it and that, moreover, coil-tapping was something not done by any major manufacturers for the next ten years. This prototype: Rocker 1 had one pick-up. The magazine article states: "Pete Johnson had guessed the market correctly, it seems, for the new Gordon-Smiths were an instant success. The single pick-up model was quickly followed by a double pick-up version". Rocker 2 had two pick-ups. Rocker 1 was fitted with a push-pull volume control enabling the musician to vary between humbucker and single-coil pick-up, effectively giving the sound of a double pick-up guitar out of one pick-up. Rocker 2 had a double amount of variation. It was a massive advantage to be able to go from one to another on one instrument. However, if you get a guitar and change the pick-ups, no matter what the owner thinks, the value is diminished because buyers want the original and then do their own modifications.

For the uninitiated, pick-ups are the things under the strings that pick up and amplify the sounds. The more pick-ups there are on a guitar, the less the sound. Humbucker pick-ups are double pick-ups that increase volume and sustain sound. They have been available since the Fifties and are two singles strapped together. They were originally called "Hum-cancelling" pick-ups but the name used is much more rock 'n' roll! A single coil sounds good in certain situations where you want a clear, clean sound. It is the startup default mode giving almost a country sound. The humbucker pick-up is associated with the rock guitar; it gives more sustain and a 'dirty' sound. A lot of jazz players favour the humbucker because it gives more tone quality. In the Eighties there were some clever new designers in pick-up technology. They stacked the humbuckers one on top of the other. This device could be fitted to a Fender guitar without altering anything, so it could easily be put back to standard again.

Pick-ups can be expensive items, especially vintage ones such as "patent applied for" pick-ups which are worth £200 plus. People express surprise that I have such items lying around in wooden boxes with other paraphernalia. "I bet you'd lose your finger before I lost a pick-up," is my grim reply.

Reputation

My involvement with the innovations described took place some years ago but I'm still surprised to find references and to have my advice sought. For example I was recently leafing through *The Guitar Magazine*, 8 June 1997 and came across this letter:

MULTIPLE RESONATIONS.

The resonator feature [TGM vol 7 no 6] as an overview on these guitars was, as usual, excellent. As you say – once played and the slide mastered, they are totally addictive.

One minor point: National and Dobro branded guitars are not exclusive to The Acoustic Centre in this country – you can also buy them off the shelf from Frailers Guitars in Runcorn [01928-573087]. There is also Custom Amplification in Crewe [01270-214779], where Pete Johnson (alias Snakey Jake) stocks used vintage resonators. In addition, Pete has to be rated as one of the UK's top slide players!

Otherwise, your feature was on the ball, as always.

R. Davies, Wrexham. (14)

Sometimes at twilight you look into lighted properties and there are people gathered together, at ease with one another and united by a common interest on which their minds are focussed. You find this in bike shops; you find this in workshops where people are gathered round a vintage car that's being renovated and you find it in music shops. The single-minded interest of the people in what is happening in that particular place excludes the rest of the world and creates a little world that is self-contained, and from which all the other things happening in people's lives are excluded for as long as they are in this particular pool of light.

Notes: Section Six

(1) Wayne Davies (Slim) interviewed by Sandra Gibson 30th January 2007.

(2) Dec Higgins aged 16 years, interviewed by Sandra Gibson at Brine Leas School, Nantwich, January 2007.

(3) Wayne Davies (Slim) interviewed by Sandra Gibson 30th January 2007.

(4) Zoe Johnson, interviewed by Sandra Gibson 26th April 2007.

(5) Matthew Johnson, from a conversation at Custom Amplification, 19th March 2009.

(6) Pete Johnson: Georgia Journal.

(7) Ibid.

(8) Wayne Davies (Slim) interviewed by Sandra Gibson 30th January 2007.

(9) Jim Farmer, interviewed by Sandra Gibson June 2006.

(10) Phil Doody, from a conversation at Custom Amplification, 19th March 2009.

(11) David Rushworth, the rep. from Inter Music, from a conversation at Custom Amplification 15th May 2007.

(12) From International Musician and Recording World February 1977.

(13) Guitar & Bass, February 2006.

(14) Guitar Magazine, vol.7, no 8. June 1997.

SECTION SEVEN

A View From The Verandah

It's not very rock 'n' roll to survive until you're sixty – I thought I'd die a young man's death. Living to experience an old-life crisis puts you into contemplative mode. For the first time in my life I was keeping very still: looking back in order to move forward. How had my past experiences and key decisions prepared me for the old age I never thought I'd reach? What had sustained me and what had I sustained? What would sustain me? Having seen so many untimely deaths what did I think about the prospect of a timely death?

No. It's not very rock 'n' roll.

Up Yours

By 2005 the edginess of my life had been amplified by circumstances which pressurised me materially, creatively and emotionally. I was hard up, the music scene had dried up and my hands were fucked up. Zoe wanted us to sell up. Sell up and cast our fates to the canal waters in a less than viable boat.

For quite a while I was immobilised on a metaphorical verandah: finger picking tunes, drinking cider and assessing. I've come to the conclusion that the three main things that have sustained me have been music, friendship and sex. Of these, music has been the most important because it has been the constant factor. The other issues: wealth, fame, hard work, taking risks, having fun, innovating, learning have all contributed in varying degrees and at various times.

Immaterial

Wealth was important to get things moving but I was never taken in by wealth *per se.* It facilitated things; it bought experiences but it didn't make me happy. Having it in abundance did me an unexpected favour – it taught me that it was worthless! But it did leave me in the enviable position of having bought that, been there and done that whilst I was still young enough to enjoy it all so I have no lingering aspirations to make me feel dissatisfied. And I have enough to get by. Meeting some of my musical heroes has meant more to me than anything money could buy and developed my economic and political views as well as my musical vision.

I had no romantic notions of starving in an attic for my music either; there was no need.

Sustaining The Ego

I never achieved great fame, though a lot of people know me and I have been praised for my work by good musicians and by people who share my musical tastes. There's a photograph of me with two of the most successful and esteemed guitarists in the business: Woody Mann and Bob Brozman, taken at Lichfield. One time at my Acoustic Night at Square One in Mill Street, a tall silent man sat through my first set without taking his eyes off me. He then congratulated me on my work and it turned out that he was also familiar with the work of Mann and Brozman. "But you're better," he said. Praise is nice, though not essential. Whilst in Georgia I received fulsome praise. Hearing my radio interviews on WRFG, fans travelled long distances to see me. Many asked me to put my hands on their guitars – some brought two or three – and one man asked me to sign his. I declined. It would have been almost sacrilegious.

But fame doesn't impress me in myself or intimidate me in others. One night I was gigging at Alexander's Jazz Theatre in Chester. The place was full of actors who had just finished their last night and they were making a noise. I spoke to them: "It may be your last night but it's my first night and it'll be my last night if this row doesn't stop." It stopped. I spoke to one of the actors – Gerald Harper – at the end of the evening. I didn't know him but it wouldn't have made any difference if I had. As actors they would expect their audience to be respectful. The fame that comes from being an entertainer seems trivial and it only sustains you in the moment.

Friends

I've had the good fortune to have friends. My friendship with Whitty was based on music and on his good company – when he wasn't too pissed. He was a loveable, creative and intelligent man and we shared a sense of humour and many a convivial time, and I was prepared to look after him – feed him, keep him from getting too drunk – in order to preserve that. We never had to discuss things conventionally; our communication was intuitive, musical and direct. Whitty was a soulmate. I tried to minimize his self-destructive tendencies, believing that there was enough light in him to dispel his demons and just as this was happening – his letters from Australia were so full of hope – the bastard died. I lost more than a friend. There was no way of replacing that precious musical compatibility we had. It transcended everything else.

I've never got over the loss of my musical brother.

But I've been sustained by the company and efforts of many people over the years. Bert Bellamy opened doors to the world of blues where I made some inspirational musical friends and I'll never forget the musical help I had from Son House. People with generous hearts like John Billington and Keith Bellamy appreciated my music and helped me financially. Others like Graham Roberts and Tom Jackson helped further my professional standing. I had an extended musical family: Melvyn and Deanie and Plum and Moggsie and Bootie and JD and Dave and Shep and Slim that made up for the depleted home life of my younger days. Keith Brammer and Count Bartelli were sporting companions. Both of my brothers could be counted on in survival situations. My mother was an enormous support to my musical success and my father became one of my role models, the others being Eugene Van De Hoog for his zest for life and Mike Slaughter for his courageous quirkiness.

My friendship with Des is more balanced than the one with Whitty and has endured for over thirty years. I'm used to looking after people and I used to try to look after Whitty but this is a friendship where I have been the one looked after. Des helped me get through some bad bouts of depression, especially when I was worried about my hands and he has recklessly confronted me to make me see sense. It's been reciprocal – I've been there for his bad times too.

This friendship isn't so strongly based on musical compatibility, though we do admire one another's musicianship and we do perform together so the compatibility is there. Des still says he's the apprentice! We have different approaches to preparation and performance. He plays it by the book whereas I favour a more fluid, intuitive approach. I find it difficult to compromise what I do to accommodate him and he must find it equally difficult. I can't relax into the music and lose myself; I can't spontaneously change the verse order or introduce an alternative ending as I could with Whitty. I am aware that Des is someone else whereas with Whitty we were the same. The banter between us is spontaneous but the songs are worked out and I don't blame Des for that. With Des there has been an enduring love more than a musical compatibility.

My relationship with Des is based on shared values and there is a sense of easiness between us, an acceptance of each other, a social compatibility that means we can sit in silence.

It's a spiritual bond if you want to so-call it. Pete has kept me away from the rock 'n' roll machine. We're actually an odd couple Pete and I. We shouldn't be friends at all.

Des Parton. (1)

We're best mates. The best.

I Just Always Loved Being Loved

I've had some good friendships with women too. I did experience the sex and drugs and rock 'n' roll *cliché*, though not to the point of excess. I need women because I lost my mother, because of my libido and because I like them. Without a woman I'm back in the despairing time when life felt empty. I've just always loved being loved. There's a song line: "I've never been to bed with an ugly woman but I sure woke up with a few" and I can honestly say this has never applied to me. There were plenty of women: all beautiful and I remember every one of them, no matter how brief the encounter. I'm not a womanizer and although I have been out on the pull there have been many times when women have taken the initiative with me.

Kenny Rogers I Presume?

As a musician I was always going to live the bohemian life of experimentation but it's hard to recapture the unique carefree simplicity of those times of sexual freedom we had in the Sixties and Seventies. The disillusionment caused by the withering of Flower Power and the moral panic fuelled by the AIDS epidemic obliterated all that. The Pill separated sex from pregnancy so it could be enjoyed without fear of consequence. Women became more assertive now they were free to experience their sexuality and I met girls who released me from the necessity for pursuit: a thrilling innovation.

I had an important advantage: I was a musician and front man in a locally esteemed band and girls are drawn to performers. They equate your confidence with sexual potency; they're wooed by the sentimental or sexy songs performed. They are actually relating to a fantasy, not a real human being but often the combination of confidence and fantasy-induced arousal works. As far as I was concerned it would only work if the girl was also intelligent.

Fantasy works both ways, of course. I was having a drink with Des at a pub that brewed its own beer – Sunrise or Sunset – and we were having a good time. I couldn't help but notice an attractive dark-haired woman and she was noticing me as well. As the drink flowed and we kept looking at one another I began to fantasise about her. She was probably Spanish. Definitely. An *au pair*. I wondered if she would play with my castanets. She leaned forward – I could smell her musky perfume. She leaned forward with her unlit cigarette like someone in a film. This was my moment – she was leaning closer and closer until she was looking in my eyes. Gazing.

"Fuckin' 'ell! I thought you were Kenny Rogers!"

I don't know what deflated me the most: the broad Stoke accent exploding my fantasy or being mistaken for a performer ten years older than me.

Dress Down

A theme runs through my experiences, on stage and off: the other side of dressing up has been dressing down – to the point of nudity. Amongst the women, that is. I've been very fortunate: many of my fantasies and fetishes have become reality. On holiday in Germany with my girlfriend, one of her breasts became exposed. This is called a wardrobe malfunction these days. An officious knobhead at another table felt it his duty to point this out: "Excuse me – I think your dress has slipped." "I'm sorry – is it embarrassing you?" she replied, slowly, very slowly, covering up. The covering up was as sexy as the exposure! It wasn't embarrassing her. Another time I was out with a girl who was wearing a *basque* and a similar thing happened. Damn it all – these things would just keep on happening. One of our companions mentioned that the tops of her nipples were showing. "Oh! Don't you like it?" was the reply. Both women challenged a man's right to make them cover up by handing the embarrassment back to him. I applaud them.

A woman has the right to dress as she wants, as far as I'm concerned. I think a lot of women would like to wear sexy clothes but are in repressive relationships. One of my ex-girlfriends appeared in a hairdressing display wearing not very much see-through chiffon over no underwear. I had bought her the not very much and she provided the rest: you could count the dots round her nipples! It was difficult to focus on the hairstyle. Her soon-to-be boyfriend was in the audience. Fast forward to the wedding photos: she's dressed like Mary Poppins! I rest my, er, case.

I think my liberal attitude to self expression is unusual for men of my generation. I'm more likely to be upset by sexual infidelity or betrayals in friendship than by exhibitionism. If someone reveals their breasts for fun, or the pleasure of others or just for themselves, what's wrong with that? Some sexual expressiveness is independent of observers. Perhaps the wild rock chicks exposing their breasts in salute at biker gigs would behave in a more outrageous way than the 'conventional' person, though this is not necessarily so. I've been to some *very* posh parties, professionally and socially, that ended up with all the women naked in the swimming pool.

I asked one of my partners about the liberated behaviour of my girlfriends. She agreed that it was because I was always supportive and never censorious: "Jealousy pushes a woman away. Men must be afraid you'll run off if people can see you but it's the jealousy that makes you go." I asked my first wife too: "You've got to put yourself on the line if you want to have fun," she said. We used to go to Cornwall in an open-topped sports car and she would enjoy the opportunity to wear unrestricting clothing. She was a political activist and feminist like Zoe and I've come to realize that the nudity, especially the discarding of the bra, was an important political act for women. The tabloids trivialised it, of course.

I think Pete wants his women to be something he can be proud of. He's envious of a woman's ability to be sexually powerful. He feels they have an advantage in a way men can't have.

Zoe Johnson. (2)

I have photographs of my parents on a barge and in a cycling party: evoking a countryside long since diminished and a culture of fresh air and physical training popular in the Thirties throughout Europe. My mother is wearing cycling shorts and riding a bicycle with a cross bar. Apparently, this caused a stir although looking at the photograph it's hard to understand out of the context of the interwar years. I think this was the equivalent of women in the Sixties discarding their bras. My mother is the prototype for all those girls who wanted the freedom to express themselves by dressing or undressing in a certain way. It isn't just a question of exhibitionism; it's a matter of individuality. It's political. Women I went out with carried on the tradition.

I do believe that what a woman wears should be appropriate to the occasion, though; dressing appropriately is a matter of social intelligence. If a girl is at a cocktail party in non-cocktail clothes and she has a reason and is confident, that's all right. If her choice of clothing is based on ignorance or lack of intelligence, it's not all right as far as I'm concerned. If you're socially intelligent you don't break the rules but you can as well!

Consequences

Of course, my sexual experiences had consequences of one kind or another. I have two fine sons for a start.

Attraction is fairly simple with men, whereas with women it is more complicated and I know this is a *cliché* but it seems to me that every bloke has to learn this for himself, unfortunately. Although I was conventionally married by my early twenties, my lifestyle as a musician gave me a lot of freedom of movement and opportunities for extra-marital relationships: serious or fleeting. My wife appeared to tolerate my other relationships as long as she and I had a relationship that was not affected. But in the end it was affected. Perhaps from her perspective it always was but this remained unspoken. I was the transgressor and my ultimate transgression was with regard to my responsibility as our son's father. I failed to show up when I should have.

There came a time when the balance changed. Matthew was born and I no longer wanted the excitement. Also, someone had to stay at home with Matthew and Pete was not very reliable when it came to this. He was having a ball. We lived parallel lives and Matthew and I waited many times for Pete to appear but something always turned up to grab his attention. His excuse would be that the arrangement hadn't been firm. I was very unhappy, increasingly so, but I didn't make a noise about it because I didn't want Matthew to experience domestic tension. I had expected Pete to leave me. He was so part time that we'd been split up for several weeks and Matthew hadn't noticed. I had to tell him that daddy didn't live here any more. I suppose I had realised things had to change when I went on holiday and found that I didn't want to go home. What I really experienced was the feeling that I didn't want to go home to Pete. People have asked me why I put up with this unsatisfactory life for so long. Even in happier times I often found myself in a role I didn't always enjoy – ferrying partying people about, for example. I would be the sober sensible one feeling excluded and fed up.

The reason I did put up with things was because of a secret vow I had made when I was nineteen. Pete's paternal grandmother looked after him when his mother was ill. They were very close. Once when we were on holiday in Cornwall, driving about in the car, I became aware of an impression – it wasn't an image – it was an impression of Pete's grandmother standing totally upright: younger and not bent as she was in old age. "You look well," I said to her silently. "Yes. I'm dead," she said. I wasn't sure what to do about this. I didn't want to upset Pete unnecessarily; I didn't want him to think I was mad. I found that I had promised his grandmother I would look after him. This happened on the middle Friday of our two week holiday. When we arrived back we found that

Pete's grandmother had died around the time I 'saw' her. After that I had a strong loyalty towards Pete because of the promise. But I am naturally a loyal person, sometimes to a silly extent. Much later, when Pete was going through a particularly bad time after he had split up with Lynn, I felt guilty.

I did have an exciting time with Pete though I think I should have ended the marriage earlier. It would have been better for both of us. I don't find it emotionally draining to talk about him. I really couldn't give a damn – it's too long ago. I've sorted things in my own head and I can live with them ok. I should have talked more to him about how I felt. I have been happier since he left. I had developed independence and I can't imagine wanting to do any more of all that again. I can't imagine sharing my space with anyone else. My mother says I should be married to a merchant seaman!

I have kept in touch with Pete over the years. He's Matthew's father and I always liked Pete's family. The Billingtons were just like my own family and I have gone to their funerals. At our wedding the two families really got on and at one point they were queuing up for the piano-playing. I play and so does Matthew.

Linda Johnson. (3)

Things remained unspoken until it was too late in another long-term relationship. I more or less lived with the girl in question until one day I arrived home for tea and found that she had ironed and folded my clothes. Me and the dog (whom she adored) were both sent packing. She claimed she wanted to spread her wings; I had perceived no sign of this. All our friends were astounded: they didn't think she'd have the bottle for it – we were regarded as inseparable – but everyone was wrong. I offered to marry her but she said it was too late. In retrospect I realize that a lot of this was down to me: she had always been fun to be with; I had not. I didn't realize how depressed I was after the death of Whitty and Brammer. She was a lot younger than me and if she wanted freedom she must have felt stifled by something. This split was the most hurtful of any of the broken relationships I've experienced but neither she nor I could have predicted the devastating effect it would have on me.

I hit the bottle for a while.

I knew it was important to go to new places and do new things. The most help getting over the heartbreak was Dave Evans. About this time I started giving him lessons in blues playing and I ended up sharing Dave's flat and we used to go to the pub together. I went from being a married man with a mistress to being a married man with a bachelor!

This was the time of the topless piano-playing and what I thought was a simple relationship for fun. I underestimated two things: the girl's emotional attachment to me and her dependence on alcohol. Why didn't the bottles of spirits she carried in her handbag ring alarm bells? But the relationship was a bit on-off and I was in party mode too. What alerted me to her feelings was an incident concerning my younger son. We had been invited to a high-profile birthday party – a fairly respectable affair – at which I was behaving with restraint because I was taking my son Matthew somewhere the next day. You have to make a commitment if you want to retain involvement. Miss Topless Winifred Atwell was behaving much more flamboyantly and refused to leave when I did. So I left her at the party. According to friends she ended up in some kind of a frolic involving Johnson's Baby Oil. The humorous reference is obvious. She was furious with me because my priority was Matthew, not her fun and because I didn't contact her. The relationship did not recover although she kept in touch.

This beautiful, vivacious woman died of alcoholism aged thirty-four. Three months after her death her parents returned the guitar I gave her as an eighteenth birthday present when her life seemed full of opportunities. It looked sad in its case. I have no photographs and I don't know where her remains are. The piano now plays in a minor key. But we had a dynamite time.

Would things have been any different if I had been more aware? I doubt it. At the end of the day I wouldn't have stayed with anybody for any length of time at that period.

I had a chance relationship with another girl who kept gin and vodka in her handbag but she did a detox and then opened a temperance hotel on the North Wales coast. I don't think I'll be visiting!

My horse-riding girlfriend with whom I spent five years was a complicated mixture of fun and trouble. I admired her independent spirit: she drove a Bedford CF utility wagon and survived in a career dominated by men. We had some tremendously good times together but the relationship began to deteriorate. She had some strange, boring men friends and started seeing a counsellor. I don't know if this was the cause or effect of the downturn in things between us. Wanting her freedom, she took the hippie route: counting thistles in fields in search of something. She grew away from me and it became hellish to live with her. As far as I was concerned, this seemed to come out of the blue. Again! She said she was emotionally upset – it was like a breakdown – and became inappropriately attached to her counsellor. We would part and I would stay at the shop but then she would turn up at the shop. The emotional fallout was extremely debilitating and I ended up going to live there permanently. Literally. John Darlington and his girlfriend occupied the upstairs flat so I had to sleep behind the shop counter. But it wasn't long before my strange, estranged girlfriend was knocking at the door again, seeking refuge from a random addict with whom she had become involved. So some nights we both slept on the shop floor until I could take no more of the see-saw life I was living. I had tried to retrieve the relationship and failed.

As before, it was a bachelor friend who pulled me out of despair. I took myself off on an uncomplicated boat trip with Des which clarified things and sorted my head out. When I returned I took possession of my territory: I gave the tenants notice to quit, took a bath in my own bathroom and felt lighter. Des moved in, heralding two years of relative harmony. Shortly after this sea-change my girlfriend left for Ireland.

In retrospect I realize that she had brought a lot of baggage to our relationship. I suspect, from things she said, that there had been some past sexual abuse and that she was ripe for unsuitable relationships of one kind or another. Why didn't she just stick to horse-riding with me? So many of my girlfriends opted for a deterioration in emotional stability. One married an alcoholic after rapidly spiralling down from one unsatisfactory relationship to another; someone else ended up in an abusive situation in Holland; a third one had to flee from a heroin addict and some unpleasant publicity. There must be some reason they left the relative stability I provided. Perhaps it was boring.

Soft spot isn't the right phrase for how I've felt about Zoe. She's my friend and my wife. She shares some of the qualities of my other partners but there are important differences that gave the relationship its durability.

Zoe is a socially and sexually confident woman. She's so photogenic! There are some stunning portraits of her: Zoe is a natural when it comes to posing for the camera, having the professional's poise and a strong sense of the effect she is aiming for. Her first husband was an artist and she had been brought up with a liberal attitude towards erotic art. Photographs I took of Zoe in her fifties compare favourably with the photos of previous partners in their twenties. I remember with pleasure an occasion when she dressed in basque and suspenders to my World War II fighter pilot outfit. Arriving back at Zoe's flat she said, referring to her basque, "You can take it off if you want." It's one of my biggest regrets that I didn't but it was early on in our relationship and I couldn't quite believe it was happening again.

I have thought about how Zoe fits into the pattern of my relationships with women. She has the sexual confidence, translucent skin, slim body and nice breasts that I'm always drawn to but she doesn't have the self-destructive tendencies some of my girlfriends have had. She has enormous optimism and enthusiasm for life – her father described her well: "She's like a sponge; you can't hold her down," he used to say. Zoe is her own person although there have been times with other partners when she has had to fight for this. I haven't had to encourage her to do and be as she wishes. She knows what she wants and where she's going and although she will take risks she has boundless confidence that she can survive. As a mother and grandmother she is a matriarch who knows where life's priorities are. She just does it; I support it; she reciprocates. Many of my girlfriends have been more timid and hesitant. I applaud the fact that she has a life separate from mine, that she is successful and publicly confident in her work for Tanzed – a charity that supports primary education in Tanzania – and is able to face the rigours of third world living. I can't.

I had lived in a very oppressive relationship and was used to fighting like a fiend to do what I wanted. When Pete and I got together again we were both surviving failed relationships and understandably concerned about entering a new one. But it was very comfortable. There was a coincidence of objects we both brought to the relationship which made things seem auspiciously compatible: small leather suitcases, old-fashioned coal-scuttles, wind-up gramophones and the same school photograph with both of us on. We knew everything about one another; there were no skeletons. When we were deciding what to do about our relationship it was established that we would both do the things we wanted to do. I have a caravan in Wales, for example; I like to go to Tanzania with my charity work. Pete has just restarted trial biking; I supported his going to Georgia. The relationship wouldn't work if we didn't have this mutual freedom. If I stayed long enough in Tanzania he'd come and visit me, even though he didn't enjoy it that much.

Zoe Johnson. (4)

Zoe will confront my tendency to be depressive, and to be dejected if things are not going well. I have always needed a safety net and she challenges this because she believes it gets in the way of living spontaneously.

I think Pete needs to find a way to keep his assets without being trapped by them.

Zoe Johnson. (5)

In this respect she is a hippie, a gypsy, and I don't quite go along with this. Zoe does have a safety net: she has mine. I don't know whether she needs it though. I've a feeling that Zoe would survive no matter what.

Zoe is curious and sexually aware and like the other women in my life she has enjoyed wearing alluring clothes. I have some photographs of her that I took at her Nantwich flat which show she is aware of her attractiveness – a combination of temptress and schoolgirl. She has been happy to initiate sexual behaviour irrespective of circumstances: in spite of the shock of my first sexual encounter, a public glimpse of pubic hair no longer frightens me!

Yet it took Zoe and I thirty-odd years to get together as a couple, though we had been friends since the age of nine at primary school. This is how it happened. Whilst performing at The Wheatsheaf in Stoke in the early Nineties, I met Zoe again. Throughout the years we had remained good friends even though we were with other partners. It was not a chance encounter; Zoe had heard I was playing there and went to see me.

A few meetings later Zoe invited me back to her flat for coffee, "no strings attached". Not a chance. Part way through the evening when Zoe had left the room, I leapt into her bed and in true rock'n'roll fashion didn't leave it for several days. We lived in Zoe's Nantwich flat together and got married four years later. Then we lived partly in the flat above the shop and partly on our canal boat. Nowadays we have a new boat on which we live permanently.

I have learnt that I can be naïve and blind when it comes to the complexities of relationships, especially with women and at times I must seem arrogant but I am basically quite a shy, reserved person who has learnt to be straightforward by being a performer. Although I have sought fun this didn't mean I was superficial. I have felt grief when relationships have ended; I need companionship and I fear loneliness. Sexual relationships have sustained me; they've also scarred me. With Zoe things never go unsaid and I have found some balance. Our marriage works because we were first friends.

Sustaining Music

Where Else Will It Be Represented?

Given that music has been at the core of my life and being, I feel depressed about the status of the country blues and my position as its champion. I knowingly chose a *genre* with a limited following, with no regrets because it certainly helped me, and you'd think I'd be used to it by now but what do you make of an event advertised as the "Nantwich Jazz Blues & Music Festival"? (6) Have jazz and blues been re-categorised as something other than music?

It doesn't surprise me though. Playing authentic country blues for which I have been praised and congratulated hasn't earned me the right to a suitable venue in this festival or a commensurate fee. Now I know I'm not a mediocre musician so why when festivals promoting jazz and blues come round am I only offered a pub venue? I play blues. Where else will it be represented for fuck's sake?

Is this about style over substance? Is this about success being measured in terms of wealth and fame? Why, as a well-known acoustic musician was I not invited to the recent local acoustic festival? Most of those performing had made their achievements through pop music and then transferred it to the acoustic guitar. So I can only conclude that this acoustic pop is preferred to music I've interpreted from the acoustic tradition of early blues.

I've also encountered some professional jealousy. Some people thought I made the Georgia trips up and that I'd done the recording at home. If only.

I made choices I don't regret and I have to accept the consequences – it isn't this I'm ranting about. I suppose I've been naively surprised by the narrow acceptance of mediocrity and the pervasive power of commercialism.

Rejected Flautist

There's certainly a lot of narrow-mindedness in musical circles. Like all the instruments I own or have owned, the lap steel awakens a musical memory. In 1991 a friend invited me to a bluegrass club in Chester. On arrival I was confronted with a very big notice: ONLY FLAT BACK MANDOLINS AND SLIDE GUITAR. MUST BE PLAYED FLAT ON THE KNEE. I had my wooden National with me and dutifully conformed to the club's musical rules when I played along and all went well.

Towards the end of the evening a couple of students arrived; one asked if he could play his flute. His request was denied. I met up with them at the bar and it appeared that the flautist was just back from Ireland where he had been playing with James Galway. I said he could play with me if he wanted. Even allowing for the fact that musicians often tell lies I was impressed when he didn't even ask me what key we would be using. I did "Stormy Weather" as a blues song with the student accompanying me. Afterwards I was asked not to attend the club again. My musical heresy had me ejected from the bluegrass fraternity but I didn't care. You have to rebel against musical fascism, especially when such inflexibility would deny an audience the pleasure of hearing two good musicians playing together. There was no nastiness, though.

I knew that this would be the consequence. There is a narrowness in bluegrass music that isn't present in jazz and blues. I can appreciate it's very clever but it never seems very deep – it seems mechanical. I don't like that pedantic monotonous beat through the whole tune; bluegrass music doesn't swing and this is its deficiency. Like heavy metal, it's a question of who can fit the most notes in.

I just don't like big notices with the word MUST in them.

Is It Because I is White?

I'm aware that a white boy playing the blues is anomalous. I'm a highly educated white westerner born into the privileges of the post-war welfare state. We have allotments but we don't go in for much sharecropping in Crewe. I haven't had a life of rural poverty and oppression, with no education and very few prospects. I haven't been hungry; I haven't jumped on freight trains; I haven't been treated as a second-class citizen. Though things get a bit rough in Crewe on a Friday night I haven't feared the lynch mob or the nocturnal drive-by shooting. The musicians who were my role models lived in a totally different world and that is why it amazes me that the path of a Crewe lad with a racing bike crossed the path of a man from a Third World shack in Tennessee who went on tour carrying a cardboard suitcase.

I have two main points to make. Being white is bound to have an effect but I play the blues as well as I can, with as much authenticity as I can. It's all about communicating our common humanity. Feeling has no colour. Secondly I think I have done a good job as a bridge between the country blues and a white audience. Perhaps I have made it more accessible – without watering it down – than a black performer could.

But my reservations about being white have prevented me from composing any music with lyrics, though people have remarked on the vivid quality of descriptions in my Georgia journal. Any lyrics I attempted seemed to lack authenticity; it didn't feel right; that's why compositions such as "Blues In A", "Just Jazz", "Magnolia And Honeysuckle", "Minor

Chill" and "Deaf Jake's Blag" are essentially instrumental doodles. Perhaps I needed the detachment of expressing my emotions through the words of others rather than my own.

I've been asked where I would place myself in relation to the history of music. I'm a folk musician: part of the country blues oral tradition – a tradition that changed and evolved with each new interpretation of the songs that were held in common.

I've never considered myself to be a great guitar player: I'm a singer, an entertainer, a communicator. Woody Guthrie and Bob Dylan are not good musicians but the eloquence of their words cancels this out. I love their stories even though I don't necessarily like their voices or musicianship. Dylan's lyrics are poetry; Guthrie makes a complex political story accessible to an ordinary person.

It was a long time before I accepted my own skills as a musician; I didn't feel worthy of even carrying the guitar cases of my musical heroes. And I still don't. This gives me the impetus to practise and practise and practise. My career has been forty-five years of musical hard graft and ten minutes of musical luck. You can continue to learn by changing your style but you never get past a certain point. I wouldn't want to change the style; I need help to take it further. I do pick up the odd chord or note from other people – they might be a student or someone not very good at all but you have to be open and humble to spot the opportunity to learn.

Sonata In E And Other Compliments

External appraisal of your musicianship can give some measure of your musical standing in spite of personal doubts.

When I was thirty, John Aaron – a highly regarded classical musician – rated me enough to approach me to do some concerts, the idea being that different aspects of guitar music would be displayed in classical and blues. I recall the incongruity in the programme: on the one hand, "Sonata In E" and on the other hand, "Down 'n' Out Blues" and so on. The first concert in Chester was well attended by guitar freaks and it went well. By the second concert in Newcastle-under-Lyme I have more confidence: I'm running in the race. John had also changed the running order so that he ended the gig whereas I had ended the first gig and that had worked. The second running order did not work: John could not hack the last spot. In retrospect changing the order was a crucial mistake.

Mixing the musical *genres* was innovative and courageous but although I enjoyed the experience and liked playing in decent venues I feel it didn't quite work. The small, select audience was a bit biased in my favour. Perhaps the musical combination was too radical for most tastes. We continued to visit each other's houses and play music together though.

My father-in-law Donald Purcell gave lessons on his grand piano in the shop when it was closed in the evenings. Our fascinating musical conversations began because this classical pianist loved my music. He could appreciate the subtle musical differences made possible by picking rather than strumming a guitar: we both spoke the same musical language. Donald said Beethoven changed music more radically than anyone else. I recorded him playing Beethoven's "Passionata". He was about seventy-six and although he apologized for the odd mistake, the dexterity still there in age gave me the optimism to carry on playing. I took Donald to the Victoria Hall, Stoke, to hear Elgar. What he kept from me, as a surprise, was the fact that Yehudi Menuhin would be conducting.

I know very little about classical music but these experiences with my father-in-law encouraged my latent interest in it. I had attended a Beethoven concert in Manchester in the Sixties. What with the choir and the orchestra, it was louder than a rock concert. The next minute you could hear a pin drop. "Will the audience refrain from coughing and sneezing, thus creating a pianissimo?" it said on the programme. If you listen to Beethoven with a fresh ear it's a very simple melody line expanded by complex harmonies and different registers: instruments like piccolos having a high register whilst the cello has a low register. It takes the mind to other places, like the time Tony Hatch made Des listen for the quarter tones.

Sometimes people ask me if I am a "musician's musician" and the answer is a conditional yes: I can also turn on a party when I want to.

Non-musicians have also rated me enough to try to further my career. Graham Roberts is a dynamic person who has lived all over the world. He wrote to the BBC about me and gave us a signed David Shepherd print for Zoe's work for Tanzed. I was very touched by his appraisal of me.

Lurking in South Cheshire is a well-kept secret, for at 80 Edleston Road is a shop called Custom Amplification which, apart from selling amplifiers, has its walls lined with electric and acoustic guitars including Gibson, Dobro, National – wood and steel bodied, 12 string, etc. Presiding over this Aladdin's cave is a 51 years old bearded guru called Pete "Snakey Jake" Johnson – a South Cheshire gentleman, full of character. He is also the best British country blues guitarist I have heard – he plays bottleneck/resonator as well as straight steel acoustic. Whilst there are many accomplished blues players in Britain, Pete has that rare quality that Abdullah Ibrahim always looks for: "you can hear the 'cry' in his voice".

I think that Pete would make a great guest on either Paul Jones' Thursday show or Bob Harris' Saturday show, both playing and reminiscing about the old American bluesmen that he has met – these include Sleepy John Estes, Jimmy Witherspoon, Mississippi Fred McDowell, Roosevelt Sykes. Sister Rosetta Tharpe and John Lee Hooker (some of the old bluesmen used to stop over in Crewe). (7)

I also appreciated John Darlington's tribute.

Pete Johnson has been the fulcrum for music in the area. I remember him saying, "I'm not looking for a piece of immortality; I'm not looking to educate people. All I want is for you guys to take my music to other places and make it your own". He had more influence on any musician around here than any pop star. Pete Johnson washed over you gently and with the force of the sea. Without being forceful, he left an impression. For everything he hasn't done there's stuff he has done. People are playing Pete Johnson's music all over the world – people who haven't even heard the originals. (8)

Given our diverse musical backgrounds it's hard to believe that Andy Boote and I found common ground.

I'm unimpressed by the cold virtuoso performance. There's an academic approach: almost over-the-top virtuosity. Speed is OK but you need heart. I like speed but it must be melodic. In this, I agree with Pete's view of musical performance: heart is all. Pete was once asked to play Hendrix's Purple Haze. He got some of the notes wrong, but he got the essence of Hendrix.

So, the friendship between me and Pete Johnson is based on a mutual passion for certain kinds of music, a respect for one another's specific musical knowledge and a shared belief that a musician must play from the heart. Friendship with Pete Johnson increased my admiration for him. God this man has got passion!

Andy Boote. (9)

I like that country blues and that South Side Muddy Waters stuff. I don't think blues should be polite. It might be about feeling good about feeling bad and it might be about swagger and in your face. I do rate Pete Johnson very highly. I'd always turn out to hear him play that BK Turner number: he does a great, great thing.

Ade White. (10)

A couple of years ago I had a phone call from Ray Bernard who lives in Alsager and collects, buys, sells and mends instruments. His original interest was in banjos and that is what brought him into contact with me because I used to collect them. Ray is the country's leading authority on the ukulele, playing both pop and classical. A lifetime's hobby. He was a friend of George Harrison – the connection being their common passion for the ukulele. Ray Bernard was ringing to ask me for some advice about a ukulele with which he was having a problem. I was a bit surprised.

So, although I am a white musician I have established some credentials for my claim to be taken seriously as a bluesman and made a sustained effort to uphold the importance of the country blues.

Who And Where And What?

When I look at the local live music scene I feel quite depressed both for the future of country blues and for music generally. I suppose I'm a grumpy old man but I'm disappointed by the current generation of young musicians, partly because they don't seem to have any fight in them. You wouldn't catch them balancing their amp on their bike or playing a home-made guitar! I started my first band at the age of thirteen on the proceeds of part time jobs, playing mainly for school functions and in village halls before graduating to youth clubs and then pubs. Early rock 'n' roll music – three chords and you're the main guitarist – spelt sophistication to an enthusiastic youthful audience; all you needed then was someone with a bass guitar and then someone who could afford a drum kit. Then, if you could get beyond the falling out, you were on your way.

My band is starting up. We're waiting for our drummer to get a drum kit. My best friend asked me to be in it – he came up with the name, Omblivious. The name must have come into his head. There was another band he was in called Inslave but it fell apart because everyone kept moving places – falling out. The bass guitarist decided he wanted to be the guitarist; the guitarist wanted to be the drummer. And they weren't very good. I wasn't part of that.

Sam Molony. (11)

I entered the pub scene already fairly confident, competent and with an established fanbase. At the same time I was innovating: reinterpreting the music, mastering slide guitar, finger picking blues and experimenting with jazz-inspired music. I owned a van, three amps and various instruments before I was twenty and I would soon buy my own house. And throughout all this I had fought my father's opposition.

I think it does you good to have to fight for something. The passion to circumvent all obstacles has to be there. I haven't observed a similar drive in the current lot. I'm unimpressed by the "Me" generation funded by indulgent parental credit – they're soft, feeble and too old. They should be thirteen not twenty. Twenty is too old! They just haven't got the balls and I'm not saying any of this scornfully – more in a resigned way. Young people coming up don't have the attitude to succeed. It doesn't bode well if your parents pay for your equipment and then you refuse even to carry it out to the car, does it?

As an established musician and source of all amps I used to enjoy the company of people younger than myself. An experienced musician has useful knowledge for an aspiring musician. As the Skunk Band changed and evolved it was the young musicians who helped keep it vibrant. But the up and coming musicians no longer up and come and this saddens me. Perhaps this generation is more concerned with the paraphernalia of DJing or with the seductive power of electronic music. People buy their instruments on eBay these days; I can't understand this – I would want to handle the instrument; I would want to talk about it in a music shop with someone who knew about it.

There are still a few lads who want the music passionately – of course there are – but far fewer than I remember.

I'd never heard of the blues guitar and then the electric guitar introduced me to the blues. I wanted to hear more of it. One of my friends was into Hendrix – that introduced me to the blues, really.

I would always choose electric guitar over everything, really. It's just the feeling; it gives you a really good feeling. It's just a way of expressing yourself; it's a way of getting your noise out and your noise is only something you know, and only you can express it in your way.

Dec Higgins. (12)

I'm into blues but I started off into heavy metal, then acoustic, jazz and swing: Hendrix, Stevie Ray Vaughan, Rory Gallagher, Tommy Emmanuel, Frank Sinatra and Metallica still. I find Nirvana depressing. I think you grow out of it. You think the swearing's cool at that age then you learn music isn't just that. It's about good music.

Our band, The Riffs, plays blues. We have written blues-inspired and acoustic songs. We try to bring in keyboard, harmonica and percussion. I'm looking for a musical career. Dec wants to be a dentist who plays guitar.

Josh Bailey. (13)

To be fair, the venue situation is against them. Kids don't go to youth clubs to play their music so where's the audience coming from? The pub scene is now largely dominated by old lags playing Sixties, Seventies and (some) Eighties music, proficiently and as well as the original artists. Essentially it's a closed shop. No publican is going to risk putting on something new when his customers expect the familiar bands. How can young innovative musicians compete against musical conservatism and the reign of the cover band?

And one by one the pubs are closing down!

Synchronised Holidays

At one time you could do a gig every night because there were so many working men's clubs. So many have closed over the years that now you're lucky to get two gigs a month. In the Sixties and Seventies a band could make £100 a night. Bands were so much in demand that you had to tell the agents in advance when you were going on holiday – and the whole band had to go at the same time! These days a soloist can only get £80. I got £30 the other night: not enough to cover drinks and petrol. Now pubs are closing one by one.

Phil Doody. (14)

Though it seems you can't entirely keep the music down.

As far as the local music scene goes, although The Limelight has closed – it took a dive when Ray & Karen Bispham left – in one way it's been good for the local pubs such as The Imp, The Brunswick, The Express, The Box, as they have bands on every week. It seems to be going well for them, when you hear how many pubs are closing. The Box is good for original material / young bands. There is a very good music scene in Crewe as there always has been, since I came to Crewe in the mid Eighties – then it was all happening at the Leisure Club in Edleston Road.

Andy Smith. (15)

Style And Substance

There's a guitar in the shop that somebody's ruined by sticking three dice on it. I can't get them off and anyway someone will like them. They won't depress the price like they depress me. When I look in the accessories catalogues I despair – am I going to start stocking pink knobs? I'm so far out of touch that what I would call bits of plastic are called Demon Plectrums worn as a fashion statement round your neck.

It's symptomatic of a general trivialization, a substitution of style for substance. We've gone through the good, creative times and now everything is on a decadent slide. Look at what has become of the musical: we had Gershwin and Rogers and Hammerstein – now we've got Lloyd Webber.

I've been looking at Blueridge Guitars in the Gremlin catalogue. They're getting a good write-up but the Historic Series has cutaway. As far as I know cutaway isn't historic. There's also some brash abalone work on the machine heads. That isn't historic either. When it was done it was done by hand and all over. Blueridge has established itself as the leading guitar brand in the US after Martin and Taylor. Why is it offering tradition but not following it?

The hype of the guitar world offers much more than a musical instrument: it offers technology and adventure, status and power, limitless variety, a wide price range and sensuous experiences. Like the food in some restaurants, guitars are described as if they will guarantee an orgasm. Directed at young people, they offer a fantasy far removed from the reality of hard work and continual practice. But today's young people can afford them – or their parents can. And I'm not saying that style and fantasy and fun have no place in musical performance; of course it does – the Skunk Band demonstrated that – so I don't want to be too scathing about this. Owning a beautiful object is important and everyone has a different idea of beauty.

My guitar is a BC Rich Beast. It's black and white and it has two spikes going up like horns at the top and one big spike on the left at the bottom and a smaller one on the right. It's off a website from a guitar shop in Surrey.

I just saw it. It looked really nice. Straight away it was the one I wanted. When I first picked it up I just felt surprised that I had it because it was such a nice guitar. It's got sharp notes; it's really nice to play.

It cost £240 including an amp and a limited edition BC Rich plectrum and a guitar strap. With it I also bought a stand because with such points to a guitar you need a stand because they might get chipped.

Sam Molony. (16)

It's great to have abundance of choice. There was so little in the Fifties and early Sixties, it was expensive and had to be ordered. You had to wait! Nowadays guitars are abundant and absolutely dynamite quality for the price: a decent guitar for a hundred pounds made by the Chinese ready for you to take away.

But sometimes I just despair when it's nothing but *faux* leopard skin guitar straps and guitars with annoying embellishments. Stylistic razzmatazz can't replace musical substance.

I was recently shocked that Radio Four pundits had narrowed down the field of 'great' guitarists to two: Clapton and Hendrix! I was surprised by the narrowness and ignorance of the discussion. One panellist had selected Jimi's "Red House" as his best. This is nonsense. It's his worst track: twelve bar blues in the easiest key. Trite with no surprises. What is this obsession with the most popular?

Discussion about style over substance would have to include the tribute band. A tribute band allows time to stand still at the point when the group in question was at its height. The popular songs are reproduced as faithfully as possible without deviation and it has to be admitted that some tribute bands are very good and do their work with respect, paralleling their originals without even waiting for them to retire! Everybody covers songs but it's so deadening to slavishly copy a song without adding something of your own. But this is very popular as a swift glance at local venues will confirm. Crewe's Limelight Club was the subject of a BBC 2 *Arena* tribute to the tribute band filmed in December 2006. Free At Last, Limehouse Lizzie, Cobain, T-Rextasy, Stairway To Zeppelin, Demon, Pink Fraud, Are You Experienced, Fred Zeppelin, AB/CD and Purple Snake were all on offer.

The Australian Pink Floyd sent me tickets and a backstage pass to see them at the National Indoor Arena in Birmingham: a stunning performance. Stunning. In terms of virtuosity and theatricality it transcended the original Pink Floyd. Of course, these days the technology is more sophisticated but I liked the touches of humour reflecting the Australian theme. It's much more than a tribute band and anyone who loves this style of music would have been transported to another world. APF are now so popular they're considering assembling an Australian Pink Floyd Two with another set of musicians. It was good to see Gareth Darlington – he's the sound man – and Damien Darlington (guitar, vocals, keyboard) backstage, though I must say the post-gig socialising was sober compared to my old Jack Daniels days.

Pink Floyd and the Australian Pink Floyd parallel one another. They're both still communicating something across the generations; we're going to see them and our sons and daughters are going to see them as well. The two bands work together: Pink Floyd have sanctioned what the Australian Pink Floyd does and APF have played at Pink Floyd's parties. They have the Pink Floyd pig and some of the Pink Floyd road crew working with them but they are also acclaimed in their own right – APF did two nights at the Royal Albert Hall.

A mere tribute band can't continue to communicate like this; there has to be true feeling. Pink Floyd have asked APF to lay off a few high profile venues to give them a chance! So it's all good-humoured and has life in it.

Substance.

Talking Of Age

In terms of my musical prospects things are not looking too good. Through my damaged hands there's a physical impairment to my performance and a psychological issue regarding confidence. I'm never going to be able to say I'm too old to play the blues; lack of eyesight, lack of digits, lack of sobriety, lack of an instrument, lack of liberty, lack of sanity has never been an excuse for any of the old men of blues. But I've had to come to terms with the fact that my right hand probably won't stand up to sustained playing though it is healing slowly. I'm back doing a few gigs with Des: it's gentle and it's fun. I also went solo at Square One recently. I was pleased with my performance that was partly fuelled by anger at some unjustified criticism.

Talking of age, as well as the epidemic of tribute bands there's been a recent trend for the resurrection of famous groups from the Sixties or Seventies – some look as if they've come from beyond the grave. "Codger Rock" or "Zimmer Frame Rock" has been very successful and what emerges is that fans want to remember their favourite groups exactly as they were. One of the claims regarding Jimmy Page of Led Zeppelin was that he had not diminished: he was exactly the same as he ever was. At a fairly recent Bob Dylan gig a fan – domed head and a long straggly curtain of hair – was beside himself because Dylan had changed his early songs out of all recognition. The fan couldn't tolerate the change; he wanted things as he remembered them. I'm with Dylan.

Heavy Metal is back: I saw Whitesnake – still good, David Coverdale – originally with Deep Purple, a band called The Answer – got the essence of the music – not just covers – bang on. It's because their parents are into it. My lad Jordan is a brilliant guitarist. He plays Seventies rock; he's never listened to anything else.

Wayne Davies (Slim). (17)

Always Something New To Learn

There are positives to counterbalance the down sides. A musician always has something new to learn. Why be repetitive? Complacency is the enemy. During the summer of 2006 I spent some time learning new chords with Andy Boote. I felt enthusiastic. I'm a non-musician; I have to relate everything back to a keyboard because that's the instrument I did have formal training in. But when someone presents you with a jazz turnaround that can be repeated up the neck as you can with barre chords, then it opens up a whole new field of Django Reinhardt /Charlie Christian style music. They evolved it in the first place so that they could play guitar with jazz ensembles and change key easily by using the chords in different positions on the neck, rather than changing chord shapes. Changing the finger configuration rather than moving the hand up and down the neck enhanced the speed of playing.

It led me to think about Lonnie Johnson and Scrapper Blackwell and the jazz influence in their blues – Leroy Carr obviously being a link – and I decided I wanted to extend my playing by learning Andy's jazz and rockabilly chords, which in time I'll be able to embellish by finger-style playing. Hopefully it'll enable me to play more complex blues as well as doing this thing with Andy on the jazz side.

I Saw The Line From Tampa Red

I made an important discovery about the provenance of jazz: I saw the line from Tampa Red – the pioneers of jazz were there in the blues men. I started talking to Pete Johnson about this – common ground had opened up through my interest in jazz and historical musical development generally which we both shared. I can easily transcribe music through listening to it and Pete asked me to do the introduction to "Shine". I listened to the whole number and made another important discovery: it had a jazz chord sequence; it was not straight twelve bar blues. I realized that I, in my own music, had been playing rock 'n' roll in a jazz style. Eight chords in it rather than three. The chord sequence moves out of key; jazz goes out of the key centre. Jazz players negotiate key changes. I love that. The twelve bar blues is a very simple structure over which to improvise.

On the strength of this musical understanding of the jazz sequences in "Shine" and another number Pete Whittingham had played in which I praised his brilliance, the friendship between Pete and I was finally forged. Studying Pete Whit's improvisational musicianship led me, via Charlie Christian, further along the jazz path and Pete Johnson was able to provide another pioneer: Scrapper Blackwell. My appreciation of jazz guitar continued and continues to grow.

Andy Boote. **(18)**

So – I'm still keeping faith with the music I first heard when I was thirteen. It has sustained me and I hope I have done what I can to sustain it.

Non-sustaining Opiate

The thing that hasn't sustained me is religious belief.

Being Human

But not believing I'll be rewarded or punished after death doesn't mean I've lived without values nor have I allowed my hedonism to dominate.

I think most of the Ten Commandments are sound but I don't want to associate this with religion. I'm a humanist and I've been sustained by friendship and by my music and by challenging bullying in all its forms. I've helped people in a musical sense and in an economic sense; although I can be physically threatening I've tried only to use violence in self-defence or in defending others, or I've deflected it into objects to make my point. It's true I've done some wheeling and dealing that was a bit on the edge and some sexual philandering, and then there's some illegal substances to be taken into account but on the whole I sleep at night. I hold the conviction that human life has worth and that you should react in a simple way to the needs of others. At a party once a woman came and asked me to dance. "Put your hand right on my arse," she said. Afterwards she said, "My mother died; that's the best I've felt since."

As far as I'm concerned we're just animals that evolved into the human race – and into a mess. We have the capacity to get ourselves out of the mess; we don't need God: we just have to stop being so greedy. The science I've read seems more logical than any religion – no matter which religion. In more frivolous moments my rational mind has wondered about daft things like how would there be room for everybody in heaven and could I play a guitar instead of a harp. On an emotional level I also think I've had enough once round; I don't want there to be any more! And if I'm wrong and I do meet God, I'm going to headbutt him for getting so much wrong!

Religion

It's easy to see why religions evolved though. The human mind can't accept that at death the consciousness stops and that's it. It can't accept the unfairness that involves some people having long happy lives and others having short tortured lives. It offends our sense of fair play! Religion illustrates man's inability to face his own stopping. It gives a better ending to the story, as long as you're good. The old spirituals gave comfort to people with wretched lives, promising a better life after death. Religion: "the opiate of the people" according to Marx, made the unacceptable acceptable.

I believe heaven and hell is what you leave behind, not what you aspire to. It's something to do with how you feel at your demise. With your last breath your conscience is what you die with. If you have led a horrible life you know and perhaps regret that in the moment of dying. Other people inherit your little footprint: heaven, hell, a bit of both, some shared laughter, some recognition, some musical togetherness. If you've spent your life trying to do your best there will be fewer regrets. Besides, it's easier to be nice to people but the evidence for religion encouraging this is not convincing.

None of my experiences of religion have done anything to convince me. Each religion believes it has the correct world view, the only way to live your life. To me all religions are clubs and I don't like clubs. If there is anything at the end of the day, who's to say which club is right? In my view a man from Papua New Guinea, who has a collection of skulls – people he's eaten out of respect and because of his beliefs – has as much right to heaven as anyone else, if God is magnanimous. Differing beliefs have led to horrific practices such as witch-hunting, torture, and wars – all with 'god on our side'. Religion has too many conflicts about a similar story and people are prepared to die – and kill – for their own version.

I was brought up in a family with strong religious beliefs – though never pressurised to sign up – so I was able to observe closely the effects on people's lives of believing in an afterlife. I was neither tempted by my father's self-blaming puritanical faith nor my mother's cheerful belief that we would all meet again in heaven. Anticipating this celestial reunion made my mother happy and confident in spite of her difficulties and able to die with a joyful conviction. On the other hand, my father felt God had dealt him a bum card and didn't believe he deserved to go to heaven. His experiences must have tested his belief in a compassionate god. He was extremely poor and fatherless in his childhood; he felt disappointed with himself: a conscientious objector who went in the army and although his war experiences were hardly mentioned at home, I know he had the harrowing job of liberating concentration camps. When my mother became an invalid and he himself faced an early death from cancer, his faith and sense of justice were further tried. The awfulness of his experiences communicated itself to me and I still carry it around. His death has affected me in a different way than that of my mother. She was positive and accepting and although I was sad I didn't feel that her life had been lacking in joy and hope. I wasn't sad for her; I was sad for me. But I absorbed my father's suffering and it's part of me. I still suffer in a very raw, unresolved way because of the tragedies of my father's life.

Contemplating Mortality

For some people the contemplation of their own death is debilitating. People get scared and make every effort to prolong their lifespan through careful diet and exercise and medical checks; others take the escapist route into drink or drugs or the pursuit of experiences. From early on I've had plenty of opportunity to look at death, including my own. I'm not afraid of coming to a full stop – dying – though apprehensive about the way it happens. Having spent my life being able to rely on my mind and body doing what I wanted them to do I would certainly fear being dependent. I'd only cope with that for a short time then I'd die. I'd just decide and die: while I'd got the strength I'd take a bottle of whisky with aspirin. I'd have a pact with Des, whichever one of us went first. What better way to go than getting drunk with your best mate?

In spite of my atheism people have found something spiritual in me and have tried to involve me in spiritual matters. A guitarist friend, whose wife is a spiritualist and who is into Transcendental Meditation, wanted me to meet his guru – an Indian man. I never did. He said something quite strange to me:

"I'd like to know how you've done it."

"Done what?"

"Achieved karma without meditating."

The way I've explained this – and I presume he meant I had some inner calm and acceptance – is that music sustains me in the same way that religion sustains others. When my mother died it was my music that helped me – not pious words. Music took her place.

Anyway, I went to a spiritualist church three or four years after my mother died because my friends invited me – not because I had any real interest. The medium said, "There's an A and three Bs" and considering that my mother's name was Albina Betsy Boswell Billington it seemed like a link but I didn't respond. I don't believe in it though bizarre things have happened to me from time to time. Whilst I was staying with Mike Slaughter I decided to take my girlfriend for a walk. Mike told me to watch out for The Judge: a formidable individual sporting a black eyepatch and very aggressive towards anyone on his land. At one time he would have been called a "hanging judge". Anyway, we did meet him. He had an eyepatch and carried a gun. Forewarned, I spoke with him in a very civil way and there was no problem about our walk to the abbey.

Once we reached the abbey we were approached by a woman with a very posh voice and a man with a black eyepatch. This was not the same man we had already met. There must be an explanation but I don't know what it is.

Losing Control

But if my fear of death isn't great I do have other fears. I have a complicated fear of heights. I've parachuted from a plane – the waiting was awful but once I'd taken the plunge it was fine and I'd do it again – yet was debilitated by panic on a circular balcony in a basilica in Prague. If I'm on a motorbike or riding a horse I can go closer to the edge than if I were walking. Having to concentrate on riding a horse or a machine diverts my attention from the fear. Horses aren't stupid – they won't go too close, whereas if there's only me on foot, there's only me stopping me. In those circumstances I'd trust a horse more than myself.

And I'd rather go downwards, hanging on a rope into a black cave – it doesn't matter how far down – than upwards.

I don't know if death or fear of death is like this – losing control, being out of control. Whilst some control is there you feel scared of losing it; once there is no possibility of control and you're falling, then you also let go of the possibility of control – the thing you were scared to lose. Then you don't have fear. Perhaps my mother, secure of her destination, had no difficulty letting go, whereas my father clung on to life for longer than was believed possible because he was more pessimistic about his fate.

When you're asleep your rational mind is not in control and your subconscious mind – the one that deals with unresolved hopes and fears – starts playing up. In my early years my sleep was troubled by vivid dreams and sleepwalking. I used to wake up, upside down or under the bed. Once, when we were staying with my aunt in Lancaster they called the police because I was missing. I was found under the bed.

I often suffer in my dreams; themes recur. One dream I had was after a hospital trip with my parents where I had been x-rayed on my hips. I remember being in the brightly lit x-ray department. In the subsequent dream there was an amputated leg standing by the side of a bed occupied by me. I could actually see down into this leg, as if it were a tree trunk or one of those scientific models. Strangely, the amputated leg is a recurring *motif* in my life. My brother Ralph had a motorbike accident and this was a possibility for a while; years later my son Nathan also had an accident where there was a chance that amputation might be needed. I suppose a Freudian would say that the amputated leg was about fears of powerlessness and as I get older I have to face this.

My earliest nightmares bombarded me with huge, intensely colourful shapes and loud unmusical noises, all crowding in on me. As I got older the sound decreased and these coloured abstractions were translated into concrete 'realistic' situations impossible to negotiate, equally terrifying and always unresolved. There I would be: trapped in a canal lock or at the top of a mountain without any means of descent. You could say these dreams were prophetic: my life has contained heightened experiences – often dangerous or complicated or ludicrous or impossible to resolve – and loud, though not usually unpleasant sounds of one kind and another.

I want the epitaph on my gravestone to say: "That's resolved".

My survival instinct is well developed and I can be aggressive but I haven't been troubled by hating people. If there was a problem I would deal with it straight away. Incensed by the behaviour of a man who claimed to be my friend but then slept with my girlfriend, I drove my Suzuki 850 through the man's plate glass front door and, still on the motorbike, pinned him up against his kitchen units. Then I rode off again. It wasn't just about sexual loyalty, which wasn't necessarily *de rigueur* in my circles at that time. It was more to do with his friendship with me. I had bigger expectations of him. The anger I felt didn't hurt him physically; it was absorbed by the glass door. I remember kicking another door down. A bloke owed me money so he moved house. It wasn't so much the debt but the lying and deceit, the lack of straightforwardness that upset me.

There was one time when I absolutely lost it. Absolutely lost it. It was an occasion when I was challenged by two men on two fronts: a territorial matter and a question of protecting my girlfriend. My training had given me the confidence rarely to have to fight – that and my loud voice. When I was in my thirties I was still pretty handy and going out with a girl who was eighteen years old. We'd been to The Cheshire Cheese and there had been a bit of aggravation between a local musician and a couple of Hell's Angel types. The musician was scared so I said I'd escort him out to his vehicle.

When we went to leave – my girlfriend was driving – the two big blokes were in the next car, opening the passenger door to prevent her getting into the driving seat. It was humiliating for her and maddening for me. The Incredible Hulk is such a good expression of what happens to me when the adrenalin starts working. If the two blokes had read the signs in me they would have avoided a bad experience. But they didn't. (19)

The next thing I realized was that the police were trying to pull me off someone. Someone whose face I was grinding into the car park with my elbow. "There's another bastard," I said. The other bastard was unconscious. I had no recollection of hitting him. But I was covered in blood: none of it mine.

But you never forget the ethics of what unarmed combat is – it's about winning a competition within reasonable ground rules. I'm not sure how this incident squares up.

Heroes And Heroines

If you don't have a god to inspire and sustain you, you have to find human examples: heroes and heroines if you like. Hero status isn't always earned. When Eugene Van de Hoog was serving in Cyprus, he left camp illegally and was walking past a bar when a bomb exploded. Something was hurled through the air and Eugene found he was holding a child whose legs had been blown off by the explosion. He took him to hospital but he died. The child had protected Eugene from the effects of the bomb and saved his life. The anomaly was that Eugene got a medal for bravery. But he never claimed it was an act of bravery. It was a convergence of events in which one person died and the other survived. There was no intention in the moment, though Eugene did act to try to save the child in the next moment.

I have a photo depicting a shared moment with a gaunt-looking, whiskered man in a rather formal dark suit with a white shirt and tie: my friend Eugene. Eugene Van de Hoog, originally from Bournemouth, had lived in Guernsey during the German occupation and had found his way to my shop via a honeymoon walking the Arctic Circle – part of the time with his wife – a spell in the Royal Marines, a period of study at Loughborough where he became an arts graduate in filmmaking and eventually life on the Shropshire Union Canal. Here he emerged as a top-hatted entertainer who looked like something out of an old medicine show. He owned two Dobros and his talents included the seven string guitar and Appalachian mountain harp.

A mutual friend brought this legendary eccentric to the shop to see the instruments – we had similar tastes in music and we became friends; I was forty and Eugene was about ten years older. Apart from everything else, he had the distinction of having appeared on the BBC's *Six-Five Special*. He didn't become famous but had a small band of devotees. The man had style; everything he did was over the top. When I knew him he was doing the pubs up and down the Shropshire Union. His music was a cross between country and blues and he made folk music fun. He did clever parodies like a version of "Deck Of Cards" in which the subject became a bottle of Guinness. There was another song he wrote called "Banal Canal". He was resourceful and intelligent; artistic and practical. I admired his storytelling – all based on true experiences – and his practical skills. He had picked up a number of crafts on his travels, including carving whalebone! Like Whitty, he painted a tie for me. He also entertained children with puppet shows out of the side of the boat and made all his own puppets. He had such an enthusiasm for life and gigging.

Eugene Van De Hoog requests that
the assembled company participate
in a little group therapy by oscillating
their vocal chords in unison
and oscillating the aural orifice with
verve. This will assist in the restoration
of the whole. (20)

I've always admired the way my friend Eugene lived his life and approached his death; we had a very brief time together but it was fun as well as being poignant. Eugene was special; when Des shook his hand he said it was like having an electric shock. Shortly after meeting Eugene, I received a phone call from him. He had terminal cancer. Echoes of my father. I rented a boat, moored it next to Eugene and Dianne's boat at Nantwich and travelled with him, looking after him in practical ways and taking him to gigs.

Eugene had the distinction of having three wakes – two whilst he was living. The first one was upstairs at The Railway pub in Nantwich, where he performed. The second one was arranged by me at The Leisure Club in Crewe a few months later. Being a positive person, Eugene had lived longer than anticipated. I was planning on providing a solo entertainment but the shop being the shop, all rumours came back to me: Eugene had a strong sense of mischief and was planning a parallel entertainment behind my back. He was busy gathering a set of musicians together. A sort of competition formed and I was doing the same: the Skunk Band was on again. To add to the fun I actually dressed up as Eugene in this good-humoured battle of the bands and a good time ensued, with both sets of musicians playing and Eugene jiving with two beautiful girls.

Eugene eventually ended up in a hospice in Winsford. Des and I used to kidnap him and take him for a smoke at the local round the corner. We would sneak drinks into the ward for him. The time came when the nurse told us he didn't want to see anybody. I couldn't accept this. "Tell him it's Snakey Jake," I said. The reply was so frail it was almost imperceptible. "I don't want to see anybody."

And that was it. Eugene died on 29th January, 1992.

The funeral was touching: heaving with people. A testament to his impact because he had only been in the area for the year of his dying. We went drunkenly to scatter his ashes at Norbury. After this, my memory fails me. Fortunately for me, Lorraine Baker from the Boat Band somehow got me back to Nantwich and onto my boat.

Before his death, Eugene had asked me, as a promise, to look after his wife Dianne and this I did to the best of my ability. She had an 1890s boat called *Gerald* that was quite well-known in boating circles. I helped her with it and taught her the jobs conventionally done by men. She eventually bought a Dutch barge and moved to Europe.

Funerals create heightened emotion: not only sadness but also anger and laughter. Although I won't actually be around for it, when asked about songs for my funeral, "Don't Get Around Much Anymore" by Louis Armstrong comes to mind! I'd want Matthew to do something about the terrible sound system at the crematorium as well. There's always plenty of scope for gallows humour at funerals. A chemist in Nantwich who used to play the saxophone left a tape to be played at the crematorium. It was "Smoke Gets In Your Eyes"! Mick Shenton told me about it because he helped the widow with the funeral arrangements.

Plum died of a heart attack. His funeral reflected things about him. He used to deal in cars; I called his firm "Kerbside Motors" and when his hearse came I said, "That's strange – there's no For Sale sign on it!" The other thing was that they'd actually closed Crewe crematorium because someone had stolen the lead off the roof. It was all of a piece with Plum somehow and I know he would have laughed. At Moggsie's funeral I was a bearer. The family plot was opened up and found to be full of paupers. So they buried him next to the dog cemetery. He wouldn't have minded.

Some of the most difficult performances I've had to give have been at funerals. I was asked to arrange and learn "Abraham, Martin And John" – a song written by Dick Holler after the assassination of Martin Luther King and recorded by various people, including Smokey Robinson and Marvin Gaye – as a tribute at Eugene's funeral. Des and I fell out and I was left on my own with it. I slowed it right down and gave it funerary dignity with guitar punctuation on the line "the good die young" using slide. I personalised it by inserting "my special friend" in one of the lines. Gut-wrenching bass notes. The effect was cumulative then I faded it at the end.

I don't have any solemn feelings about the body of a dead person – a bin bag and cart the body off as far as I'm concerned. Funeral services help the living, not the dead.

To me Eugene was a hero because of the positive way he lived. He had the courage to embrace life. There are those whom I admire for other reasons. There's a scene from the BBC 2 1973 series *The Ascent of Man* in which Doctor Jacob Bronowski stands in a pond and holds mud from it in his right hand. It's a very emotional moment. He is at Auschwitz and ash from people exterminated there will be mingled with the earth and water.

We have to cure ourselves of the itch for absolute knowledge and power. We have to close the distance between the push-button order and the human act. We have to touch people.

Doctor Jacob Bronowski. (21)

Members of his own family had died at Auschwitz.

I was impressed by Doctor Jacob Bronowski's erudition and humanity. A friend of my wife wrote to him and received a handwritten letter back. I was moved by this personal gesture.

When I visited Auschwitz-Birkenhau I thought about all the people classified by the Nazis as freight who had worked and died there, and about all the people who had been dehumanised and transported from Africa to work and die in the New World, and saw no difference. Racist bullying on a vast and organized scale. And I thought of Doctor Bronowski and wondered how he personally dealt with what had happened to the Jews. Having seen the claustrophobic 1940s newsreels of the camps, what strikes you when you visit Auschwitz is its vastness. With its much documented purpose-built railway line, Auschwitz is itself a big place. Built originally as a barracks; it has tangibility that Birkenhau, the extermination camp, lacks. Birkenhau is the size of a small town. The Germans tried to obliterate it so all that is left is an empty space filled with your worst imaginings.

In 1984 Sir Michael Tippett's oratorio *The Mask Of Time,* like Bronowski's work an overview of the history of humankind, was inspired by *The Ascent Of Man.*

Nelson Mandela and Mahatma Gandhi both sacrificed their personal freedom for the liberation of others and their different approaches have interested me. Mandela and the ANC had resisted apartheid peacefully until the Sharpeville Massacre, after which they resorted to sabotage.

During my lifetime I have dedicated myself to the struggle of the African people. I have fought against white domination and I have fought against black domination. I have cherished the ideal of a democratic and free society in which all persons live together in harmony and with equal opportunities...if needs be it is an ideal for which I am prepared to die.

Nelson Mandela. (22)

How could Gandhi have achieved so much by being passive? It must be the total commitment that made him a formidable force. Passive doesn't mean inactive. But as someone who has been so active I find this intriguing and almost impossible to imagine.

Keep your thoughts positive, because your thoughts become your words. Keep your words positive, because your words become your behaviours. Keep your behaviours positive, because your behaviours become your habits. Keep your habits positive, because your habits become your values. Keep your values positive, because your values become your destiny.

Mahatma Gandhi.

One of the women I have admired is the American entertainer Josephine Baker, who fought for emancipation on several fronts. She was a spectacular presence: famous for erotic dancing, stage nudity and her diamond-collared pet cheetah that used to escape and terrorise the musicians. She was the first African American to star in a major film; she insisted on integrated audiences; she helped the French Resistance, receiving the *Croix de Guerre.* She worked for the Civil Rights Movement and was held in such high esteem that she was offered leadership of the Movement after the death of Martin Luther King. Josephine Baker used her talent and her sexuality courageously and her life was a testimony to her ideals. She adopted a "Rainbow Family" from all over the world to live in her chateau in France.

On a smaller scale than any of these outstanding acts of freedom-fighting, I've come to realize that even fairly mild acts of individuality can have a strong reaction. Some people are very scared of any threats to the status quo. There are times in your life when you have to do something. I remember Mike Slaughter, a fellow blues enthusiast, one-time lawyer and full-time philanthropist walking down Oxford Street distributing hundreds of pounds.

He was arrested. "Ain't bad for a pink!" I thought.

Notes: Section Seven

(1) Des Parton, interviewed by Sandra Gibson, May 2006.

(2) Zoe Johnson, interviewed by Sandra Gibson, 26th April 2007.

(3) Linda Johnson, interviewed by Sandra Gibson 4th November 2008.

(4) Zoe Johnson, interviewed by Sandra Gibson, 26th April 2007.

(5) Ibid.

(6) Brochure for The 14th Nantwich Jazz Blues & Music Festival 2010.

(7) Extract from letter sent to the BBC by Graham Roberts, 24th July 2000.

(8) John Darlington, interviewed by Sandra Gibson 3rd January 2007.

(9) Andy Boote, interviewed by Sandra Gibson 4th September 2006.

(10) Ade White, from a conversation with Sandra Gibson at The Oddfellows, Nantwich. 27th February, 2010.

(11) Sam Molony, 13 years, interviewed by Sandra Gibson at Brine Leas School, Nantwich, in October 2006.

(12) Dec Higgins, 16 years, interviewed by Sandra Gibson at Brine Leas School, Nantwich, January 2007.

(13) Josh Bailey, 16 years, interviewed by Sandra Gibson at Brine Leas School, Nantwich, January 2007.

(14) Phil Doody from a conversation in Custom Amplification, 19th March 2009.

(15) Andy Smith: e-mail sent to Sandra Gibson, 19th February 2010.

(16) Sam Molony, 13 years, interviewed by Sandra Gibson at Brine Leas School, Nantwich, in October 2006.

(17) Wayne Davies (Slim) interviewed by Sandra Gibson 30th January 2007.

(18) Andy Boote interviewed by Sandra Gibson 4th September 2006.

(19) It's all in the body language and there's a look in the eye. Perhaps the two guys were too drunk to notice or too arrogant to take heed. You have to be either stupid or extremely confident in your own powers to put yourself in physical danger. This reminds me of an occasion when I watched in fascination while my roadie was playing about with one of those karate weapons called a nunchucks. Now this irritated another bloke – an ex-mercenary who had been kneecapped – so he grabbed hold of the device and snapped the chain. He must have been confident in his hardness to do something so provocative because he wasn't going to be able to run away!

(20) From the tribute in the Middlewich 3rd Folk & Boat Festival Souvenir Programme, June 1992.

(21) Doctor Jacob Bronowski: The Ascent Of Man: Knowledge Or Certainty. BBC.

(22) Nelson Mandela, 20th April 1964: opening defence statement in Rivonia Trial.

Acknowledgements

The telling of these stories is an acknowledgement to all those who created them. The following are mentioned for their actual contribution to the writing of the book, with apologies to anyone missed.

Andy Boote, John Darlington, Dave Evans, Zoe Johnson, Melvyn Allen, Fred Watts, Andy Smith, Slim (Wayne Davies), Linda Johnson, Des Parton, David Rushworth, Phil Doody, Ian Moore, Ade White, Jim Farmer, Matthew Johnson, Sam Molony, Geoff Edwards, Dec Higgins, Josh Bailey, Barry Bray, and Jonty Ellwood.

This has been a long, extensive project. What began as a booklet grew into a book and it couldn't have happened without generous support. We would like to thank everyone who gave time, effort, humour, inspiration and intelligence to create the light and life of this kaleidoscope of memories. Let's raise a glass to absent friends. Let's raise a glass to those phenomenal musicians whose rhythmic songs of joy and sorrow inspired rock 'n' roll.